S0-BIJ-722

BRADFORD
COLLEGE
LIBRARY

REVERSAL THEORY
MOTIVATION, EMOTION, AND PERSONALITY

REVERSAL THEORY

Motivation, Emotion and Personality

MICHAEL J. APTER

ROUTLEDGE
London and New York

First published 1989
by Routledge
11 New Fetter Lane, London EC4P 4EE
29 West 35th Street, New York, NY 10001

Typeset by Photoprint, Torquay, Devon
Printed and bound in Great Britain by
Mackays of Chatham PLC, Chatham, Kent

British Library Cataloguing in Publication Data

Apter, Michael J. (Michael John), *1939–*
Reversal theory: motivation, emotion and personality
1. Man. Behaviour, Reversal theory
I. Title
155.2

ISBN 0–415–01581–2
ISBN 0–415–01582–0 pbk

Library of Congress Cataloging in Publication Data also available

Contents

To Ivy, with love

Preface

What *is* reversal theory? It is exactly this question which the book you hold in your hand is designed to answer. In order to do so, all the main concepts are introduced in a step-by-step fashion and illustrated with examples from everyday life, research generated by the theory is reviewed, and applications of the theory to clinical practice are outlined.

Although the starting point of reversal theory is an analysis of the different ways in which people experience their own motives, this analysis forms the basis for an argument which develops into a broad and integrative theory of motivation, emotion and personality – the three fields indicated by the subtitle of the book. In the process, fundamental assumptions in these fields are challenged, and the resulting approach is therefore not one which will please everyone. But it does raise a number of important and unavoidable issues for psychology.

Since the theory is general and integrative, it relates in principle to an enormous research and clinical literature. In an introductory text, however, it would clearly not be possible to attempt to link all the relevant published material to the argument. Instead, therefore, I have for the most part focussed on the published research of those working within the reversal theory framework itself. In order to place the theory in context, however, I have also, at various points, contrasted its principal ideas with those of other recognized theories and approaches; and the final chapter is devoted to a systematic examination of such contrasts.

The basic ideas were originally put forward in the mid-1970s by Dr K. C. P. Smith, a consultant child psychiatrist, together with the present writer. They were then developed by the present writer into a full systematic theory. Although a number of papers were published in the 1970s, the first book-length account appeared as *The Experience of Motivation* (Apter 1982a). Soon thereafter, and reflecting the interest in the theory which was rapidly developing among researchers and practitioners in a number of fields, it was possible to hold a first international conference. This took place in Wales in 1983. A selection of papers from this conference was published in Apter, Fontana, and Murgatroyd (1985). Since then, two further international conferences have been held (in Canada in 1985 and Holland in 1987) and a selection of papers based on contributions to both these conferences will be found in Apter, Kerr, and Cowles (1988). The present book not only provides an accessible account of the theory as a whole, written with the student and non-specialist very much in mind; it also brings the story up to date by incorporating recent conceptual developments and by reviewing all the empirical evidence that has been generated by the theory so far.

I would like to take this opportunity to record my sincere appreciation of the enthusiastic support I received from Mary Ann Kernan and David Stonestreet at Routledge – it is good to have editors who care. It is also my pleasure to thank Sven Svebak for his helpful comments on parts of the book, and Mieke Mitchell not only for typing the manuscript with ferocious efficiency, but also for her invaluable advice on matters of style and presentation. Finally, I wish to thank my wife, Ivy, for her understanding of the fact that writing a book is a kind of illness which, like all illnesses, requires sympathy, understanding, a little peace and quiet, and plenty of good food.

1

The Structure of Experience

I would rather shape my soul than furnish it.

Essays
Michel de Montaigne (1533–92)

Contemporary psychology has many problems, not least of which is that characteristic which has been designated by one writer, in a phrase as ungainly as the phenomenon itself, 'accumulative fragmentalism' (Kruger 1981). One is even tempted to call it 'bloated accumulative fragmentalism'. What this comes to is that there is a great deal of it – more than can ever be properly digested or assimilated; and still it continues to grow apace. Like the rider who was said to 'jump on his horse and ride off in all directions', there is about the subject, through nobody's fault in particular, a tendency to do many increasingly divergent things at the same time. Now certainly any flourishing science needs diversity of interest and opinion, and nothing could be worse than the straitjacket of some theoretical orthodoxy, or a Ministry of Research Topics. But at the same time every science, and not least psychology, needs some of its practitioners to devote themselves to the broad view, to develop, in however tentative a fashion, large-scale theoretical views which, even while clashing with each other, help the cause of synthesis and integration. For some reason the psychology of recent years has not encouraged such developments. 'Grand theories' have been widely sneered at and dismissed as 'old-fashioned', while the fashion which came in with the mini-dress and the mini-car (and which, unlike these, is still with us) has been for the mini-theory.

All this is by way of justification of the subject matter of the present book, which deals with a new general approach to psychology, and a theory generated from within this approach which *does* attempt some degree of breadth. The approach has been called 'structural phenomenology' (Apter 1981a, 1982a), and the theory derived from it is known as 'reversal theory'. In this first chapter I shall set the scene for the rest of the book by saying a little about structural phenomenology; the remainder of the book will illustrate this approach through a more detailed account of reversal theory. In case you are one of those readers who become restless with discussions of methodological issues, be assured that, starting in the next chapter, the focus will be on substantive psychological problems.

Something which bedevils discussion of phenomenological psychology is the fact that the term has a range of meanings, and that this is not always realized even by those who avail themselves of it. These meanings extend from that special kind of psychology which is derived from the specific ideas of the German philosopher, Edmund Husserl (1859–1938), to a broader sense which we could define as any form of psychology which is centrally concerned with subjective experience. The term 'phenomenology' in 'structural phenomenology' is intended to reflect this latter (and more Anglo-American) sense of phenomenological psychology. So conceived, there is no implication that this type of psychology rejects any interest in objectively observable behaviour; indeed, the relationship between experience and behaviour will often be a significant concern. But it does imply a rejection of any approach which attempts to explain human behaviour without any reference to experience, or which sees experience as no more than a by-product or side issue. It is thus totally opposed to behaviourism in any of its forms, regarding it as a kind of methodological vandalism.

This is not the place to justify this stance at length, or to enter into one of the most longstanding debates in psychology. Even so, one reason for adopting this position may be of interest here, since it actually constituted the starting point of the development of reversal theory. This was the observation in a child guidance clinic that different children with, behaviourally speaking, the same problem, can nevertheless perceive what they are 'up to' in diametrically opposed ways. A good example is that of truanting. For some children it turned out that this was an escape from the threat which school represented for them, for others it was an escape from the monotony of the classroom. In one case the meaning of the action for the child was that of flight from danger, in the other that of search for stimulation and challenge and risk. Clearly the appropriate therapy for one would be likely to be counterproductive for the other. It would be no good taking the nervous, frightened child and convincing him that there were sources of risk and challenge of which he had not previously been aware in the school context; neither would it be likely to be particularly helpful to persuade the more ebullient adventure-seeker that there was nothing to fear in the safety of the classroom, or to teach her techniques for overcoming anxiety. In the case of truanting, then, and many of the other problems faced in the clinic, it became clear that a knowledge of the subjective meaning of the problem behaviour was an essential preliminary to treatment. This may seem obvious but is frequently overlooked by many clinicians, especially by those who take a narrow partisan position, whatever their professed mode of intervention.

Having touched on phenomenology, we can now turn to the 'structural' component of the term 'structural phenomenology'. In doing this we are led directly to the basic premiss of the approach. This is that experience has structure. In other words, the different aspects of subjective life are systematically related to each other. Experience is not so much a bag of beans – it is more a finely spun web. If we think of the totality of an individual's experience at a given time as constituting her 'phenomenal field' – the way she sees the world and herself in it, including her perceptions, thoughts, feelings, and emotions – then structural phenomenology can be defined as *the study of the structure of the phenomenal field.*

Since part of the phenomenal field will be the individual's own actions, structural phenomenology is concerned with behaviour as well as mentation. Although the initial focus of interest here is the way the person sees his own actions, this may lead into interesting questions about the relationship between the subjective and objective views of these actions, and the objective effect of the actions in the real world. While this can be seen as a natural extension of structural phenomenology, however, the starting point and the pivotal centre of interest is always the phenomenal field.

The use of the word 'action' here, rather than 'behaviour', is significant. The concept of action, which also has a long history in psychology, contrasts with that of behaviour precisely in that an action is behaviour plus subjective meaning. To describe someone as stamping his feet would be to describe a piece of behaviour; to describe him as stamping the dirt off his shoes, stamping out a fire, or dancing, would be to describe an action because it implies something about what the actor saw himself to be doing. In its concern with the subjective meaning of behaviour, especially the intentions of the person performing the behaviour, reversal theory could therefore be regarded (Apter 1979) as a type of 'action theory'. (For some recent accounts of action theory, see Clarke and Crossland 1985; and Harré, Clarke and De Carlo 1985).

Returning to the phrase 'structural phenomenology', 'structural' here is emphatically *not* to be understood in the sense of Wundt's structuralism, that early type of psychology which was primarily concerned to analyse the individual elements of conscious experience. The structuralism of structural phenomenology is about the way in which features of experience cohere or relate to each other, and can be seen rather as a branch of contemporary structuralism in the social sciences (*viz.*, Lachenicht 1985a, 1988). By this is meant the type of structuralism of Lévi-Strauss in anthropology, or Noam Chomsky in linguistics. This modern structuralism, which has become a dominant movement in a number of fields, is concerned with the 'deep' abstract structures which underlie and generate particular types of 'surface' phenomena. In anthropology, for example, it is concerned with the rules which underlie the generation of kinship systems, totem systems, myth systems, culinary systems, and other kinds of system in different cultures. This type of structuralism is essentially holistic, and in this respect is the opposite of Wundt's atomistic and misleadingly named 'structuralist' approach.

From this perspective, what reversal theory does is to apply some of the insights of modern structuralists not so much to the *products* of the human mind (linguistic systems, kinship systems, and the like) as much as to the *human mind itself*. Consciousness now becomes the complex surface phenomenon below which organizing structures are to be fathomed. (Those readers who have some familiarity with structural anthropology will, in fact, recognize in subsequent chapters of this book certain more specific influences at work in reversal theory, such as the use of the notion of 'binary opposition'.)

To say that conscious experience itself is organized and has structure is to say something more than that the *contents* of experience are organized in the sense of Gestalt psychology. As is well known, the Gestalt psychologists, in a variety of ingenious ways, showed how an essential feature of perception is the grouping of stimuli into patterns and configurations which have a life of their own over and above the elements which enter into them. In structural phenomenology, however, the interest is in the way that *experience itself* is structured. This is the starting point for all that follows in this book, and there will be many concrete illustrations of what must, at this point, seem a somewhat obscure and uselessly abstract statement. But to impart some sense of what is meant, here straightaway are a couple of obvious examples of the way in which experience itself may be said to be structured.

First of all, we can recognize that conscious experience has what has been called a focus and a fringe. On the one hand there is whatever it is that we are interested in or concerned with, at a given moment, and on the other there is the rest of experience which is more peripheral. If I am playing chess, then the focus of my attention is the chessboard and the pieces on it, but I am also marginally aware of other aspects of my situation: the fact that the board is on a round table, that my chair is a little uncomfortable, that I have an itch on my left shin, that I can hear it raining outside, and so on. It seems to be intrinsic to normal experience that we concentrate on something and relegate the rest to the background – although it is always possible that what is in the background will suddenly come into the foreground, for example if the itch on my shin gets worse.

Secondly, experience is divided into self and not-self: there are all those parts of my experience which are contained within my self-boundary, and all those parts which are external to it. In the example just given, the chessboard, chair, table and rain are experienced by me as cohering to make a world 'out there', whereas the itch on my shin I perceive to be part of that cohesive inner world I call 'myself'.

Both these aspects of the structure of experience, the focus/fringe division and the self/not-self distinction are problematic in a number of ways that I do not intend to pursue here. The point is simply to give some idea of what is meant by 'the structure of experience' and to show how this is different from 'structures within experience'. In both these examples of the structure of the phenomenal field, the basic structure will normally remain the same in its essential features even if the content changes. Thus the itch which is part of my inner world may disappear, but I may instead become aware of some other aspect of my self, such as that I am thirsty; I may get up from the table to get myself a drink, in which case the focus of my attention will move away from the board and on to the drinks cabinet. This distinction between form and content in experience is not unlike that between, to use a modern metaphor, computer programs and data. The same program can be used on as many different data sets as one cares to enter, and the same data can be processed by different programs.

As well as structures which can be identified at a given moment, there are also temporal structures, patterns of qualitative change in experience over time. If we cut across experience at a given moment, we can see certain kinds of basic structure, such as those which have just been described; if we do this at different times we find certain kinds of change in these structures, and these kinds of change may also be patterned. The situation is like taking cross sections of a stem to examine under a microscope: each cross section has a structure, and this structure varies in a systematic way down the stem, sometimes gradually, sometimes abruptly.

Thus the focus of the phenomenal field may grow narrower or broader, rather like the pupil of the eye dilating and constricting, during the course of everyday life. Or, more dramatically, one type of structure may give way completely to another. For example, the focus/fringe structure may disappear completely in sleep, and then in dreams the focus alone reappears, to disappear again in sleep and be replaced eventually by the full focus/fringe structure on waking.

In this respect, consciousness is seen as polymorphous – as having different shapes or forms. This is shown particularly clearly in special states of consciousness like hypnotic trance or meditation or drug-induced hallucination. But this protean quality can also be discerned in the course of everyday life. If consciousness is, to use William James's famous metaphor, a stream, then it is one whose contours change as it runs towards the sea, and at different points on its downward path it may even become a lake or waterfall.

We are now in a position to give a slightly fuller definition of structural phenomenology. It is the study of the different ways in which the phenomenal field may be structured and the dynamics of transition from one type of structure to another over time. It thus deals systematically with the nature of experience itself at a given time and the changes it undergoes over time.

Mention of the dynamic aspects of structural phenomenology brings in the relevance of systems theory (or, as it used to be called, cybernetics), since the study of the dynamic aspects of structures is essentially what systems theory is all about. That is, it is about the ways in which structures maintain themselves or in which transformations occur from one to another. In particular, it involves the development of general principles of control which apply to all control systems, be they mechanical (e.g. the room thermostat), electronic (e.g. the computer monitoring an industrial process), physiological (e.g. the maintenance of body temperature), mechanical/psychological (e.g. a man driving a car), social psychological (e.g. the maintenance of group norms), or of any other kind. Such systems theory notions as those of homeostasis and negative feedback can be developed in rigorous mathematical terms, and applied to a wide variety of systems, whatever 'fabric' they happen to be made of, be it metal and oil, flesh and blood, or transistor and plastic. There is a sense in which modern structuralism and systems theory are closely related to each other, at least at a formal level, the one exploring and emphasizing the logic of form and the other the logic of function, but both of them searching for deep abstract principles which underlie a diversity of superficially dissimilar phenomena. Some writers, most notably Jean Piaget (1971), have in fact gone so far as entirely to equate structuralism and systems theory. In any case, as will become apparent, reversal theory has been strongly influenced by systems theory as well as structuralism, and it therefore forms an important part of the intellectual background to the theory. By relating systems theory to phenomenology, it can be shown how phenomenology need not be restricted to those arid and static descriptions which form such an unfortunately large part of the phenomenological literature, but can, as it were, be 'brought alive'.

It will be realized that there are many different aspects of experience which could in principle be examined from the perspective of structural phenomenology, as I have described it here. In the development of reversal theory, however, one aspect was taken as being of overriding importance in understanding human action. This was motivation. Motivational experiences were regarded from the outset as the hub around which everything else is organized in the phenomenal field, and the necessary starting point for any thoroughgoing attempt to understand the vicissitudes of experience and behaviour. It would be quite possible to practise structural phenomenology without this assumption, and from other starting points, and no doubt it would be possible in the process to produce theories different from, or complementary to, reversal theory within the structural phenomenological framework. (For instance, Lachenicht (1985b) develops a structural phenomenological account of social relationships.) But is was from this standpoint that reversal theory itself did in fact develop. Incidentally, in making motivation primary in this way, reversal theory flies in the face of what has undoubtedly been the major trend in psychology in the last twenty years or so: the trend towards increasing emphasis on cognition. As cognitive psychology has developed, so the study of motivation has increasingly taken a back seat. In this respect, one of the aims of reversal theory is to help to put it back where it belongs – in the driver's seat.

Reversal theory, then, starts with motivation. But it does not end there. As a theory of motivation it inevitably also becomes a theory of the emotions. In turn, both these aspects of mental life become part of a more general theory of personality, and this theory broadens itself to include the abnormal as well as the normal. From there it is but a step to extend the account to cover therapy as well as pathology, and to provide an orientation for the clinician. At the same time it becomes possible to start asking research questions about the relationships of the mental structures identified in the theory to psychophysiological variables, to observable actions (including social interactions) and to performance of different kinds – and to search for evidence which might bear on the universality of these structures and to test hypotheses about the underlying mechanisms. In these ways one can see the beginnings of a potentially cohesive research programme which would cut across a number of the traditional subfields of psychology.

From all that I have written so far, two major features of the methodology of structural phenomenology should be evident. The first is that research is 'theory-driven' and in this sense the approach is what has been called a 'top-down' approach. That is, the theory – in this case reversal theory – guides the search for evidence, rather than data being gathered in the hope that it might lead to a theory. The second feature is that the development of the theory itself is 'experience-driven'. In other words, the theory derives not from previous research results, or the development of some new type of instrumentation, or certain abstract ideas (like drive, intelligence, repression) – although all of these may quickly be drawn into the process of both theory development and experimentation. Rather, the principal starting point is that cool, clear source of everything we know about ourselves: our own consciousness.

The general approach of structural phenomenology is therefore not just 'top-down' but is also what one might call 'inside-out'. It starts from subjective experience and interprets behaviour, or physiological processes, in the light of this experience – rather than starting with external observation and measurement and then (possibly) making inferences about the experience which may lie behind it. Thus in dealing with arousal, instead of starting with an objective measure of cortical or autonomic arousal and then (perhaps) asking how far the subject is feeling aroused, reversal theory does things the other way round. It starts from the question of whether the subject feels aroused, and then looks to see what the physiological concomitants of this feeling might be, and therefore what might be the best physiological indices. This is a seemingly subtle distinction but one which has far-reaching implications for research.

It can be seen, then, that there have been many influences at work in the formation of structural phenomenology, especially structuralism, phenomenological psychology, action theory, cybernetics and systems theory. Despite what some people would see as conflicts between aspects of some of these – for example the experientialism of phenomenology and the mechanistic basis of cybernetics – they all come together in structural phenomenology to produce what I believe is a distinctive and coherent approach to psychology. The question is: How useful is it? The reader will be able to judge this for himself or herself in the chapters which follow.

2

The Experience of Arousal

The doors of heaven and hell are adjacent and identical

The Last Temptation of Christ
Nikos Kazantzakis (1883–1957)

AROUSAL: THE NATURE OF A PROBLEM

Motivation, as it is experienced, is a complex phenomenon with a number of aspects. One of the most salient of these, and the one which we shall be looking at in this first chapter, is the feeling of *arousal*. By this I mean the degree to which one feels oneself to be 'worked up' or emotionally intense about what one is doing. Thus one might be highly aroused in an argument, especially if it is about something one believes in passionately, but low in arousal while sitting with one's feet up doing nothing in particular after Sunday lunch.

We should be clear from the outset that this sense of arousal is phenomenologically different from two others which are often confused with it. One of these is one's feeling of being wide awake or sleepy. This is obviously not the same since one can be wide awake but not particularly worked up about anything, or sleepy but emotional. (Indeed, one can actually be asleep and worked up, as one is during a nightmare.) The second is the feeling of how much energy one has available, how 'pepped up' one is. Again, this does not necessarily go together with arousal in the sense of 'worked up'. After all, it is perfectly possible to feel energetic but composed, or to feel worn out but shaken. So we must distinguish the emotional/calm dimension of interest here from that of both awake/drowsy and energetic/tired. These may often go together, but they do not necessarily do so, and would in any case appear to be phenomenologically distinct.

It should also be emphasized that the analysis at this stage is experiential and not physiological, representing as it does the approach of 'structural phenomenology' described in the previous chapter. This is not to exclude physiology, and physiological aspects of the processes identified here, including arousal, will be examined in a later chapter. But it is based on the argument that it is most meaningful to start with subjective experience and work outward into physiology and objective behaviour.

To give the following discussion some concrete focus, let us consider four everyday situations of a kind with which we are all familiar, and examine how our feelings of arousal might be experienced in each:

1. Waiting at the dentist for an extraction to be carried out.
2. Watching a thriller film at a particularly tense moment.
3. Soaking in a hot bath at the end of a hard day's work.
4. Waiting for a bus with nothing to read and no one to talk to.

Obviously if you think about it, there are two major components of these experiences, two variables which differentiate between them. First, there is the intensity variable – just how worked up one feels oneself to be, that is how high or low one is in arousal. For most people the value of this variable will presumably be high in the first two situations listed, and low in the second two. Generally, we get worked up going to the dentist or watching a thrilling film, but not having a bath or waiting for the bus. The second variable is that of how pleasant or unpleasant the arousal is – its so-called hedonic tone (to use a term introduced by Beebe-Center (1932)). This is presumably pleasant for most people in the second and third situations – after all we voluntarily engage in them – and unpleasant in the first and fourth – people do not generally entertain themselves by going to the dentist or hanging around for public transport.

So now we come to a basic question in the psychology or motivation: How are these two variables of felt arousal and hedonic tone related? Clearly the relationship is not a straightforward linear one. We cannot say that the greater the intensity the greater the pleasure (situation 1, waiting at the dentist, would be an exception). Nor can we say the opposite: the greater the intensity the greater the displeasure (situation 2, watching a thriller film would be an exception). Somehow we have to account for the way in which high arousal can be pleasant or unpleasant, and likewise low arousal. In fact, the English language provides us with four words which exactly describe each of these combinations of arousal level and hedonic tone: anxiety (unpleasant high arousal), excitement (pleasant high arousal), relaxation (pleasant low arousal), and boredom (unpleasant low arousal). The four situations listed above then exemplify each of these four emotions (in the same order). So the question now becomes: How can we incorporate all four of these emotions into a structure which relates felt arousal level to hedonic tone?

OPTIMAL AROUSAL THEORY

There is in fact a classic answer to this question, which has been around since the mid-1950s and which provides what is today still the most widely accepted account. Indeed, it has become almost a kind of orthodoxy. It is called optimal arousal theory, and one of the first statements of it was made by Hebb (1955). There have been many variants, but they all agree on the essential fundamental idea: that there is a single optimal level of arousal and that this is somewhere around the middle of the arousal dimension. If this idea is represented graphically, we get the famous inverted-U curve shown in Figure 1. By 'optimal' is meant both optimal in terms of performance (i.e. the best amount of arousal for most successful task performance) and optimal in the sense of hedonic tone – most pleasant. Since we are here concerned with the *experience* of motivation, we shall restrict our discussion to the latter aspect, and accordingly Figure 1 shows the curve of optimal arousal theory in a space defined by arousal level and hedonic tone.

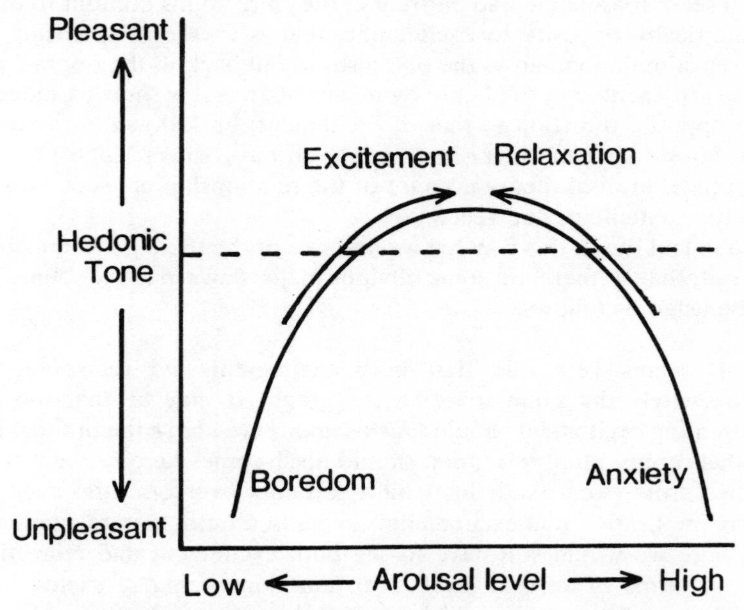

Fig. 1 The relationship between arousal and hedonic tone according to optimal arousal theory (Hebb 1955).

It is not always clear when optimal arousal theorists are defining arousal in physiological and when in subjective terms, but since they frequently use subjective words like 'anxiety' and 'reward', it is reasonable to assume that their account is supposed to relate to subjective experience as well as to objective physiology. Certainly Hebb (1955) uses such subjective terms, and we may take his account as prototypical. So how does Hebb deal with the four basic arousal emotions which I have identified?

The main thrust of Hebb's argument in relation to hedonic tone is that at low levels an increase of stimulation may be rewarding, whereas at high levels it is a decrease that rewards. Although he does not in this paper use the term 'boredom' to refer to low arousal, it is clear from his descriptions of his well-known sensory deprivation experiments summarized in his paper that this is how subjects feel when they do not have enough stimulation. He also seems to go along with those who use the concept of anxiety for arousal which is too high. So we may place the terms 'boredom' and 'anxiety' against the suboptimal and superoptimal ranges, respectively, of the curve in Figure 1. Excitement in his account arises when some mild stimulation takes the organism up to the optimal point; examples he quotes include playing bridge and golf or reading a thriller. This can be represented in the figure by means of an arrow showing movement up to the optimum level of stimulation. Relaxation is not mentioned, but it would seem reasonable and entirely in the spirit of his account to make it symmetrically opposite to excitement, that is to see it as arising when lowered stimulation allows the organism to fall back to the optimal point. This is represented in the figure by means of an arrow showing movement in an opposite direction to that of excitement, back down to the optimal level. So Figure 1 shows a construction, on the basis of Hebb's paper, of the optimal arousal theory account of the relationship between boredom, anxiety, excitement, and relaxation.

When laid out in this way the weaknesses of the theory are immediately exposed; that is, there are some obvious major flaws in the account. These can be listed as follows:

1. It seems very odd that both excitement and relaxation share approximately the same space in the graph. It may be that the arrow representing excitement should finish somewhere *above* the optimal point, and that representing relaxation should finish somewhere *below* it, so that the two cross over. And this would certainly overcome the even more bizarre implication that excitement is lower in arousal than relaxation. But even here we would still have to see both excitement and relaxation as close in terms of arousal level, both emotions being restricted to that central part of the curve which lies on the upper, pleasant side of the horizontal neutral line between pleasant and unpleasant hedonic tone.

2. Excitement is seen as arising from only mild stimulation, with strong stimulation in this view leading to anxiety. But surely it *is* possible to feel strong excitement, as a result of intense stimulation? A strikingly obvious example is that of sexual excitement which surely can be as high in arousal as anxiety, and just as pleasant as anxiety is unpleasant. Life is full of examples of highly exciting activities, including watching thriller films (the excitement situation listed at the beginning of this chapter), taking part in dangerous activities (such as parachuting or mountaineering), enjoying rides at the fairground like the roller coaster, gambling, watching sport –

even on occasion playing bridge and golf and reading thriller novels, the very examples of excitement cited by Hebb.

In a similar vein, it is possible to argue that relaxation can be extreme and not just mild. Think of the example cited earlier in this chapter: relaxing in a hot bath at the end of a busy and tiring day. Surely this can take one much further down the arousal dimension than the middle range?

All this may seem obvious and commonsensical. But if data is required to demonstrate the point, the present writer presented a list of fifty varied situations to 67 subjects who were asked to rate each in terms of arousal and the hedonic tone of the arousal (by means of two 7-point rating scales). Of the eleven situations which subjects judged to be the most pleasant in terms of felt arousal, four turned out to have a high average and four a low on the arousal dimension (the remaining three having a moderate average). The pleasant, highly arousing situations were 'arriving on holiday in a foreign country', 'playing in an important game when the scores are level', 'building up to an orgasm', and 'reading a particularly tense chapter in a thriller'. Those highly pleasant situations which were low in arousal were 'just before going to sleep', 'having a bath', 'relaxing after a hard day's work', and 'just after eating a good meal' (Apter 1976).

The implication of all this is that somehow we have to be able to get well up into the top left and the top right quadrants of the graph shown in Figure 1.

3. Not only can excitement and relaxation be experienced at relatively extreme points on the arousal dimension, but anxiety and boredom can, surely, be experienced somewhere near the centre of the dimension, which is to say that they can be relatively mild. Surely it is perfectly possible to feel only a little anxious about something (and experience this as quite different from excitement). Waiting at the dentist's for an examination rather than an extraction might produce such feelings of only moderately intense arousal, experienced as mild anxiety. In like manner, it is possible to experience mild boredom, in which arousal is still reasonably elevated, as well as extreme boredom, in which arousal is particularly low. (And such mild boredom would appear to be qualitatively different from relaxation.) When you have been waiting for a bus that does not come – our situation 4 above – you will presumably experience only minor boredom to start with, and this will only become more extreme as time passes and arousal continues to diminish.

4. As if all this were not enough, there is another obvious problem with the optimal arousal account. If these four emotions have unique ranges along a single curve, then one must pass between them in an unvarying order as arousal increases, and again as it decreases. (Refer to Figure 1 if you are not sure about this.) Thus as arousal increases from the low point of boredom, it will eventually give way to excitement and then in turn to anxiety. This implies that excitement is *always* felt before anxiety if arousal

starts to increase from a relatively low point. But there is no evidence for this of which I am aware; nor is it consistent, I would suggest, with everyday experience. Do we really always experience excitement on the way to the dentist before we start to feel anxiety? (And this is assuming that relaxation can only be experienced as a result of some change in a *downward* direction; if it is its absolute position on the curve which counts rather than a change of position downward, then this would make the optimal arousal account even less convincing – since relaxation would always have to be experienced, as arousal increases, after excitement and before anxiety!) Exactly the same kinds of considerations apply to arousal which decreases from anxiety to boredom, and hardly need spelling out. When it comes to looking at changes from one of these emotions to another, optimal arousal theory is as inadequate as it is in describing the emotions themselves. As a theory, therefore, it is far from optimal.

REVERSAL THEORY AND AROUSAL

All this makes it clear that a different approach altogether is needed in order to have a chance of solving the problem of the relationship between these different emotions. Let us approach the problem in a new way, then, by following the structuralist technique of laying out the material we are trying to make sense of in the form of a table (Apter 1981b). If we do this with these four emotions, using high and low arousal and pleasant and unpleasant hedonic tone as the axes, we finish up with a simple table (Table 1).

Table 1 A basic set of four contrasting emotions.

	LOW AROUSAL	HIGH AROUSAL
PLEASANT	RELAXATION	EXCITEMENT
UNPLEASANT	BOREDOM	ANXIETY

On inspection, a pattern immediately becomes evident here – across the diagonals. That is, excitement and boredom are related by being opposite to each other, and anxiety and relaxation are similarly related. In structuralist terms, we have a pair of 'binary opposites'. Thus excitement is what we want when we are bored, and boredom is what we experience when we cannot achieve excitement. Relaxation is what we want when we are anxious, and anxiety is what we feel when we cannot obtain sufficient relaxation. *And both of these apply over the whole arousal range*. This

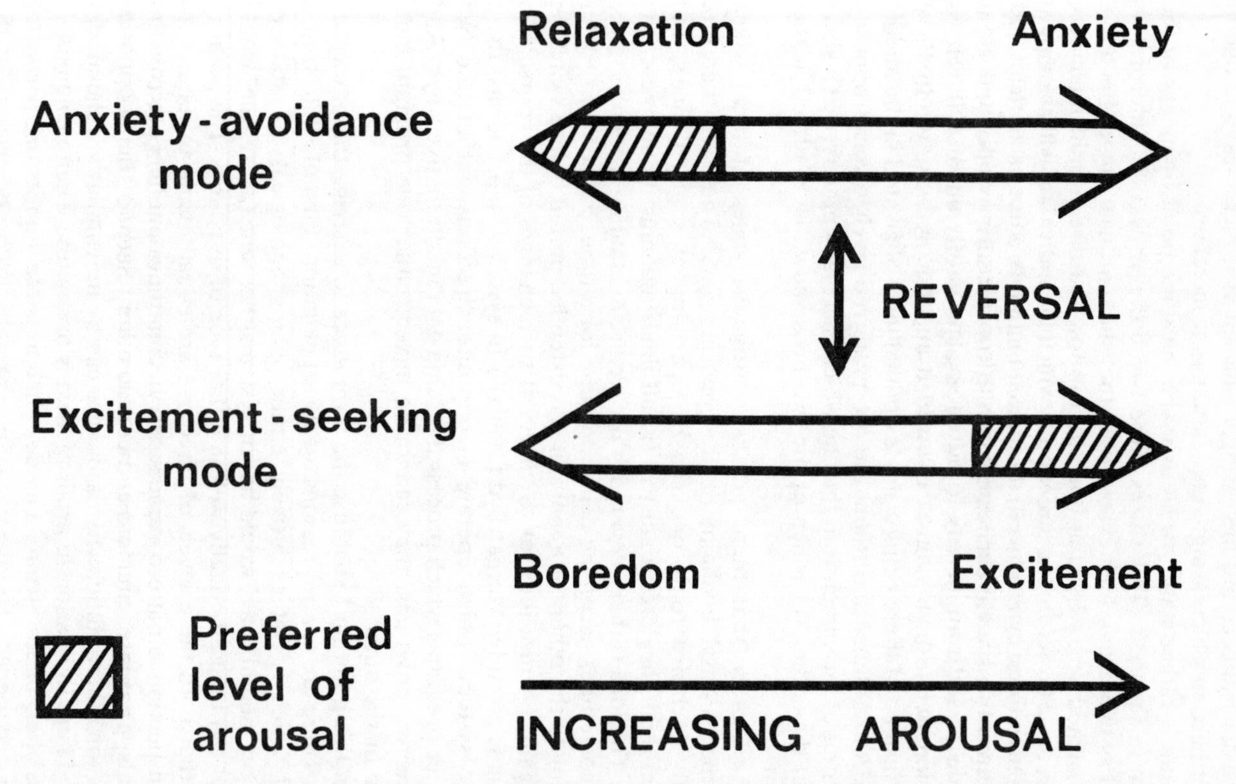

Fig. 2 The two opposite ways of experiencing arousal suggested by reversal theory. Each horizontal bar represents one of these 'modes', the direction of preferred arousal change being depicted by the hatched arrow-head on each bar. The possibility of reversing from one mode to the other is represented by the double-headed vertical arrow.

means that there are two totally opposed ways of experiencing arousal, one in which arousal becomes increasingly pleasant as it increases, and one in which it becomes increasingly unpleasant as it increases.

A table is rather static, so let us make the same point by means of the diagram in Figure 2. This shows these two different ways of interpreting arousal as two lines which extend over the whole arousal range. Each line has a hatched arrow-head at one end to show the direction of increasing pleasure, and therefore the direction in which the individual will attempt to change his arousal level while in that state of mind. In one case, high arousal is preferred and is felt as excitement (while low arousal is avoided and felt as boredom); in the other case, low arousal is preferred and is felt as relaxation (while high arousal is avoided and felt as anxiety). In these terms, instead of there being a single optimal level of arousal in the middle of the arousal dimension, there are *two* preferred levels towards opposite extremities of this dimension, the one which is actually preferred at a given moment depending on which of the two lines shown is 'in effect' at that moment.

Hence we see that there are two distinctive states of mind which experience arousal in diametrically opposite ways. They are therefore mutually exclusive (only one can be operating at a given time), and between them they are exhaustive (at all times one must be in one or the other). The idea is that in everyday life we are fluctuating from one to the other, sometimes becoming delayed in one for a time, but sooner or later switching to the other for a more or less extended period before switching back again. (A nice illustrative 'diary' of such changes in the course of a morning is given by Murgatroyd (1985a).) In systems theory terms, there are two systems which operate in opposite directions, rather like two computer programs which process the same data in alternative ways. And just like two programs, they cannot be mixed: either one program must operate or the other.

From this point on I shall use the term *mode* to describe these 'ways of being'. There are several reasons for this appellation. First of all, a word is needed which is not exclusively either phenomenological (as 'state of mind', or 'mental state' would be) or systems-theoretic (as 'system' would be), but can be used equally well in either type of discourse. The point of this is that both these levels of discourse are equally valid in relation to reversal theory, and are complementary; sometimes one is more convenient or appropriate, and sometimes the other. Second, the word *state* implies something static, whereas modes can be moving, as are the modes depicted here in relation to arousal. That is to say, there can be a number of types of experience *within* a mode, whereas 'state' implies one particular type of experience. To give a specific example, in the psychology of the emotions, anxiety is frequently referred to as a state. But for the analysis given here, anxiety is simply one way of being in a certain mode, which, as we have just seen, covers a complete spectrum from anxiety to relaxation and can involve movement from one to the other without change of mode. So in relation to the diagram in Figure 2 there are two modes, which we can label the anxiety-avoidance mode and the excitement-seeking mode – or, more simply, the arousal-avoidance and arousal-seeking modes.

More terminology is needed here in order to be able to say what kinds of modes these are. Certainly they are to do with motivation, but they are not themselves motivational. Rather, they are *about* motivation, they involve different ways or organizing or interpreting motivation. Technically, therefore, they are *meta*motivational in the same way that one language which talks about another is a metalanguage, or a communication which comments on another communication is a metacommunication. In all such cases we have two levels, a level of content and a level of reference to this content. Accordingly, arousal is motivational; a mode which interprets arousal in a particular way is metamotivational. The arousal-avoidance and arousal-seeking modes therefore constitute a pair of *metamotivational modes*. It is important to grasp this distinction between motivation and metamotivation at this stage because we shall be returning to it throughout the book.

Since the two metamotivational modes which have been identified here are opposite to each other, switches from one to the other can be seen as *reversals*. And it is because of the importance of such metamotivational reversals in the explanations of reversal theory, as we shall see, that the word has been used in the title of the theory itself.

To allow a more direct comparison with optimal arousal theory, let us put the reversal theory account which has just been given into the form of a graph, using as axes, once more, arousal level and hedonic tone. The result is shown in Figure 3. It will be seen that we now have *two* hypothetical curves which cross over each other in the graphical space which was formerly occupied by the single hypothetical curve of optimal arousal theory, and that we have replaced the inverted-U curve by what might be termed an X-combination of curves.

It can now be seen how this simple but radical step overcomes at one stroke all the flaws of optimal arousal theory:

1. Excitement and relaxation no longer share roughly the same space but have been shifted apart, as they should be, towards opposite ends of the arousal dimension.

2. Excitement and relaxation can now both be extremely pleasant and not just mildly pleasant. In other words, we have managed by this arrangement to extend the curves well into the top right and left quadrants of the graph.

3. Both anxiety and boredom can now be mild, and only mildly unpleasant, as well as intense and intensely unpleasant.

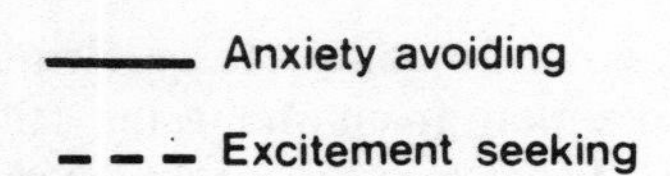

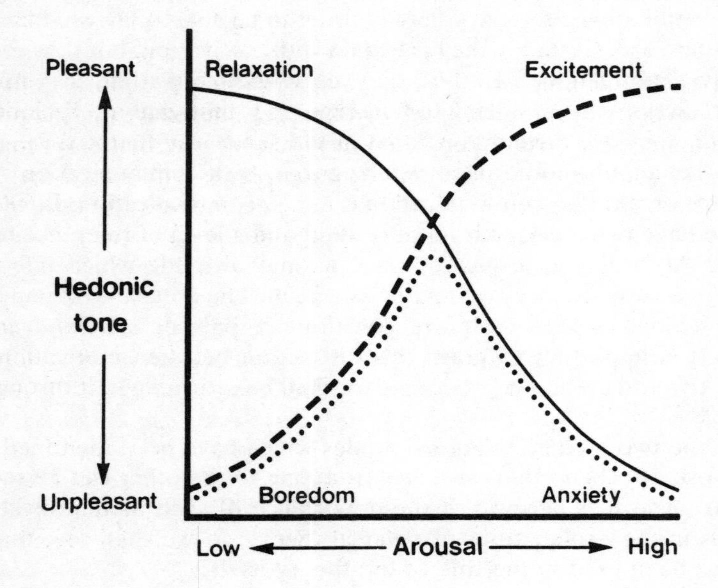

Fig. 3 The relationship between arousal and hedonic tone according to reversal theory. The two hypothetical curves represented by a continuous and a dashed line depict the two modes postulated by reversal theory. For comparison, the dotted line making an inverted U-curve represents the single mode of optimal arousal theory.

4. It is no longer the case that anxiety can only be reached through excitement as arousal increases, or that boredom can only be reached through relaxation as arousal decreases. There is now complete flexibility in the sense that, through a suitable transformation (change of arousal level, or reversal, or both of these), any of the four emotions can move directly to any other in this set without one of the others having to occur on the way.

At the same time, this account retains the satisfactory aspects of optimal arousal theory, in particular the fact that arousal can be felt as unpleasant, and even extremely unpleasant, when it becomes too low or too high. Furthermore, if the arrangement of the two curves takes the form which it does in Figure 3, then it is also possible for moderate levels of arousal to be pleasant. In other words, the inverted-U is still there (and indicated by a dotted line in the figure), but it now forms only a part of the total picture.

Since in reversal theory there are two modes and two curves, this means that a further advantage accrues over optimal arousal theory. This is that the principle of reversal, of instantaneous switching from one curve to the other, allows reversal theory to explain a number of phenomena which otherwise remain enigmatic. For example, why do people undertake dangerous sports of different kinds, and expose themselves in the process to quite unnecessary risks? People do not usually *have* to attempt to climb mountains, go down potholes, jump from airplanes with parachutes, race motorcycles, or hang from hang-gliders. Yet every day many people voluntarily and gladly do these things, and some even become addicted to them. Why? The answer to this question suggested by reversal theory is that people who do these things confront themselves with real danger in order to raise their arousal levels as high as possible, probably experiencing anxiety in the process, but then master the danger or come into control of the situation. This switches them onto the other curve so that, to the degree to which they previously experienced anxiety they now experience excitement. (Remember that the higher the arousal level, the higher both the anxiety and the excitement, depending on which mode is operative. In terms of the graph in Figure 3, a reversal from one to the other involves a vertical switch upwards or downwards from the curve representing one mode to the curve representing the other.) Since the arousal may take a while to subside, the resulting excitement should be experienced for a relatively prolonged time. One must assume that the payoff is such that for a relatively short period of anxiety a relatively long period of excitement is gained, making the activity as a whole worthwhile. (Some interesting autobiographical materials concerning dangerous sports are cited by Kerr (1985a) in support of this interpretation.)

In the opposite direction, it is possible for high arousal to be carried over from excitement to anxiety, converting a situation which should be enjoyable into one which is, involuntarily, a highly disagreeable one. Consider the case of sexual dysfunction (impotence or frigidity). The problem here appears to be that a reversal takes place from the arousal-seeking mode, which is natural to healthy sexual behaviour, to the arousal-avoidance mode, at some point during sexual interaction. The result for the person to whom this happens is that sexual excitement now becomes transformed into (sexual) anxiety, and this in turn acts to inhibit sexual performance (Apter and Smith 1978, 1979a.) Note that this is different from the conventional account of what happens, which has it that anxiety inhibits sexual excitement. The reversal theory argument is that the anxiety *is* the sexual excitement experienced in the 'wrong' mode. Among other things, this explains the paradox that the sexually dysfunctional person may feel highly excited before the dysfunctional moment occurs and that the greater the sexual excitement, the greater the subsequent anxiety appears to be and the greater the disruption to the sexual behaviour (e.g. see some of the cases in Kaplan (1978)). All this is exactly what reversal theory would expect. (The different reasons for reversing from one mode to the other will be dealt with in a later chapter; for the moment all that is necessary to the argument is that reversals should occur, for whatever reason.)

Three points are in order here. The first is that one cannot necessarily tell, from outside observation, which mode someone is in – at least not without asking them questions which would disclose their frame of mind. Of course sometimes it is reasonably evident from their behaviour, but the point is that we can never tell for sure, and are always open to be mistaken if we simply make guesses. And often behaviour in itself is completely ambiguous with respect to mode. Imagine two people driving fast up a motorway. One of these may be speeding because he is late for an important appointment, and is trying to reduce his *anxiety*. The other may be deriving *excitement* from the feeling of speed, from testing his car and his expertise to the limits, from chancing arrest, and from taking the risk of having an accident. Just observing them driving would probably not allow us to decide which mode was actually prevailing at the time.

The second point here is a linguistic one. Although I have chosen four arousal words to represent four primary types of arousal, each of these is really a 'label to a box' which contains a number of other words representing different degrees of intensity of the emotion, different durations of the emotion, different kinds of causation and context, and so on. So in the excitement box we would also find such words as *passion*, *fascination*, *thrill*, *exhilaration*, *elation*, *euphoria*, and *ecstasy*; in the anxiety box we would find *apprehension*, *worry*, *fear*, *terror*, and *panic*, among others; in the boredom box we would find at least *monotony*, *restlessness*, and *ennui*; and in the relaxation box we would find such words as *relief*, *calmness*, *tranquillity*, and *serenity*. The advantage of using just the one chosen word to represent each batch of emotions, wherever we want to talk about pleasant and unpleasant low and high arousal, is that it helps to bring out the unvarying pattern underlying all the varieties of felt arousal. But we shall certainly not always want to restrict ourselves in this way and sometimes it will obviously be preferable to take advantage of the full richness of natural language.

The third point starts from an objection which might be made to the idea that boredom is low in arousal. Some people might say that they feel *intensely* uncomfortable when they are bored, and even tense and agitated. So how do we reconcile the unwanted low intensity of the arousal with the intensity of the unease? The answer must be that there are two different aspects of the situation. The first is that of arousal proper, the second is that of the possible awareness of a discrepancy between the amount of arousal one wants and the amount of arousal one has. Let us call such a discrepancy 'tension'. Then tension represents the feeling that things are not as they ought to be, and that one will have to do something about it. In these terms, tension will be felt any time that arousal is outside its preferred level. Anxiety and boredom therefore have in common that they are both forms of tension, but the tension is produced in opposite ways, in one case because the arousal is too high, and in the other because it is too low. Boredom can, in this way, be quite properly perceived as low in arousal but high in tension.

The concept of tension as defined here is essential if we are to be able to differentiate, as we want to, between arousal level and the comfort or discomfort, pleasure or displeasure which is associated more or less intensely with a given arousal level. The concept of tension also becomes essential when dealing (as we do in later chapters) with other motivational variables, and is therefore one of the central concepts of reversal theory.

A STUDY OF AROUSAL PREFERENCES OVER TIME

One way of exploring the way in which people's arousal preferences actually change over time would be to choose some type of stimulus which, when varied, is either arousing or de-arousing to some degree or another. Then one could trace out their preferences for different values of this stimulus variable, and hence their different arousal preferences, over time, and see whether these are characterized by the fluctuations one would expect on the basis of reversal theory.

One stimulus variable which fulfills this criterion, and which is easy and convenient to use, is that of colour. There is growing evidence that 'hot' colours (i.e. colours like red and orange which are at the long-wavelength end of the spectrum) tend to increase arousal, whereas 'cool' colours (i.e. colours like blue and indigo which are at the short-wavelength end of the spectrum) tend to decrease it. (The evidence is reviewed in Walters, Apter, and Svebak 1982.) So if we were to present people with a range of colours chosen from across the spectrum and ask them to say which one they found the most attractive at a given moment of time, we would have a good indication of the degree of arousal they wanted at that time. And if we repeated this at regular intervals we could map out the way in which their arousal preferences changed over time.

A study along these lines was carried out by Walters *et al.* (1982), using as subjects 75 office workers who were asked to make their colour preference choices at regular periods during their working day. Most of the subjects were asked to do this every quarter of an hour, some for as many as eight working days. The same set of colours was used throughout, these colours being chosen at roughly equal intervals from across the colour spectrum. At the end of the study each subject was asked to rank the seven colours along a scale from the most arousing, through a neutral point, to most de-arousing. Subjects had no difficulty in doing this, and by and large the results across subjects bore out the expected relationship between wavelength and arousal value. However, the point of asking subjects for this assessment was so that each subject's personal colour/arousal rankings could be used in mapping his or her particular arousal preference changes.

The results from this study can be said to provide strong support for the reversal theory position, in contrast to that of optimal arousal theory. For one thing, fluctuations in choices were more obvious than stability, and choices tended to be at or towards one or the other end of the colour/arousal dimension – so that switches from one to the other could be regarded as reversal between opposing levels of arousal preference rather than simply minor adjustments and shifts (which also occurred). Although there were strong individual differences in that some people spent more time at one end of the dimension (e.g. the arousing end) and others spent more time at the other end (e.g. the de-arousing end), and some people reversed more than others, nevertheless this general pattern of change could be observed in most subjects. In Figure 4 the choices of two typical subjects are shown, both of them displaying the characteristics just described, with reversals more frequent in one subject than the other. (In interpreting this figure, it must be remembered that we are dealing here, as intended in this study, with arousal *preference* rather than actual arousal level.)

From the point of view of optimal arousal theory, one would expect frequent distributions of arousal preference choices to be unimodal, that is to peak around a single optimal level somewhere roughly in the middle of the arousal dimension. In contrast, reversal theory would predict a bimodal distribution, with two peaks towards the two ends of the dimension. The data from this study clearly support the reversal theory rather than the optimal arousal theory position in this respect. The frequency distribution of choices for each subject was generally bimodal (the two subjects shown in Figure 4 exemplify this). Although, for statistical reasons, adding bimodal distributions to each other does not necessarily produce new bimodal distributions, nevertheless in this case distributions obtained from grouping those subjects who had been studied over the same periods of time and with the same frequency, were indeed bimodal. This shows clearly the tendency for colour choices to be polarized along the arousal dimension; in fact, and remarkably, on only four occasions was the neutral point on the arousal dimension (represented for most subjects by green) chosen by any of the subjects at any time during the whole period of testing.

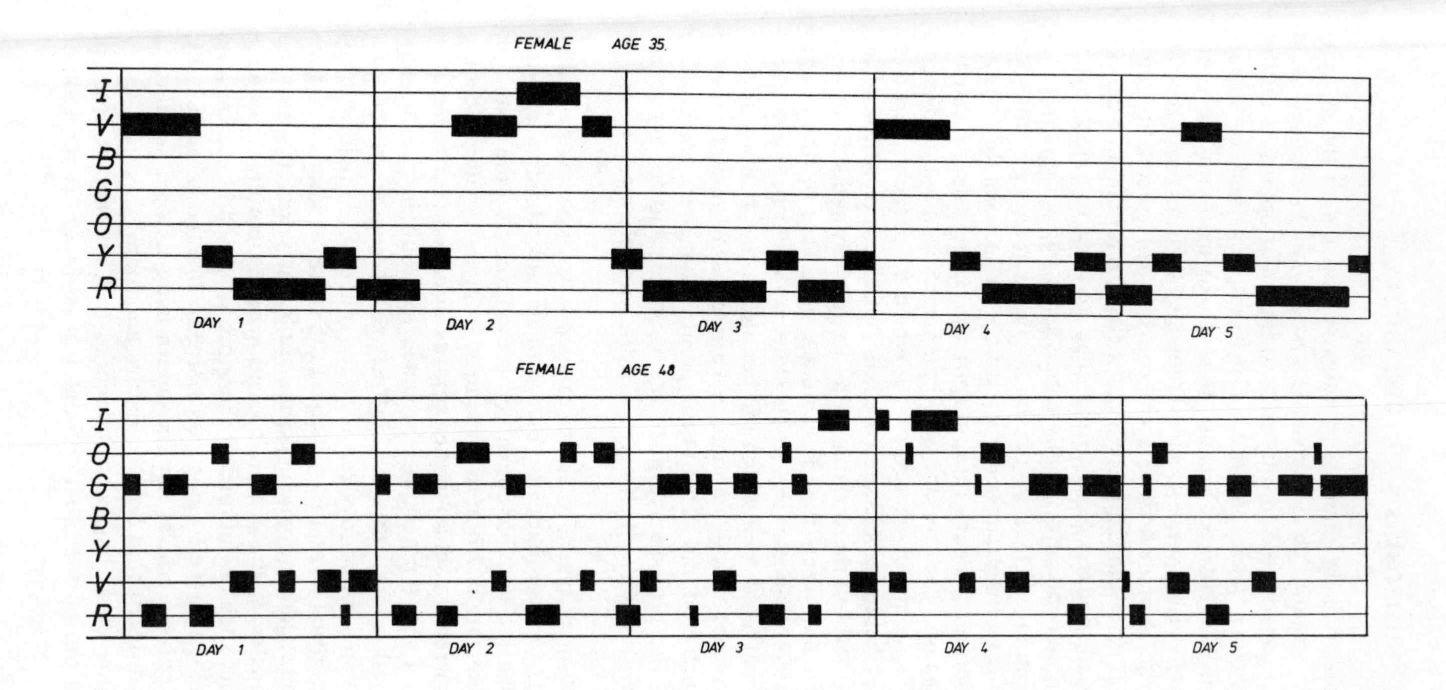

Fig. 4 The colour preferences (and by implication the arousal level preferences) of two different subjects over five days of testing. The position of each of the colours on the vertical dimension is determined by each subject's own rating of each colour in terms of its arousal value, the colour which is most arousing being at the lower end of the dimension, and the most dearousing colour being at the higher end. (These subjects were tested every quarter-hour during the working day.) (After Walters, Apter, and Svebak 1982.)

HOMEOSTASIS AND BISTABILITY

Optimal arousal theory is an example of a theory which is, in the systems theory sense, homeostatic. A homeostatic system can be defined as a system which is so constructed that it tends to maintain one of its output variables within a given range of values. For example a thermostatically controlled room is homeostatic because it tends to maintain the room temperature variable within some specified range, so that the room is never too hot or too cold. A man driving a car can be seen as constituting a homeostatic system since the tendency is for the car to remain in a certain position on the road, not too close to the edge and not too close to the centre markings. The concept originally comes from physiology, where it was coined by Cannon (1932) to depict all those many physiological systems which tend to maintain some variable at a reasonably constant level: body temperature, heart rate, respiration rate, rate of calcium metabolism, and so on. The concept was then generalized within systems theory to cover *all* systems, of whatever type, which act in such a way as to tend towards a specifiable stable state (the range of values constituting the so-called preferred level of the variable). Physiological systems of the type studied by Cannon and others then became a special case of this general type. Of course, maintenance of this stable state can never be guaranteed. There may be a freak cold spell which the heating in the thermostatically controlled room is not strong enough to counter. An animal may be exposed to too much cold and die. But the point is that there is an innate tendency towards the preferred level of the variable, and to counteract changes in the environment which may push the variable away from this level.

This counteraction is typically achieved in control systems (whether naturally occurring or man-made) by means of negative feedback. What happens here is that the variable concerned is monitored by the system in some way, any deviation from the required range of values leading automatically to corrective action in the opposite direction (hence *negative* feedback). Thus, if the temperature becomes too high in the thermostatically controlled room, this will affect some sensor which will automatically turn on a cooling system; if on the other hand the heat drops below the lower required level, this will affect the same, or another, sensor which will turn on the heating. Such systems are 'error actuated' – it is the errors or deviations from the required levels which themselves produce action to counteract such deviation and therefore to maintain the variable at a preferred level within a changing environment. It is the variable itself, therefore, which plays a crucial part in determining its own stability: a clever arrangement discovered both by nature and man.

The idea of homeostasis has been influential in a number of areas of psychology, and it can be seen that optimal arousal theory is yet another homeostatic psychological theory. The variable in this case is arousal level, the preferred level of the variable is somewhere in the middle of the arousal range, and deviations above or below this range prompt activity in the individual designed to shift the arousal back up, or back down, to this desired level. Hence, if arousal falls too low the individual will look for more stimulation; if it goes too high she will attempt to avoid stimulation. In this way there is a strong tendency for the arousal to remain within the desired central range.

Now we have seen that this homeostatic account of the experience of arousal is psychologically inadequate, and an alternative account has been proposed here which appears to fit the facts better. Does this mean that we are proposing something which, from the systems theory point of view, is odd or unlikely, not conforming to the notion of homeostasis in control systems? Far from it. In fact, there is another class of control systems known as *bistable* systems which exactly cover the case of that type of system which reversal theory proposes is involved in the control of arousal levels. Here, instead of the *unistability* of homeostasis (where there is a *single* range of preferred values of the variable) we now see systems of the next degree of complexity in which there are *two* distinct ranges of values which are acceptable. (Indeed, there are more complex systems again with even more ranges of values, all of these together with bistable systems constituting, in contrast to homeostatic systems, what are called *multistable* systems.)

A simple example of a bistable system would be a light switch, since this is constructed, for obvious reasons, in such a way that it tends to be in either the on or the off position, these two positions being stable and other positions between the two being unstable. Thus, if one pushes such a switch it will tend either to fall back to the position it was in before or, if the push is hard enough, to go over completely to the opposite position. Similarly, an automatic door will tend to open completely or remain closed, and intermediate positions will be no more than temporary and move quickly to the open or closed position. In contrast to a thermostatically controlled homeostatic heating system we have the bistable system of British Rail: either the heater comes on, in which case there is an unbearably high temperature in the compartment, or it does not come on at all, in which case one may freeze. Again, there are two stable states, towards one or other of which the system tends to move at all times.

There are plenty of examples of bistability in the psychology of perception. Consider the Necker cube (Figure 5). This figure can be seen in opposite, equally stable ways: as if from slightly underneath, or as if from slightly above. So while one inspects this figure, a reversal occurs from time to time from one way of looking at it to the other, the seeming front plane of the cube moving to the back and the back plane coming forwards. The whole time one looks at it, it appears in one way or the other. There are no

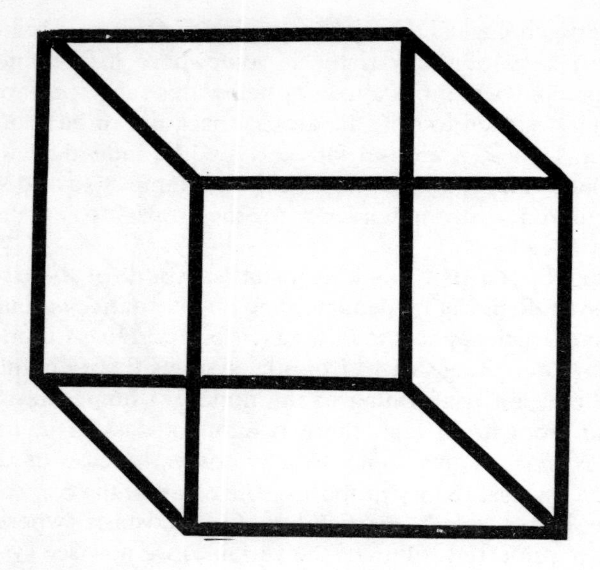

Fig. 5 The Necker cube.

real intermediate positions or mixtures of the two positions, and when a reversal occurs, it occurs rapidly.

Another kind of perceptual example is that of the figure–ground reversal, such as the version shown in Figure 6. Again there are two different ways of looking at the diagram, each of them stable, one in which the white disc is the figure (seeming to sit on top of the hatched background) and one in which it constitutes the perceptual ground (seeming to be an opening through a hatched surround). But from time to time one reverses from seeing it one way to seeing it the other; and the whole time the diagram is seen in one way *or* the other.

These psychological examples remind us that this reversal phenomenon is one of the propensities of the nervous system, and that we should therefore not be surprised to find it in areas of psychology other than perception. Indeed, there is a sense in which there is a direct relationship between this perceptual phenomenon and the metamotivational reversals: in the latter case we see opposite ways of interpreting ambiguous information from the body (i.e. interoceptive information, in this case concerning arousal); in the former we have different ways of interpreting certain kinds of ambiguous information from the outside world (i.e. exteroceptive information which in this case is visual).

Bistable systems come in a variety of forms, and can involve more complicated control mechanisms than homeostatic systems do. This is not the place to go into these technicalities (for which see Apter 1981c; 1982a,

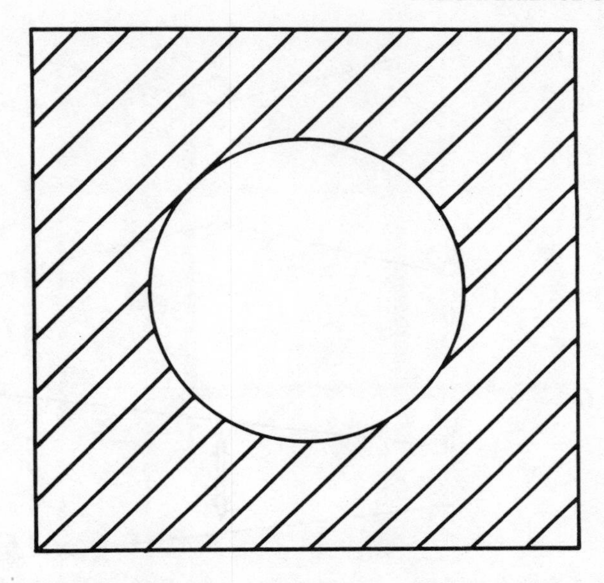

Fig. 6 A figure-ground reversal figure. If you look at this long enough you will see the circle as alternatively in front of, or behind, the hatched area.

Chapter 2). But, specifically, the type of bistability proposed in reversal theory is one in which the two preferred levels are alternatives in the sense that only one is preferred *at a given time*. This contrasts with the light switch where both positions of stability are available at all times. To clarify this, imagine a 'landscape' with a ball which can roll over it, as shown in Figure 7. In (i) in this figure, we see homeostasis represented: there is one stable position, and the ball will tend to come to rest in this position every time after it is moved. In (ii) we see the light switch situation. Here there are two different positions of stability, and hence bistability, and both these positions remain available. Which position the ball in fact comes to rest in will depend on the direction and force of the movement which is imparted to it. In (iii) we see the type of bistability involved in metamotivation. Here the whole landscape takes one form *or* the other, like a seesaw, so that at any given time there is only one stable position, but over time there are two such positions. Each landscape here represents a metamotivational mode, and each metamotivational mode covers the whole area. This corresponds to the way in which the arousal-seeking and arousal-avoidance states each cover the whole arousal dimension, so that even when arousal is at the opposite extreme on the dimension from the preferred level (e.g. boredom), it will tend to be drawn towards the preferred level (e.g. excitement) and to counteract forces which tend to prevent this.

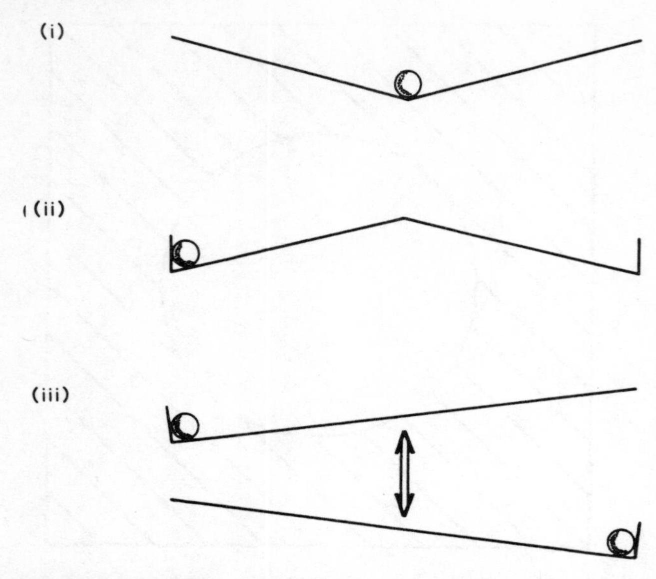

Fig. 7 Three types of stability represented by a ball which can move over a contoured landscape. (i) This represents homeostasis since there is a single resting point. (ii) Here we have bistability, but the areas of stability are fixed. (iii) This is the type of bistability referred to in reversal theory: the whole landscape assumes one shape **or** the other.

For both types of bistability there are two levels of bistability. At one level the landscape is bistable, having two different points of stability. At the other, the position of the ball on the horizontal dimension is also bistable, because it will tend to follow the contours of the landscape. However, at this lower level the bistability cannot be guaranteed, because the external pushes which cause the ball to move may be sufficiently strong to overcome the effects of the landscape. There is a slightly more technical, cybernetic, way of putting this by distinguishing between the level of control and the level of regulation. Control is the process of deciding where the preferred range of values of the variable will be. Regulation is the process of actually bringing the value of the variable into the preferred range. For example, with the thermostat, control is setting the thermostat to a particular desired temperature; regulation is what the system as a whole does to attempt to bring the actual temperature up or down to this desired level. Now in the type of bistability being posited for metamotivation, control is bistable (there are two different, alternative settings) and regulation is also bistable since, over time, the variable will tend to take up these two values rather than others. The control level here corresponds to the level of metamotivation and the regulation level to the level of motivation.

The final points in this chapter, concerning bistability, may seem rather abstract, not to say abstruse. But they are essential to a full understanding of the reversal theory account of the dynamics of conscious experience as they relate to motivation.

3

The Experience of Means and Ends

This contrast between Heinrich's carefulness
and Teddy's easy-goingness, come to look at it,
is I suppose one of the most fundamental in the
world. It reaches to everything.

Mr. Britling Sees It Through
H. G. Wells (1866–1946)

TELIC AND PARATELIC MODES

When we experience our own motivation, an important part of this experience is the amount of arousal which we feel. But it is of course not the whole of it. We also normally experience some particular goal which we have in mind, together with one or more possible ways of reaching it. In other words, the content of the experience of motivation includes not only an intensity component – arousal – but also a directional component consisting of means and ends. We are usually aware of what we want, and how we might get it, as well as of how worked up we are about the whole situation.

In exploring felt arousal, we considered some imaginary situations. Let us now follow the same procedure in relation to means and ends, and think about some cases which fall more or less within everyday experience. Imagine, if you will, the following four situations:

1. You are studying for an examination which it is important to you to pass.
2. You are jumping out of the way of a passing car.
3. You are playing a game of tennis.
4. You are sitting on a beach throwing pebbles into the sea.

Now in each of these cases there is a goal. In the first case it is to pass the examination, in the second to avoid being run over, and in the third to win. The fourth case is perhaps a little more problematic, but if you were asked while you were throwing pebbles into the sea what your goal was, you would no doubt be able to provide some such answer as, 'I am seeing how big a splash I can make', 'I am trying to throw the pebble as far as possible',

'I am trying to hit the wave before it breaks', 'I am attempting to make the stone bounce off the surface of the water', 'I am trying to hit a tin can which is floating there', and so on. And in each case there are also activities undertaken to achieve these goals – activities too obvious for me to need to enumerate them. All this would seem to be thoroughly consistent with the conventional view – or perhaps we should say 'assumption', so little is it examined – that the goal comes first and is primary, while action succeeds it and is secondary. The organism has a goal imposed on it (for example, the biologically imposed goal of eating or drinking) and then selects from its repertoire some activity designed to achieve the goal. To the learning theorist, the animal in the puzzle box has the goal of escaping, and tries a variety of behaviours to achieve this, one of which is eventually successful. To the ethologist, the predator has the goal of finding food, which sets off certain hunting activities which are continued until the prey is caught. There is no need to labour the point: means are selected to achieve ends.

But are they? Or rather, I should say, 'Is this necessarily the case?' Certainly, there is a sense in which most behaviour has a goal. All except the most obviously reflex activity, or (arguably) the most bizarre psychotic behaviour, can be seen as directed towards some goal. But is it true to say that every goal when it appears is primary? Consider again our examples. It would undoubtedly appear to be the case that swotting for an examination is brought about by the need to pass the examination and would not otherwise occur. And in jumping out of the way of a car it is reasonable to suppose that one is doing so for no other reason than to avoid danger. After all, one does not normally hop around in a busy street. But the other two of our four examples raise problems for this assumption of 'goal-primacy'. Take the activity of throwing pebbles into the sea. Surely one does not necessarily first of all say to oneself something like 'I must make a big splash', and then look for a way of doing so. Rather it is more likely that in looking at the pebbles, and perhaps toying with one, the idea of throwing it in the sea arises, and later, having thrown a few pebbles in, and to add to the fun, the idea of making as big a splash as possible arises. But this 'goal' remains arbitrary and dispensable. One might even go so far as to conjecture that it is possible to toss pebbles in the sea without having any real goal at all, that is in an entirely aimless fashion. But even without going this far, one can see that any goals there might be are likely to be highly contrived. In this case, surely it is the activity which is primary and the goal secondary. Rather than being unavoidably forced on the organism in some way, like the goal of finding food, or the human case of filling in tax forms, it emerges freely out of an ongoing activity and serves to develop and extend this activity.

Now let us turn to our remaining example, that of playing tennis. Surely here too, when we come to examine it, the activity is primary and the goal only secondary. To be sure, the goal does not emerge out of the activity in the way making a big splash may emerge out of the activity of pebble throwing. We do not, every time we go onto the tennis court, hit the ball backwards and forwards and then stumble on the idea of scoring points and trying to beat each other. The goal of winning is intrinsic to competitive games like tennis, and is what lends such games their spice. Indeed, such games could hardly be said to take place at all as 'games' without the goal of beating an opponent within the context of an agreed set of rules. Nevertheless, for the player out to enjoy himself on a Sunday afternoon, the goal *is* secondary. The real point of playing is to have some fun, not to beat an opponent. Our notional player did not presumably wake up in the morning with the urge to beat someone, and then decide over breakfast that the best way to do it would be to play tennis. And if he were to lose the game, he would not thereby think that the whole thing had been a waste of time and effort. Nor would he necessarily have refused to play if he thought he would almost certainly lose. In this, the situation is totally unlike that of the person preparing for and taking an examination. For this unfortunate, passing the examination is what counts, and if the examination is failed then this means that all the work leading up to it was indeed wasted. The same may be true of a professional tennis player who loses: the whole episode becomes a total loss, and one which may have important implications for him beyond the game. But for the true amateur the game itself, win or lose, is its own justification. The goal of winning is certainly an essential ingredient of the game, but it is there to provide the organization and direction of the activity, an excuse for the effort and aggression, not as an overriding purpose going beyond the activity itself.

What all this comes to is that not only can the activity serve the goal, but the goal can be used to serve the activity. Sometimes the end is primary and the means are secondary; sometimes the means are primary and the goal secondary. The conventional psychological view, then, is only half right. It overlooks all those occasions when we do things for their own sake or 'for the hell of it' – occasions on which the goal is no more than an excuse or pretext for the activity, or a way of organizing, elaborating, developing or enhancing it. Two of our examples – swotting for an examination and avoiding being run over – exactly fit the conventional view of the goal coming first. The other two – playing tennis and throwing pebbles in the sea – when considered phenomenologically as they are here, provide instances of an inversion of the usual assumptions. Hence, we are confronted with two alternative 'ways of being', one in which the end justifies the means, and the other in which the means justify the end. In other words, as in our exploration of the feeling of arousal, we find that there are two opposite ways of interpreting an aspect of motivational experience, only one of which applies at a given time, with the possibility of switching between one and the other over time. Putting it in this way should make it evident that, once more, we have discovered a pair of metamotivational modes – modes which each interpret in their own way the same motivational content (in this case the relationship of means and ends). And since these interpretations are opposite, the switch from one to the other can again be thought of as a *reversal*.

Let us call the metamotivational mode in which the goal is primary, the 'telic' mode, after the ancient Greek word *telos*, meaning 'an end' or 'goal'. And let us call the opposite mode, in which the activity is primary, the 'paratelic' mode, adding the ancient Greek word *para*, meaning 'alongside', to the word *telic*. Note that the word for 'goal' is still included in the term *paratelic*, which is as it should be, since there is no implication that there is not a goal in this mode. The implication is rather that there is an alternative mode 'alongside' the telic mode, in which goals have a different function.

A good way of determining whether someone is in the telic or paratelic mode would be to ask: Would you give up what you are doing in exchange for having already achieved the goal of what you are doing? In the telic mode the answer would be yes. In working for an examination the work is what has to be done to achieve the end, and if one could pass without it, then in the telic mode one would do so. In the paratelic mode the answer would be no. One would not give up a good afternoon's game of tennis just for the sake of ensuring a win. (And if one would be willing to do so, then *ipso facto* this would imply that the telic mode was prevailing, not the paratelic.)

The natural rewards of the telic and paratelic modes, then, derive from different sources. In the telic mode, pleasure comes primarily from the feeling of movement towards the goal, of progress and improvement, as well as from the attainment of the goal itself. In the paratelic mode, pleasure comes primarily from the activity – from the immediate sensual gratification, from the satisfaction of skilled performance and the kinesthetic sensations which go with it, from the continuing interest in seeing what will happen next, and so on. If the activity is mental, there is the pleasure to be derived from playing with ideas, from imagining different possibilities, and from looking at things in new ways. Pleasure may, of course, also derive from some activity in the telic mode (e.g. from the whiskey one is drinking while studying for an examination) or from attainment of a goal in the paratelic mode (e.g. winning at tennis). But in each case these are 'bonuses', not the *raison d'être* of the action. It is all a question of orientations, of what is most salient or important in experience, and of what is peripheral or marginal. One does not, in the normal way of things, while dancing at a disco, think, 'Strange, I do not seem to have achieved anything for all my effort.' Nor does one, on returning from the dentist, think, 'I wonder why I did that; I did not really enjoy it at all.'

If we think of what is most salient in the phenomenal field, the focus of the field, as constituting the figure, and what is at the fringe as making up the ground, then we can say that in the telic state the goal is the figure and the activity the ground; in the paratelic state it is the activity which is the figure and the goal the ground. Now one of the characteristics of the figure in the phenomenal field is that it remains constant in a changing ground, and this also applies here. If the goal is the figure, as it is in the telic mode, then this means that the activities chosen to lead to it may change but not the goal. Thus, if you are studying for an examination and you feel that the methods you are using are not working, then you can change your methods; but the aim of passing the examination remains unchanged. (Similarly, the animal in the puzzle box may try out various types of behaviour with the single unvarying aim of escape.) If on the other hand you are playing tennis and you are not enjoying the game, then you can stop and do something else instead. (If for some reason you cannot stop, for example your partner will not let you, then the situation becomes a telic one, with the goal of reaching the mutually agreed end of the game.) This kind of relationship is illustrated in Figure 8, which also brings out the way in which a switch from one mode to the other – a reversal – is a kind of figure–ground reversal, not dissimilar to the perceptual figure–ground reversals studied by the Gestaltists.

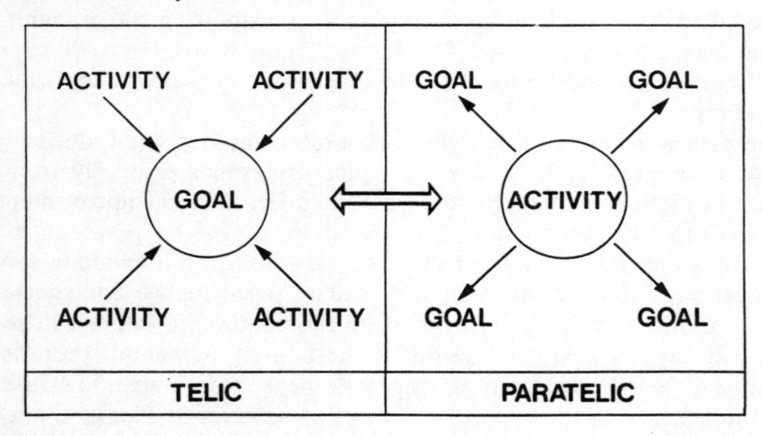

Fig. 8 A schematic representation of the contrasting way in which the relationship between activities and goals is organized in the phenomenal field in the telic and paratelic modes. (After Apter 1984b.)

Up to this point, illustrative situations have been chosen in which a given mode is likely to be associated with a given situation – for example, the telic mode with studying for an examination. But very often the *same* situation will be experienced from within different modes at different times by the same person. Telephoning a friend may on one occasion be a duty call, with the aim of fulfilling an obligation of some kind; on another occasion – even to the same friend – it may be to enjoy a good gossip or have a laugh. In the first case, involving the telic mode, if the friend is not in, then the goal will have to be achieved in some other way, for example by writing a letter, or sending flowers. In the second case, involving the paratelic mode, if the friend is not in, then it is the enjoyment which will have to be achieved in some other way, for example, by telephoning a different friend. To take another illustration, suppose one is going for a walk. In the telic mode there will be a goal which determines the activity, for example, to arrive at an appointment at a particular time. If it starts to look as if one may not arrive in time, then some other action may be taken instead. One might decide to take the bus, for example, or a taxi. On the other hand, the walk may be undertaken in a paratelic frame of mind. Perhaps it is a beautiful day, and although the walk is for its own sake, to give oneself an excuse for it one has decided to walk to a local beauty spot. In this case, though, if it looks as if the goal is too distant in the time available one may simply substitute another goal – to walk to a park which is nearer, for example.

It is even possible to switch from one state of mind to the other in the course of a single continuous action. Using again the example of going for a walk, one may start in the telic mode, but at some point en route realize that one has more than enough time to reach one's destination by the appointed hour. At this stage the goal may temporarily recede into the background and the paratelic mode take over. Now one may start to dawdle and to enjoy the walk in itself and the scenery. But after a while one notices a clock which shows the time to be later than one thought, with the result that one reverts to the telic mode and once more hurries towards one's appointment.

This last example hints at another typical difference between the telic and paratelic modes. In the telic mode there tends to be a future time orientation, since the pleasure of goal achievement lies in the future, perhaps even the distant future. And any pleasure of movement towards a goal depends on progress towards this desired future state. For this reason, too, there will often be planning ahead in the telic mode, and a continual monitoring of progress to ensure that the overall direction continues to lead towards the goal. In the paratelic mode, in contrast, there tends to be a present-time orientation, an emphasis on immediate gratification and pleasure in the here-and-now. Such goals as there are, are likely to be relatively short-term and closely tied to ongoing behaviour. Instead of the rigidity of planning ahead and monitoring progress, there tends instead to be a preference for spontaneity and flexibility, the criterion being the immediate one of 'Does it feel good to do what I am doing?' rather than the more earnest 'Does this take me where I need to go?' The paratelic mode is, one might say, characterized by the three 'imps' of impulsiveness, impetuosity, and improvisation (and sometimes by a fourth: improvidence). If in the telic mode, life seems to be like a game of chess, in which one has to think many moves ahead; in the paratelic mode it is more like a game of roulette; planning is not likely to help, and pleasure (or displeasure) comes from the immediate effects of one's actions. Where the telic mode is careful and constrained, the paratelic tends to be easygoing and casual.

Even this does not quite bring out fully the radical difference between these two ways of being. In the telic state it is not just a question of looking forward towards a given goal, but of tending to see that goal as part of a route to a further goal, and that in turn as but a way-station towards something more distant and perhaps more important again. (The goal of getting dressed and looking smart becomes a subgoal on the way to arriving on time at the interview, which in turn is a subgoal of getting the job, which hopefully leads to the further goal of a better job, and so on.) Calling life a game, even a game like chess, is to some extent to miss the point: in this state of mind life is not a game, it is deadly serious. And this is another way of saying that everything one does is seen as having *significance* beyond itself, as partaking in a whole hierarchy of subgoals and goals. (Hyland, Sherry, and Thacker (1988) suggest that this characteristic of the telic state might be referred to as 'goal coherence'.)

In the paratelic mode, however, life *is* seen as exactly like a game: what one is doing has no significance beyond itself and is done for its own sake. If the telic state is serious-minded, the paratelic state is light-hearted and fun-loving. Rather than every action acquiring its meaning from the way in which it leads towards or away from some important future goal, the activities of the paratelic mode are turned inward on themselves, cut off from the rest of life and encapsulated in their own 'bubbles'. Thus we have the bubble of the tennis court, the bubble of the fairground, the bubble of the casino, the bubble of the pub or bar, the bubble of the discotheque; we have such self-contained episodes as the morning on the beach, the day at the races, the night at the theatre. It is exactly in such spatial and temporal enclaves that the tyranny of the goal is, temporarily, overthrown.

It might have occurred to the reader that what I have been talking about in this chapter is simply the difference between work and play. This is exactly right if these two words are used in the spirit of different states of mind. Unfortunately, both 'work' and 'play' are words which have become conventionally associated with different kinds of activities irrespective of the states of mind of those taking part, and often this convention runs counter to the way that the activities are experienced. Thus, one 'plays' games and 'works' in the office or factory. But for a professional sportsman playing a game, winning or losing may have the most profound significance for him, and his state of mind during play may therefore be more often telic than paratelic. (Some evidence consistent with this is provided by Kerr (1987a).) A research worker in a scientific establishment may be doing her 'work' on some problem of great significance for others (e.g. cancer research), but while actually engaged in the research problem, experience it most of the time as a kind of intriguing intellectual puzzle which she enjoys attempting to solve for its own sake. In other words, she may be preponderantly in the paratelic state of mind. Furthermore, in both cases (the sportsman and the researcher) the state of mind may occasionally switch back and forth during the activity, although *objectively* the activity continues to be seen in the same static once-and-for-all way. It was for reasons such as these that it was necessary to coin the terms *telic* and *paratelic* – to avoid the kind of confusion which would otherwise have arisen from trying to use words defined 'from outside' (and often used in this superficial way by behavioural psychologists, sociologists, and others) for important underlying mental states. In any case, the terms *work* and *play* when used in their normal conventional way cannot properly be applied to many actions, while the terms *telic* and *paratelic* will be applicable to every experience. For example, one cannot really call jumping out of the way of a car to avoid an accident 'work', nor can one really call such activities as watching television, having a drink, or going for a walk, 'play' – or at least not without putting a severe strain on the way in which normal everyday language is used.

It is, therefore, all a question of how one looks at what one is doing 'from inside'. The task itself, or the actions themselves, although they may influence whether the situation will be approached in the telic or paratelic mode, do not determine this. By the same token, it is not possible to decide from the outside alone what metamotivational mode *must* be obtaining. Even in the examples considered at the beginning of this chapter we cannot be *sure* of the individual's state of mind. He may be in the telic mode when playing tennis (for instance, if he is playing for the sake of some serious exercise schedule to improve his health). He may be in the paratelic mode while studying for an examination – if the examination is not especially important but is seen as an amusing challenge. There is no universal and unequivocal relationship between type of task or situation on the one hand and metamotivational mode on the other.

A classic illustration from literature of the different ways in which one can see the same task comes from Mark Twain's *Tom Sawyer*. In a famous scene, Tom has been set by Aunt Polly to whitewashing a fence, a highly unwelcome duty on a nice summer's day. But he has a stroke of inspiration, and as his friends and enemies come past he purports to be so absorbed in the fun of painting the fence that each of them in turn stops to watch and are soon begging to be given a turn. After much apparent reluctance and bargaining for the privilege – for example, one child gives him a piece of blue bottle glass to look through, another a dead rat with a string to swing it with – he finishes up by spending a pleasantly idle afternoon watching others doing his work and counting his gains. As Twain observes: 'If he had been a great and wise philosopher, like the writer of this book, he would now have comprehended that Work consists of whatever a body is obliged to do and that Play consists of whatever a body is not obliged to do. And this would help him to understand why constructing artificial flowers or performing on a treadmill is work, while rolling tenpins or climbing Mont Blanc is only amusement' (1959 edn., p. 22).

A more sombre literary example of the way in which an unwanted activity can be made more desirable may be found in Solzhenitsyn's *One Day in the Life of Ivan Denisovich*, which is about life in a Siberian labour camp in the time of Stalin. Under appalling conditions the prisoners are building the wall of a power station, and usually they do as little as they can get away with. But Solzhenitsyn describes how the the group containing Shukhov, the principal character in the novel, decide spontaneously to do the paradoxical: to do the most they can manage in the time available, and to do it as well as possible. In doing so, since they are now pursuing a voluntary and, in a sense unnecessary, goal they have changed the situation into one which is no longer *governed* by a goal in the way in which it was previously. As a result they start to gain a strange enjoyment from what they are doing. Again we see how the same activity can be construed as play or work depending on whether the goal is experienced as imposed and primary or as freely chosen and secondary.

It has not been my intention at any point in this chapter to imply that the paratelic mode is intrinsically preferable to the telic, or vice versa. Indeed, under normal circumstances, both seem to be essential ingredients of mental health. One should be able to treat serious matters with the gravity which they deserve, but also have a good time when the possibility for this arises. As we have seen, each mode has its own kinds of satisfaction; and each has its own kind of dissatisfaction too. Thus the paratelic mode might seem like a 'fun state', but what this means is that fun is what is wanted in this state, not necessarily that it is what is experienced. And the telic mode might seem like an 'achievement state', but this means that achievement of some goal is what is wanted, not necessarily that it is actually accomplished. This is analogous to the arousal-seeking and arousal-avoidance modes, where each has a pleasant and unpleasant outcome – excitement or boredom in one case, relaxation or anxiety in the other.

AROUSAL AND THE RELATIONSHIP OF MEANS TO ENDS

We are now in a position to be able to take the next step in the argument. Two pairs of metamotivational modes have been established – the arousal-avoidance and arousal-seeking on the one hand, and the telic and paratelic on the other – and the reader may already have noticed a possible relationship between these two pairs emerging. Thus words like *work* and *serious* seem to go with *anxiety*, while words like *play* and *fun* seem to go with *excitement*. Accordingly, the next step is to hypothesize that these two pairs of modes are in fact linked, and specifically that the telic mode is associated with the arousal-avoidance mode, and the paratelic mode with the arousal-seeking mode.

Let us think this through a little. When one is in the telic mode, which means that there is the overall imperative of achieving some goal, then anything which makes this goal more difficult to achieve – a barrier or frustration of any kind – will be likely to increase arousal and be experienced as unpleasant i.e. as anxiety. The same applies to anything which makes the achievement of the goal seem more important or urgent or far-reaching in its consequences. But once a goal is achieved, then arousal will be likely to drop away, and this will be felt as pleasant – as relief or relaxation. Hence, in the telic mode one seems to move up and down the curve defined by arousal-avoidance. Imagine you are a businessman trying to clinch a big deal. As the size of the deal grows, so you become more anxious about bringing it off, especially if there is a deadline looming. And difficulties of various kinds – for example legal hitches – will only serve to increase your anxiety still further. But the moment everything is 'signed and sealed' – your goal is accomplished – you will sigh with relief and may be able to enjoy some well-earned rest.

In the paratelic mode the general idea is to enjoy what one is doing, which means, among other things, to experience it as strongly and sharply and intensely as possible. Now a central part of the intensity of the experience will be the intensity of the arousal, and therefore one would expect the greater the arousal the better. Doing something that one really enjoys is 'exciting' or even 'exhilarating', whereas failing to be 'lit up' by it eventually produces 'boredom'. In the paratelic mode, therefore, one seems to move up and down the boredom–excitement dimension of the arousal-seeking mode. Consider the case of sexual intercourse. Healthy sexual behaviour occurs when both partners are enjoying the experience in itself as a kind of playful and exploratory behaviour. Biologically there is a goal, and a supremely import one – that of conception. But phenomenologically, functional sexual behaviour seems to require a certain playfulness in which long-term implications and serious aims are kept firmly in the background; the foreground consists of the activity itself and all the sensations and feelings which go with it. This activity is made as intense and prolonged as possible, and the increasing arousal is experienced as sexual excitement. If, on the other hand, there is no heightened arousal, then boredom will be experienced and some other means may be added to try to obtain the arousal needed – for instance, through becoming aggressive, breaking taboos, or adding elements of unexpectedness and surprise.

This relationship between arousal preference and seriousness/playfulness can be illustrated from the responses which subjects made to questions about the way in which they experienced a psychophysiological experimental situation in which their task was to play a video car-driving game successfully. (This experiment by Apter and Svebak (1986) will be described in Chapter 5.) Some subjects were clearly in the telic state during the experiment. For example, a female subject reported that 'I felt serious. Because it was an experiment I wanted to behave in a way as near as possible to real life; I wanted to do as I really would do. I did not want to treat it as a game.' She was also concerned that when all subjects were paid a week after the experiment, other subjects would know how well she had done from the amount she was paid (which supposedly related to success of performance). In this way she saw the experiment in the context of further important goals, both social (that she would have contributed to serious research) and personal (in terms of self-esteem). When asked about the arousal which she had experienced in the experiment she reported that she had felt various levels, both 'up' and 'down', but that she had preferred to feel 'down'. When asked further about how she had felt when she was 'up' she replied, 'I hated it' and followed this with a grimace.

In contrast, another subject typified those who had experienced the experiment in a paratelic state of mind. He said that he enjoyed the experiment which was, in fact, his 'nicest hour so far this week'. Although he felt anxious initially when the electrodes were attached to his arms for physiological recording purposes, after that he enjoyed feeling aroused. Indeed, he admitted that 'I tried for a period to get more excitement by just missing the cars coming towards me.' In other words, the situation (after a short initial period when he felt threatened) was simply a game for him, and the fact that he was willing to risk making errors for the sake of immediate excitement shows that he was not seeing his performance as having any important long-term significance.

This does not mean that it will always be the case that in the telic frame of mind arousal will in fact be sought, or in the paratelic that high arousal will be searched out or created. After all, in the telic mode, high arousal may be tolerated for the sake of movement towards the goal. The actor may put up with his stage fright rather than give up the aims of his career; a businessman may know that he is often going to feel anxious but accept this in the knowledge that this is all part and parcel of his way of life; a sportsman may be pleased about the 'butterflies in the stomach' feeling before going out to play, in the belief that he needs to be keyed up to perform well. As Boekaerts (1988) has pointed out, a pupil may take on a difficult learning task, even though it causes anxiety, because it is important to him. In the paratelic mode, low arousal may be tolerated if it is compensated for by strong sensations of other kinds. One may find the low arousal of sunbathing acceptable in the paratelic mode, provided there are intense feelings of heat, and perhaps pleasantly strong smells of sea and sand and other sensations. For these reasons, the relationship between the two pairs of modes is a complex one. According to this analysis, we may expect that high arousal will always be unpleasant in the telic mode and low arousal in the paratelic mode, but that, nevertheless, high arousal will not necessarily be sought at all times in the former or low arousal in the latter.

There is a sense, therefore, in which we can regard the arousal-avoidance mode as part of the telic mode. But this relationship is to be understood as dealing with the types of emotions which can be felt in each mode – some degree of anxiety or relaxation can be felt in the telic mode but not in the paratelic; some degree of excitement or boredom can be felt in the paratelic mode but not in the telic. It does not imply, however, that the individual will necessarily seek out the preferred level of arousal at a given moment, since this may be overridden by other telic or paratelic considerations.

One other small point here: it might be objected that it is perfectly possible to be relaxed in the paratelic mode, despite what I have said. For example, it might be pointed out that it is perfectly possible to play games like tennis for relaxation, or to relax by watching horror films; but this is really no more than a different use of language. In everyday usage, *relaxation* seems to have two distinct meanings. One is the meaning which I have been using above, that is, pleasantly low arousal. The other is something like being unthreatened, removed from real life problems, looking for entertainment, 'off-duty' and the like – in other words, it means effectively being in the paratelic mode. It is in this latter sense that people use the word in such phrases as 'playing tennis for relaxation'. After all, they do not intend to imply by this that the game is being played languidly from a deckchair with a drink in one hand and a racquet in the other. In this sense the supposed objection turns out in fact to constitute further support for one of the concepts of reversal theory, that of the paratelic mode.

In a continuation of the research described in the previous chapter using colour preference as an index of arousal preference, the study was repeated, but with the addition of a simple adjective checklist which was administered each time the subject was asked to make the colour preference choice. The point of this new study was to see whether the colour choice might represent the telic-paratelic distinction as well as the arousal-seeking/arousal-avoidance distinction, as it should do if the analysis just given is correct. That is, if the arousal-avoidance mode is associated with (or part of) the telic mode, then we should expect a telic adjective to be chosen at the same time as a cool colour representing a preference for low arousal. Similarly, if the arousal-seeking mode is associated with (or part of) the paratelic mode, then we would expect a paratelic adjective to be chosen at the same time as a warm colour representing a preference for a high level of arousal.

In this new study (Walters *et al.* 1982) there were forty-one subjects, none of whom had taken part in the previous study. They were all either office workers, as before, or members of the staff of a library. The same set of colour stimuli was used, and subjects were tested every quarter of an hour for a period of four hours in their place of work. As in the earlier research, the arousal value of each colour was determined for each subject individually, and it was this personal value which was used in the analysis. The adjective checklist consisted of three sets of adjectives, of which the subject had to choose one from each set to describe himself or herself at the time of the colour choice: (1) playful/serious, (2) spontaneous/planning ahead, (3) bored/excited/anxious/relaxed. The first adjective of (1) and (2) of course is the paratelic one, and the first two adjectives of (3). Because the adjective in each case is not about a preference (unlike the colour choice), but rather a description of the current state, both the desirable and undesirable emotions in the anxiety-avoidance and arousal-seeking states have to be included in list (3), since either are possible at any given time. Hence there are four adjectives in this particular set.

As far as colour preference was concerned, the same pattern of choices towards the ends of the colour/arousal dimension was observed as in the first study, with fairly frequent reversals from one end to the other, so that the distribution of choices, as before, tended to be bimodal rather than unimodal. This again lent support to the reversal theory, rather than the optimal arousal, interpretation of the relationship between arousal level and hedonic tone. The choice of adjectives showed that preference for an arousing colour was associated with either the word *bored* or the word *excited*, while preference for a de-arousing colour was associated with either the word *anxious* or the word *relaxed*. (An analysis of variance revealed highly significant F scores for these interactions.) This showed that the choice of colour was indeed related to an arousal *preference* rather than symbolizing the actual level of arousal, since both *bored* and *excited* indicate a preference for high arousal whether or not it is being experienced, and *anxious* and *relaxed* likewise both imply a preference for low arousal. It can be inferred, therefore, that the colour choices were functional in helping to change arousal levels in the desired directions, and this is why they were chosen, rather than being merely symbolic of a current level of arousal. This finding is important to the study, because it supports an assumption on which the whole investigation depended.

So far, so good. Now we can turn to the main question: the relationship between the telic/paratelic adjectives and colour choice. Here it was found that de-arousing colours were indeed preferred when adjective choice indicated the telic state, that is, when the subject chose the adjective *serious* rather than *playful*, and *planning ahead* rather than *spontaneous*. Similarly, arousing colours were preferred when adjective choice indicated the paratelic state (the reverse of the previous choices of adjective). When an analysis of variance was carried out, the F scores revealed that in both cases (i.e. serious/playful and planning ahead/spontaneous) these interactions were the most significant effect, and were highly significant. The

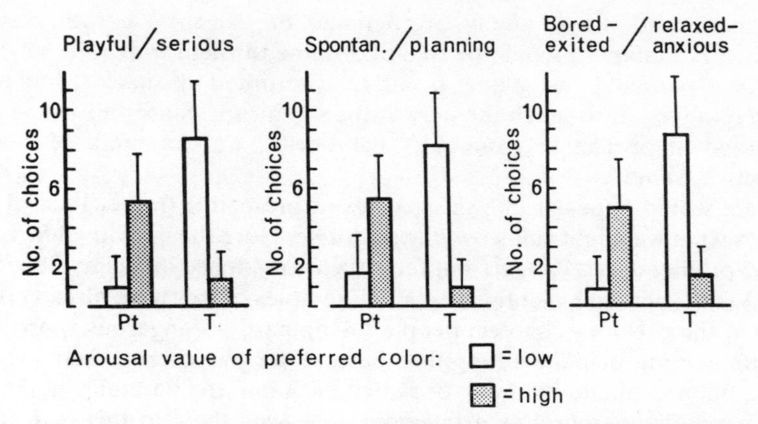

Fig. 9 The mean number of choices per subject of each adjective, when combined with choice of a low-arousal or a high-arousal colour. In each of the three histograms the paratelic adjective means (and standard deviations) in relation to both types of colour choice are shown on the left and the telic on the right. (After Walters, Apter, and Svebak 1982.)

relationship of colour choices to all the mode adjectives in this study is described by means of the histograms shown in Figure 9.

This evidence clearly provides support for the idea of an association between the telic and arousal-avoidance modes on the one hand, and the paratelic and the arousal-seeking modes on the other. That is, it shows that serious-mindedness, planning ahead, and preference for low arousal do indeed seem to go together, as do playfulness, spontaneity, and preference for high arousal.

SAFETY FRAMES AND PARAPATHIC EMOTIONS

One of the differences between the telic and paratelic modes, to which attention was drawn earlier, is the tendency of the telic mode to connect with real and important life problems and the paratelic mode to cut off from these same problems. In the telic mode one is aware of the possible long-term implications of one's actions, and one's present actions acquire significance from this wider perspective. In the paratelic mode one tends to see one's actions (realistically or not) as having little or no importance beyond themselves.

One of the metaphors used earlier to represent the paratelic mode was that of a bubble, but there is one respect in which this metaphor might be misleading. In the paratelic mode one is, of course, not cut off from the whole world, only from those aspects of the world which would otherwise be experienced as genuinely problematic or exigent. A rather more satisfactory metaphor would be that of a frame through which the world is seen in a particular way, like a pair of rose-tinted spectacles, but ones which remove not so much the ugly as the significant. Since this frame acts as a kind of protection from the 'real world', we can think of it as a protective frame.

There would appear to be three kinds of protective frame. First of all, there is what we might call a *confidence frame*. Here the individual faces up to real problems and dangers but feels such confidence in facing them that they do not seem like genuine threats. Examples of this have already been given in the previous chapter: people taking part in dangerous sports like mountaineering or parachuting use the real danger to raise their arousal levels, but are able to maintain or switch back into the paratelic mode and experience their arousal as excitement. The way they do this is through feeling confident in their own abilities, the safety of their equipment, and the reliability of those sharing their risks with them.

A second kind of protective frame can be labelled a *safety-zone frame*. Here the individual feels himself to be, as it were, encapsulated within a zone which is remote from risk and threat. Unlike the confidence frame, where risk is recognized as present but protected against, in the safety zone there seems to the individual to be no danger at all which might call for protection. In this case, arousal has to be generated in ways other than through confronting danger. In fact, this category covers all those situations in which one becomes so enthralled and absorbed in what one is doing that one becomes totally unaware of a world outside or the way in which one's activity might relate to long-term problems and issues. Illustrations might include the research worker absorbed in his exploration, the lovers with no thought for anyone or anything other than pleasuring each other, the computer addict hacking, the fisherman fishing, and the painter painting. The thrill and excitement are intrinsic to the situation and the situation is seemingly 'off-line' from the problematic world of everyday life.

There is another major subcategory under the heading of 'safety-zone frame'. Sports and games of all kinds provide both ready-made safety-zones and their own forms of arousal generation. Usually in sport there is some specially demarcated area – the cricket pitch, the tennis court, the golf course, the gridiron – and these provide clear-cut enclaves within which the problems of the rest of the world are not allowed to enter. Each sport also has its own system of rules which help to construct a psychological space within which only certain kinds of things can happen; and these are known in advance and controlled by referees or umpires. The effect of all this is to produce a kind of safety zone. Of course there can be no guarantee that the problems of the real world will not intrude – there is always the possibility of encroachment. Thus, one may be injured while playing; and for the professional, as we have already noticed, the implications of winning or losing will be likely to connect the game back to the world outside. But by and large, especially for amateur players, sports would appear to be a particularly successful way of providing a protective frame to order. Then within this frame excitement can be derived from the competition and confrontation, the surprise of novel moves, and the outcome which remains unknown until the end.

The third and final kind of protective frame is what one might call the *detachment frame*. Here the individual participates in what is going on, but only as an observer. This does not imply that she is detached emotionally, but rather that she is detached from the action. There is, therefore, no goal which she herself has to achieve, or danger which she herself has to avoid; and therefore she is protected from the need to do anything. But she can observe others attempting to achieve goals or avoid dangers. Through empathy and identification she can become aroused, but the presence of the protective frame, and consequently the paratelic mode, means that the arousal can be enjoyed.

The activity which the individual observes can be real – for example, she may slow down to look at an accident on the motorway, enjoy watching people quarrelling, or be fascinated by catastrophes on the television news. The observed action can also, of course, take place within a safety zone, as it does when the individual is a spectator at some sporting event. But perhaps the most prevalent way in which people enjoy the detachment frame is through fiction of every kind: novels, films, plays, television series, epic poems, opera. Like the safety zone of sport, some of these cases also involve a special zone: this time an observation zone. In particular, the theatre and the cinema both provide distinctive cues which turn them into their own glittering enchanted zones, seemingly detached from the real world of the mundane and the ordinary.

Thinking about the way in which fiction is experienced leads us to another of the tenets of reversal theory, and one which seems at first sight to be rather surprising, but which becomes evident once one's attention has been sufficiently drawn to it. This is that all high arousal emotions are enjoyed in the paratelic mode, not just excitement; and this is true even if these are emotions which are supposed to be unpleasant. In watching a play or reading a novel we may experience a variety of 'negative' emotions – such as anger, horror, grief, contempt, disgust – and, within the detachment frame, we enjoy them. Why else would we go to watch tragedy, horror films, family dramas, 'weepy' movies, and the rest? The negative emotions in these cases, and indeed in all of fiction, are not there simply to be tolerated: they are the principle vehicles of our pleasure. Thus the best moment in the horror film is the moment of shock; in the family drama it is the moment of disclosure of a scandal which has been kept secret; in the romantic film it is the moment of pathos when the heroine dies. Without these moments when we are moved or thrilled, however supposedly distressing the particular emotion, we would feel cheated.

It would seem that, whatever the source of arousal and whatever the emotion, in the paratelic mode it will be enjoyed if it is sufficiently intense, just as a lack of emotion of any kind will be disliked in this state of mind. If this were not true, then presumably fiction of every type would disappear from human culture, along with fairgrounds, casinos, bullrings, circuses, tabloid newspapers, and many other institutions for diversion and entertainment.

These negative emotions, which take on an enjoyable quality in the paratelic mode, are known in reversal theory as 'parapathic' emotions, from the ancient Greek *pathos* meaning 'a feeling' or 'emotion', and *para* meaning, as we have already seen, 'alongside'. (In fact, the term *parapathic* helps to emphasize their relationship to the paratelic mode.) These are emotions which exist alongside their natural counterparts in the telic mode, and go by the same name as their telic 'twins', but which, in the paratelic mode, have an inverted relationship to hedonic tone. Many of these emotions, of course, are difficult to experience at all in the paratelic mode, the cause of the emotion normally being sufficient to induce or maintain the telic mode along with the arousal of the emotion. If the protective frame is strong enough, however, it would appear that there is no emotion which cannot be experienced in its parapathic form – and there can surely be no emotion which has not been experienced and enjoyed in parapathic form through fiction. What this comes to is that the detachment frame is the strongest protective frame of all. While in principle any emotion can be experienced in parapathic form within the confidence frame or safety zone frame, it would seem that the full range of parapathic emotions can only normally be experienced with any frequency through the distancing effect of detachment. Even anxiety, that quintessential telic emotion, can be translated into parapathic 'anxiety' through the eyes of the detached observer.

4

Reversal and Dominance

. . . the present pleasure,
By revolution lowering, does become
The opposite of itself

Anthony and Cleopatra
William Shakespeare (1564–1616)

INDUCING REVERSALS

While reading the previous two chapters, a question has probably been nagging at you. If you were able to put it to me, it might take something like the following form: 'It's all very well to keep talking about reversals, as if they just happened, but what *causes* these reversals? Surely reversals themselves need to be explained before you can use the concept to explain anything else.' This is a valid question and we should therefore examine what factors might play a part in inducing reversal between metamotivational modes. Let us do so, as before, by starting from some concrete examples of an everyday kind which you should be able to recognize from your own experience – if not in the exact form presented here, at least in a closely analogous type.

1. You suddenly hear a loud and inexplicable crashing noise from the corridor outside the room you are sitting in. You rush to the door, your heart pounding, to discover that someone has dropped a tin tray and no one has come to any harm.
2. You are playing golf and having a pleasantly enjoyable afternoon. However, something has gone wrong with your putting which means that, although you are playing your other shots well, you are losing every hole. The whole thing becomes infuriating to you, and you determine that, whatever else happens, you *are* going to get your putting right before the game is over.
3. You have taken a day off and are working on something that needs doing at home, a chore that you do not enjoy in itself, but which you feel must be done – such as getting the garden into shape, or decorating the kitchen. After a while, and for no particular reason, you feel like doing something to enjoy yourself, such as watching television or having a drink.

In the first example we see something happening which is interpreted, in the lack of further information, as potentially threatening to oneself or someone else. Has there been an explosion? Has someone fallen down? Is anyone hurt? Is whatever has happened going to be repeated? The threat produces a goal which overrides any other goal or activity which you may have been engaged in before, the new goal being that of avoiding danger. This may mean finding out first what the danger is and may also include helping anyone else who may be in danger. But the result is that, if you were not in the telic mode before, you will have been switched into it by the event.

This is an example of a type of reversal which we may refer to as *contingent* – it is contingent upon some environmental event or situation occurring. Such events consist of all those things that happen, or aspects or contexts of things that happen, which, cognitively interpreted by the individual, bring either a goal or an activity to the focus of the phenomenal field.

Some events or circumstances will almost universally produce the telic mode in anyone who is subjected to them – for example, a loud crashing noise, as in our example, will presumably induce this mode in nearly everyone. Others are more dependent on individual quirks of cognitive interpretation; for example, some people seeing a large fish beneath them while swimming in the sea would feel threatened, others would not. If a threat is perceived to be sufficiently menacing, then, it will induce the telic mode. So will a duty, if it is seen as sufficiently important and unavoidable, thus bringing the obligation involved to the focus of the phenomenal field. Completing a day's work, paying back a debt, fulfilling a contract, honouring a promise, filling in tax forms, sending a thank-you letter, visiting someone in hospital, seeing the bank manager when requested to do so – these are all examples of duties which it is reasonable to suppose will normally induce the telic mode through contingent reversal.

To induce the paratelic mode we see the inverse process: the removal of threat or duty. In the first example given above, that of the loud noise which turns out not to represent a serious threat after all, we may suppose that the discovery that the loud noise was caused by something trivial will induce the paratelic state. One may even enjoy the residual high arousal in this case through laughter. (As we shall see later, humour is essentially a paratelic emotion.) Similarly, the sudden removal or completion of a duty may itself induce the paratelic state – after finishing sitting an examination one will repair to the pub or a bar.

All this discussion applies equally to the arousal-avoidance and arousal-seeking modes associated with the telic and paratelic modes. A threat will induce arousal avoidance, and with it anxiety along with telic goal orientation; but suddenly overcoming the threat may produce excitement, as discussed in Chapter 2, along with the paratelic mode. A duty will also induce anxiety avoidance, and whether anxiety or relaxation is actually experienced will depend on how far one is 'on top of' what one has to do. The lack of any duty, on the contrary, will produce arousal seeking and either boredom or excitement, depending on what one can find to do in the absence of an imposed and unavoidable goal.

As well as these obvious *events*, there may be more enduring *conditions* which tend to induce the telic or paratelic modes when they are brought to bear on the individual. These can also be included under the same heading of contingency. In other words, there are, picking up on a theme from the last chapter, all the different settings which, on entering them, exert a strong force in one direction or the other. Law courts, police stations, hospitals, dentists' waiting rooms, headmasters' studies, bank managers' offices, churches and chapels, may all induce the telic mode in most people. Fairgrounds, casinos, public houses and bars, betting shops, theatres, cinemas, restaurants, sports grounds, parks, and a host of other settings will strongly tend to induce the paratelic mode. And each individual may have his or her own individual settings which induce one or the other mode. For example, to induce the paratelic mode these may include a favourite cafe, the lounge at home, or the toilet. To induce the telic mode, they may include such settings as the office or place of work, a particular dark alley, or one's mother-in-law's house.

One further, more subtle, type of contingent effect may be the nonverbal cues people give each other in the course of their transactions. Thus, a smile says, 'I am not going to threaten you', and will therefore tend to induce the paratelic mode. Likewise, laughter in a group says 'This is a place where it is perfectly proper, indeed expected, for you to be in the paratelic mode.' On the other hand, a tense look or a frown will say, 'Our interaction should take place in the telic mode; we are dealing with serious matters.'

What these different factors have in common is that they all, in their different ways, insert or remove one of the types of protective frame discussed in the previous chapter. A sudden loud noise removes, at least momentarily, the confidence frame and the feeling of physical invulnerability which accompanies us much of our lives; but the discovery that the noise does not presage any real danger allows the frame to reassert itself. The various settings that we move into and out of during our daily lives bring to bear prefabricated safety-zone or detachment frames – or alternatively push us without protection into confrontation with duty or danger. Gestures, facial expressions, and the like also provide cues which help us to determine how we shall construe the situations we are in and whether or not we shall see them as cut off from the world of real dangers and duties.

The second of the situations you were asked to consider at the beginning of this chapter leads us to a second major type of factor in triggering a reversal: *frustration*. In the example given of problems with putting on the golf course, we see a paratelic state of mind giving way to the telic under conditions of mounting frustration. Failure to achieve what was, initially, simply one of the goals supporting the activity, builds up until achieving the goal comes to outweigh the activity itself and becomes temporarily of overriding importance. *Ipso facto*, this makes the situation telic. Along with this reversal of paratelic to telic we would expect to see the excitement of the game converted into anxiety that the goal will not be attained; that is, we expect to see a concomitant reversal from arousal seeking to arousal avoidance.

Equally, frustration can help to bring about a reversal *from* the telic *to* the paratelic mode. Imagine that you are making no headway against some serious problem. Suppose, for example, that you are arguing the case, on some issue which is important to you, at a committee meeting – but you seem to be making little progress in convincing anyone else. As the argument continues you become increasingly frustrated by everyone else's stupidity or malevolence, until a point is reached at which you suddenly find yourself fantasizing goal achievement, or playing with ideas of what you would like to do to other members of the committee, or seeing the funny side of things, or even just becoming more interested in a doodle you are drawing in the margin of your papers. All of these would be examples of a paratelic way of looking at matters in which the unachievable goal loses its centrality in the scheme of things and is replaced instead by ways of gaining immediate amusement or gratification, and even excitement.

A third major cause of reversal is exemplified in the third example given at the beginning of the chapter, that of taking time off from the chore of decorating or gardening to do something you enjoy. Here there is no obvious change in external conditions which might bring about the change, and the reversal from the telic mode cannot therefore be classified as contingent. Also, although it is always possible to be frustrated in such tasks as gardening or interior decoration, we shall assume that this is not occurring in this case. What we see is something with which we are all familiar in everyday life – a seemingly gratuitous switch from a serious mood to a more playful one. And of course such a change can occur equally in the opposite direction, from playful to serious; one can suddenly get fed up with what now seems like the trivial, the arbitrary, the time-passing diversion, and find oneself longing to 'get stuck into' something solid and worthwhile. In this case the reversal would have been from the paratelic to the telic.

It might be thought that the reason for the change of activity in the illustration we have been considering, of gardening or home decorating, is simply that one has become physically tired and needs to rest. But if this were the case it would explain only a change to a more physically restful activity which might remain telic (like sitting comfortably attending to bills), not to a more playful one. Indeed, it is possible to conceive of a change from the serious goal-oriented activity to an equally, or even more strenuous, playful one: like practising one's golf swing, or going for a run. And, of course, when such apparently gratuitous change operates in the other direction, it does not necessarily occur when one wants to do something *more* physically strenuous. One might get bored with playing tennis, and feel a need to get back to doing something a bit more important, and this might be more physically demanding (moving furniture) or less (filling in tax forms). In other words, the question of how much energy one feels oneself to have may well determine a change from a less to a more taxing activity, or vice versa, but does not explain those changes which involve metamotivational reversals. Obviously something else is at work.

This something else is postulated in reversal theory to be *satiation*. The idea is that there is an internal dynamic which leads naturally and inevitably to reversal, unless something else happens (e.g. an environmental event) to bring about the reversal sooner. An analogy would be to the waking–sleeping cycle. After one has been asleep for long enough, one will wake up – unless one has already been woken by a noise or for some other reason. And when one has been awake for long enough, one will naturally go to sleep. So the theory suggests that there is a kind of underlying rhythm which leads backwards and forwards between the telic and paratelic modes (and in conjunction with this, between the arousal-seeking and arousal-avoidance modes) – a rhythm which is typically interrupted and overridden by other forces in everyday life, but which surfaces from time to time in the absence of other agents for change. One way of conceptualizing this is to think of some kind of satiation building up over time which increasingly facilitates reversal and which, when it becomes strong enough, induces a reversal on its own. We may suppose that it then dissipates, and starts to build up all over again, in the opposite direction, eventually being strong enough by itself to produce a new reversal. The resulting reversal, when it occurs in this way, seems to be gratuitous because there is no obvious external event or change to which it can be attributed.

This phenomenon of metamotivational satiation has been investigated under laboratory conditions by Lafreniere, Cowles, and Apter (1988). Subjects in this experiment (psychology undergraduates) were asked to spend two hours using a microcomputer, ostensibly as part of an investigation of personality and attitudes to computers. Two types of materials were provided for them to use: a set of teaching programs on statistics (and the subjects were all taking an examined course on statistics) and a varied set of video games. The assumption, which was confirmed to be the case for 29 of the 36 subjects by means of rating scales administered after the experimental task, was that the statistics programs would be experienced in a serious telic frame of mind and the video games in a playful paratelic state by each subject. Changing from a video game to a statistics program, or vice versa, could therefore be taken as a *prima facie* indication of metamotivational reversal in these 29 subjects. Subjects were given complete freedom during their two hours with the computer to decide exactly which programs they would use, in which order, and how long they would stick with each program before changing to another one of the same, or a different, type. It was therefore possible to observe the pattern of changes displayed by each subject over this time period. Since the situation remained constant, and each subject worked uninterruptedly in a bare room containing only the necessary equipment and facilities, switches between types of program could not be attributed to the occurrence of environmental events, that is to contingency. What they *were* due to was elucidated by means of questionnaires (including the rating scales referred to above) and detailed interviews with each subject following the experimental task.

The results showed clearly that switches did occur between the telic and paratelic types of material under these unchanging conditions. Over all the 29 subjects used in the analysis, the range of such switches was from 0 to 9, with a mean of 2.9. (The fact that three subjects kept to the same type of material throughout indicated that such switching was not an artefact of the situation.) In response to the post-task questionnaire and interview, a few of these changes between the two types of material could be attributed to voluntary decision which had nothing to do with metamotivational reversal. For example, many subjects early in their sessions decided to look at both types of program in order to explore the alternatives – either for reasons of serious telic planning or playful paratelic curiosity. But the majority of changes did go with, and reflected, metamotivational reversal. Many of these reversals turned out to be due to frustration with the program currently in use. But many of the others could not be accounted for in any way other than satiation, and subjects' reasons for these reversals were also consistent with this interpretation: they found themselves wanting to change for no good reason and it was something that just seemed to happen to them. As might be expected, the proportion of such satiation-induced reversals tended to increase as the session progressed for each subject.

It is presumably because of this factor of satiation that one can find oneself confronting the same situation at different times in different frames of mind, for instance sometimes dealing with some unvarying aspect of one's work in a playful way while at other times being serious about it. This would appear to be an intrinsic part of the complexity of human nature, and something which is difficult to explain in terms other than those provided by reversal theory. So-called situation-specific, or 'situationalist' theories can explain why people behave in inconsistent ways – always being kind to colleagues but cruel to pets, for example – by arguing that each situation may call forth, perhaps because of previous learning, different aspects of an individual's personality. As can be seen, reversal theory goes well beyond this by explaining how people can be inconsistent with themselves *under the same circumstances*, as well as under different circumstances, something which we all recognize from our own lives. This *principle of inconsistency* is a central feature of reversal theory and one of the ways in which it paints a more lifelike and less 'wooden' picture of human behaviour and experience than other theories of personality are able to do.

There may be other types of factor which can help to bring about a reversal, but any complete account will have to make reference to at least the three major categories listed here, namely: contingency, frustration and satiation. Presumably, at any given time influences from each of these (and, in the case of contingency, influences from a number of different sources within the category) will together be acting with or against each other, to facilitate or inhibit reversal at that time. For a reversal actually to occur, the forces for change must then, together, be stronger than the forces resisting change. Often it must be the case that one particular factor will be strong enough on its own to overthrow any opposition (e.g. the contingent effect of a sudden loud noise, or satiation when it has built up to a strong enough level), but more frequently the outcome will be the result of the balance of the forces acting for or against reversal.

One implication of this analysis is that metamotivational reversal is not something which is under conscious voluntary control. One cannot change one's metamotivational mode in the same direct way that one can raise one's arm. This does not mean, however, that the reversal process cannot be brought effectively under control through *indirect* means. Just as one can make oneself perspire by going somewhere hot, one can induce a mode by confronting oneself with circumstances likely to bring about a reversal to that mode. For example, if one wants to induce the paratelic mode in oneself, settling down in front of the television set may have the desired effect; if one wants to induce the telic mode, sitting at one's desk may be sufficient. Even focussing deliberately on certain frightening or reassuring images or ideas may 'do the trick'. But one can never guarantee that one will be able to induce a reversal through such priming, since the contrary forces (e.g. coexisting environmental conditions) may be too powerful. And in any case, even if the reversal process is brought under conscious control in this way, it remains indirect and to this extent precarious.

Although it might be possible to influence metamotivational reversal through cognitive means, this does not imply that metamotivation is simply another name for cognitive interpretation or that reversal theory is really a part of cognitive psychology. Certainly reversal theory is consistent with the classic research of Schachter and Singer (1962), showing that different arousal levels (induced through the injection of adrenaline) when interpreted in different ways (suggested by environmental cues) lead to different emotions. But within reversal theory, this is a special case. From the reversal theory perspective, how one interprets arousal, and means–ends relationships, and other aspects of motivation to be looked at in later chapters, depends not so much on the cognitive interpretation of specific contents of experience, as on the *whole structure* of the phenomenal field. This larger structure *may* be induced at particular times by particular contents when suitably interpreted, such as the loud noise interpreted as danger. But it may also be induced by extra-cognitive factors – especially satiation, which is entirely independent of cognitive processes. Metamotivation, therefore, is something other than cognition, at times being influenced by cognitive factors, at others overriding cognition and even determining cognitive interpretation. For example, if one is in the telic mode one will tend to interpret some ambiguous event as threatening, while if one is in the paratelic mode it is more likely to be experienced as pleasurably intriguing.

MODE DOMINANCE

As we have seen, then, the existence of alternative modes which are opposite in their preferences and aspirations means that there is an inherent inconsistency in human experience and behaviour. Sometimes one wants one kind of thing, sometimes the opposite, and one may even switch from one to the other in the course of the very same action. When we come to look at personality, therefore, reversal theory emphasizes from the outset the essentially dynamic and changing quality of people's lives, the fluctuations and vicissitudes, the *intra*-individual as well as *inter*-individual differences. In doing so, it challenges the emphasis which has always been placed in the field of personality on traits, which are by definition static and enduring personal characteristics, labels depicting supposedly unvarying psychological qualities.

This is not meant to imply that stable personality characteristics do not exist, but simply to decry the almost exclusive concern which is paid to them in much of personality theory. Indeed, we now come to the question of the consistencies which lie behind the inconsistencies of alternative metamotivational modes. But the interest of reversal theory here is in the way in which these consistencies set the psychological context for the inconsistencies, and in the relationship between these two aspects of personality.

In the study using colour preference choices as an indicator of the arousal-seeking and arousal-avoidance modes, it will be recalled that, while subjects generally alternated in the way expected between high-arousal and low-arousal colour choices, some subjects lingered longer with a choice towards one end of the arousal dimension and others with choices towards the other end. (An example was shown in Figure 4, where one subject spends much more time with the high-arousal colours than the other subject.) In other words, people appear to display a bias towards one mode or the other. The effect of this is that, over time, a person will be liable – other things being equal – to spend longer periods in the mode towards which he is biased than the other. So here we see a kind of inter-individual difference underlying the intra-individual differences, a consistency behind the inconsistencies.

This is, however, not a trait in the conventional sense, since it does not imply some fixed and continuing quality of behaviour. Take the trait of extraversion, for example. If one is extraverted to some degree, this implies that one is always extraverted to this degree and that therefore one's behaviour will at all times be governed by certain needs or tend to have certain characteristics. The environment will not always allow these characteristics to be fully expressed, of course, and there may also be some noise in any measuring instrument which attempts to measure the introversion–extraversion variable, so there may appear to be some variability. But theoretically it remains constant. Now compare this with the bias towards one or the other metamotivational mode. If one has a strong bias towards being in the arousal-avoidance mode, this does not mean that one will never be in the opposite mode. And when one is in the opposite mode, one will presumably be as 'fully' in this mode (i.e. as fully arousal-seeking) as someone who is perhaps normally in this mode. So there is a complete swing from one way of being to another. Since the bias involved, therefore, cannot properly be thought of as a trait, this kind of personality characteristic has been given another name in reversal theory: it is known as *mode dominance*, or simply *dominance*. Thus, one can speak of someone being 'telic dominant' or 'paratelic dominant' to some degree or another.

Among other things, this whole approach allows us the possibility of breaking down the old, and increasingly sterile, state/trait debate, by positing mode as a middle term. On the one hand states are seen as particular values of modes (e.g. the state of anxiety is a particular value of the arousal-avoidance mode), and on the other, 'traits' are seen as tendencies to be in one mode or another over time. In this way we see how both concepts can be reconciled within a more complex and meaningful theoretical structure.

THE TELIC DOMINANCE SCALE

If as you read the descriptions of the telic and paratelic modes in the previous chapter you found your sympathies moving one way or the other, and felt that the 'neutral' stance adopted by the writer was difficult to understand, then you will already have some preliminary indication of your own personality orientation in this respect. You would be able to gain a more precise idea of your own degree of dominance in one direction or the other from a psychometric scale which has been developed to measure this, and which is known as the Telic Dominance Scale (TDS).

The Telic Dominance Scale is a forty-two item questionnaire in which respondents are required on each item to choose between two courses of action (or 'ways of being'). If they cannot do this, they are to indicate 'not sure'. The instructions ask the subject to choose one item rather than the other on the basis of which they would most usually prefer, or which would most nearly apply to them (rather than how they happen to feel at the time of filling in the questionnaire), and to use the 'not sure' response only if unavoidable. The inventory is scored positively in a telic direction (a telic choice counting 1, and a 'not sure' response counting 0.5). But this is a purely arbitrary convention and the scale could equally well have been scored in the other direction and called the Paratelic Dominance Scale. A high score therefore represents someone who tends to be more often in the telic metamotivational mode, and a low score someone who tends to be more frequently in the paratelic mode.

The scale as a whole consists of three fourteen-item subscales which could be regarded as measuring the means–ends, temporal, and intensity aspects of telic dominance. The subscales are labelled and defined as follows:

Serious-mindedness subscale. This measures the frequency with which a subject sees himself or herself to be engaged in activities whose overriding purpose is to achieve a goal beyond these activities, rather than activities which are enjoyed in themselves.

Planning-orientation subscale. This measures the frequency with which a subject sees himself or herself to be involved in activities which require planning ahead and an orientation to the future, rather than activities which involve spontaneity and a 'here-and-now' orientation.

Arousal-avoidance subscale. This measures the frequency with which a subject sees himself or herself to be involved in activities which tend to reduce arousal, rather than activities which tend to increase arousal.

An example of a serious-mindedness subscale item would be: 'Going away on holiday for two weeks (paratelic) versus 'Given two weeks of free time, finishing a needed improvement at home' (telic). An example of a planning-orientation subscale item would be: 'Investing money in a long-term insurance/pension scheme' (telic) versus 'Buying an expensive car' (paratelic). And an example of an arousal-avoidance subscale item would be: 'Frequently trying strange foods' (paratelic) versus 'Always eating familiar foods' (telic).

The Telic Dominance Scale therefore produces three separate subscale scores, and one overall total telic dominance score. The theory predicts that these subscale scores will be significantly correlated with each other, since they are different aspects of the same psychological processes; but they are regarded at the same time as different from each other in that they are phenomenologically distinct. Of the three, the first, serious-mindedness, is seen as the defining scale. It will have been noticed that, for the purpose of this psychometric instrument, the arousal-avoidance and arousal-seeking pair of modes has been regarded as incorporated within the more general telic and paratelic modes.

The details of scale construction will be found in Murgatroyd, Rushton, Apter, and Ray (1978). It will suffice to say that the final items that made up the scale were selected on the basis of conventional statistical methods of item analysis, that the alpha coefficients of the resulting subscales have proven to be satisfactory, and that the scale and subscales have been found to be highly reliable over periods up to one year. Murgatroyd et al. (1978) found that the inter-subscale correlations were, as expected, positive and significant, although the correlation between serious-mindedness and planning orientation was much higher than that between either of these subscales and arousal-avoidance. This pattern of subscale relationships is one which has also been found by other researchers (e.g. Fontana 1981a; Matthews 1985; Baker 1988). From the reversal theory point of view this is not entirely surprising since, as discussed in the previous chapter, although high arousal will be expected to be unpleasant in the telic mode and low arousal in the paratelic, nevertheless people will often choose activities with unpleasant arousal levels because this is more than compensated for by other aspects of the activity.

Validation studies have taken a number of forms. For example:

1. The way that subjects see themselves, as disclosed in the 'Who am I?' test (Kuhn and McPartland 1954) and rated by three judges, was found to correlate significantly with telic dominance as measured by the TDS (Murgatroyd et al. 1978).

2. Earlier in this chapter a laboratory study of reversals due to satiation was described (Lafreniere et al. 1988) in which subjects were observed for two hours interacting with microcomputers, using either statistics teaching programs or video games. The subjects were in fact selected from 311 students to make up a stratified sample of ten high, sixteen intermediate, and ten low scorers on the serious-mindedness subscale of the TDS. An analysis of variance showed that there was a significant relationship between groups selected in this way and amount of time spent on one type of material rather than the other. The high-scoring group spent most time,

and the low-scoring group least time, on the statistics programs, and vice versa for the video games. Since the statistics programs were associated by the subjects with the telic mode and the video games with the paratelic mode, the study shows that, when not predisposed by environmental circumstances to be in the telic or paratelic mode, telic-dominant subjects, as measured by the serious-mindedness subscale of the TDS, will tend to spend longer periods in the telic mode and paratelic-dominant subjects in the paratelic mode.

3. Using the Stroop colour–word interference task (Stroop 1935), it was found that, while all subjects were sensitized to supposedly unpleasant and emotive words, the paratelic-dominant subjects were significantly more sensitized than the telic-dominant subjects. This is what one would expect if increased arousal is, as it should be for paratelic-dominant subjects, reinforcing (Murgatroyd et al. 1978).

4. A study (reported in Murgatroyd 1985b) shows that paratelic-dominant subjects are more likely to have engaged in a greater variety of sexual behaviours (e.g. oral and anal) than telic-dominant subjects, and are more likely to show an interest in pornography.

5. Anderson and Brown (in press) found that regular gamblers were more paratelic-dominant as indicated by their TDS scores than the population norm. They also found that the more paratelic-dominant the gambler the greater the bet size, and the higher the heart rate when blackjack was played in a real casino (rather than in a psychological laboratory).

6. Doherty and Matthews (1978) found that opiate addicts were paratelic-dominant with respect to all three subscales of the TDS.

Correlations between the TDS and other well-known tests of personality have turned out to be much as one might have expected from the scale descriptions. Thus, of eight studies surveyed by Murgatroyd (1985b) in which both the Eysenck Personality Inventory (EPI) and TDS were used, only one shows a significant correlation between a TDS subscale (planning orientation) and the EPI neuroticism scale; as far as the EPI extraversion–introversion scale is concerned, five studies show a correlation with the arousal-avoidance subscale and only one with serious-mindedness. There is little overlap therefore between the two EPI subscales and two of the TDS subscales, but what would appear to be definite relationship between arousal-avoidance and introversion – which is as would be expected from the definition of the introvert as someone who, among other things, avoids excitement.

Matthews (1985) found a number of significant relationships between some of the factors of Cattell's 16PF and the TDS which were again as one might have anticipated. For example, there were significant correlations between Cattell's G-primary factor (super-ego strength) and the serious-mindedness and planning-orientation subscales of the TDS, and between his F-primary factor (surgency – i.e. quick, impulsive, and happy-go-lucky) and both arousal-avoidance and planning orientation. In studying the relationship between the TDS and the Motivation Analysis Test (MAT) of Cattell and others, Matthews found no relationship between TDS subscales and 'integrated' motivation variables (those which consist of consciously expressed needs), but he did find significant correlations with a number of 'unintegrated' (semi-unconscious) variables. Murgatroyd (1985b) argues that 'These findings strongly support the core proposition of reversal theory, namely that experience and behaviour are shaped by 'meta'-motives – the implicit motives for having explicit motives' (p. 28).

Svebak and Apter (1984) investigated the relationship between the telic–paratelic dimension (using the TDS) and that of Type A/Type B behaviour (behaviour related to vulnerability to heart attacks). The Jenkins Activity Survey (JAS) was used to measure the latter. The results showed both total scale scores to be unrelated over the sample as a whole, as was the main factor extracted from the JAS in this study ('speed and impatience') in relation to both the TDS total scale score and each of the subscales. This general relationship may seem surprising to those familiar with the Type A/B distinction in view of the fact that, like telic dominance, it is to do with striving and purposefulness. However, when the two dimensions, as measured by the TDS and JAS, are examined closely we find that they are concerned with quite different aspects of purposefulness. While telic dominance is, as we have seen, defined in terms of serious-mindedness, Type A behaviour is to do with impatience, competitiveness, and hostility. Now, one can be impatient and competitive in either a serious or playful state of mind, and conversely one can be serious either in a way which involves the setting of urgent deadlines and the continual comparison of one's own performance with that of others, or in a more quiet and careful way. In the latter case, although one sees oneself to be pursuing serious goals, there is little competitiveness with others involved in their pursuit, and planning ahead involves a long-term view which reduces the element of fluster over short-term deadlines. In sum, the telic-dominant individual may or may not treat life like a race, and the same is true of the paratelic-dominant person.

I will not pursue this general psychometric line further here, but refer the interested reader to Murgatroyd's (1985b) review of TDS research for data on the relationship between the TDS and its subscales and other established psychometric instruments.

The TDS as it stands is no doubt far from perfect, and in particular there are problems with the factor structure (see discussion in Murgatroyd 1985b; Hyland, Sherry, and Thacker 1988). So revisions will be needed in the future. But meanwhile it is proving useful as a research instrument and in a number of applied settings. Norms now exist for Britain (based on a sample of 945 Open University students; see Murgatroyd (1985b)). It has been translated into French, Norwegian, Swedish, Dutch, Spanish, Bulgarian, and Arabic, and is used in many countries worldwide. A children's version for use in Dutch schools has also been developed (Boekaerts 1986; Boekaerts, Hendriksen, and Michels 1988a,b).

There is a danger in the attention which the TDS has received, and this is that it will become treated in a way which is isolated from the theory which gave rise to it. In other words, it will be treated as simply another trait measure, and the dynamic aspect of personality implied by the concept of 'dominance' – as against 'trait' – will be lost sight of. The answer to this, of course, will be to develop in the future new types of test instruments for dominance, rather than relying on the conventional multiple-choice inventory. A step in this direction has been taken by Boekaerts, Hendriksen, and Michels (1988a, b) in their children's version of the TDS which has just been mentioned, since they ask their subjects to rate the attractiveness of each of the alternatives in each item, as well as choose between them.

All this will need to be supplemented by measures of other changeable features of personality, of the kind to be discussed later in this chapter. Meanwhile, an indicator of current mode has been developed, the Telic State Measure (TSM), consisting of a simple set of rating scales of different aspects of the telic and paratelic modes. We shall return to this in the next chapter.

TELIC AND PARATELIC LIFESTYLES

It is not possible to experience what it is like to be both a telic- and a paratelic-dominant personality, and therefore I cannot give examples, as I have done previously, which call on your own phenomenological reflection to check the arguments I am putting forward against personal experience. What I can do, though, to give a better 'feel' of these two tendencies, is to quote from some interviews given by Murgatroyd as part of a research study he was carrying out with Svebak in Norway (and which was published in Svebak and Murgatroyd (1985)). In this research, subjects (psychology students) had been invited by Svebak to take part in a psychophysiology experiment in which he was comparing extremely telic-dominant with extremely paratelic-dominant subjects (chosen on the basis of scores on the serious-mindedness subscale, i.e. the defining subscale, of the TDS). Blind to both the TDS scores and the psychophysiological data, Murgatroyd interviewed six subjects from both extreme groups. He asked them what they did the day before the interview, whether it was what they had planned to do, what had been the most exciting thing which had occurred, and what the most surprising. He also asked them what they planned to do the day after the interview, which might disrupt their plans, and what was likely to be the most exciting event of the day.

Here, first, is an extract from the protocol of an extremely telic-dominant subject (male), which consists of his description of his previous day:

> All of my days go into each other, they look generally the same. I try to keep them this way. I like to work in routines. I found in the army, when I was there for one year, that routines let you stay as you are and become stronger as you are. I like this. So here is my yesterday.
>
> I got up at 10.00, went to the bathroom and washed my hands, then I went to the toilet, washed my hands again and then decided to have a shower. I brushed my teeth and then dried myself very thoroughly. I went to the gym for some weights and other training, but because it was closed due to a problem with water I could not get exercise. This upset my routine. I went to the bank to collect my loan and then I telephoned my father to ask his professional advice about what to do with the money. He told me to send the loan papers to him and he will make the necessary arrangements. I then returned to my flat at 13.00 and ate an apple and drank a cup of citrus juice – people overeat, I look after my figure. People with whom I share a flat have a dog which I took out for a walk and a jog. I found this exhilarating and exciting. At 15.00 I took the dog into town to watch the final part of the student demonstration. The demonstration was about rents – I do not think such demonstrations achieve their purpose. It is better to find ways of paying your rent. On my return to the flat at 16.45 there was a letter saying that I owed the army 37 crowns for my last telephone bill. This was untrue. I had paid my bill. I wrote directly to them and jogged to the post office to post my letter. I was upset by this letter . . . I did not expect it and it is a mistake. Such mistakes annoy me a lot – they must not be allowed to happen. I then prepared and ate my dinner and did my own daily exercise. I think it is important to keep the body healthy and not to abuse it. At 17.00 I watched a TV programme – only for 35 minutes. From 17.35 to 21.00 I worked on my translation of Kretch and Crutchfield. Because my head was full of this work, which is especially important, I stopped and took a walk to the shop for a very small bar of chocolate. At the shop a lot of people were watching Norway v. Sweden at football. It looked interesting and people were excited, but I had important work to do so I went back to my flat. I started work again, but all were watching TV in the room above, cheering whenever a goal was scored. In the end the noise meant that I had to give up and join them in the football. Once it was finished I was able to get back and read some more. This I did until 01.30 when I went to bed. I slept almost straight away.

In contrast to this, here is an extremely paratelic-dominant subject (female):

> Yes, well . . . er . . . I overslept . . . hadn't felt well the day before . . . and, er, I needed to sleep . . . so, er, I just slept in . . . I don't think my clock worked . . . but I slept in. I got to the reading room at 10.00. I was supposed to go to a lecture and to two tutorial groups, but I did not bother. Instead I talked to a man who fancies me. I agreed with him that I would go to the pictures, so I went home and had a shower, washed my hair and sat in a sauna – it was good. I didn't feel guilty about missing the lectures . . . I was having a nice time. Also, I felt better – I told you, I hadn't felt too well. At about 17.00 I had dinner with the man I told you about. Then my friend came and we decided to help her by driving her to the airport. It made me a little homesick – my friend, she is from the same town and she is going back for a few days. At the airport I met with three others who were going home too – I had a coffee with them. I felt more homesickness. Then the man friend took me to the pictures to see *Fame*. I enjoyed this film because it changed a lot – lots of different threads – I like that. Then we went to his flat and had tea and played Chinese chess. We had sex and then I went home. I think he is serious about me but I am not serious about him. I got home at 02.00 . . . very tired.

The differences between the lifestyles and phenomenological worlds of these two subjects is marked and shows dramatically the difference between subjects who spend much of their lives in the telic mode and those who find themselves in the paratelic mode most of the time. Murgatroyd, not surprisingly, had little difficulty in judging which group each of the subjects he interviewed fell into, and his ranking of the subjects correlated significantly with the ranking obtained from the psychometric scores from the serious-mindedness subscale of the TDS. (Incidentally, there were no gender differences between the two groups, and it would have been equally possible to quote from a transcript of a female telic-dominant subject and a male paratelic-dominant subject.)

Svebak and Murgatroyd make a number of interesting points about the differences between the two groups of subjects. The most obvious differences, of course, were differences of content. Paratelic-dominant subjects appear to indulge in a greater variety of activities, have a more exciting time, and be less well organized and more adaptable and spontaneous than telic-dominant subjects. Telic-dominant subjects carried out more carefully planned activities, continually monitoring themselves while doing so, and appeared to spend more of their lives accomplishing tasks or moving towards longer-term goals. But Murgatroyd also comments on the fact that the telic-dominant subject's descriptive style is different from that of the paratelic-dominant subject. Telic-dominant subjects were more detailed and described what happened in the correct chronological order, often giving specific times. Paratelic-dominant subjects tended instead to be more impressionistic: to offer a generalized account with one or two key features highlighted and sometimes exaggerated, and not necessarily given in the order in which they occurred. This kind of qualitative difference also extends to the way in which language was used by the two groups. While the telic-dominant subject 'provided a descriptive account with occasional evaluation,' the paratelic-dominant subject 'offered an evaluative account with occasional descriptions' (Svebak and Murgatroyd 1985: 113).

INDIVIDUAL DIFFERENCES AND METAMOTIVATION

So far, in looking at personality from the reversal theory perspective, the emphasis has been on mode dominance, specifically in relation to the telic/paratelic and the arousal-avoidance/arousal-seeking modes. But there are many other respects in which individuals can differ from each other in relation to metamotivation, and at this stage it is worth considering briefly what some of these might be. Certainly any complete reversal theory description of personality will have to take these into account, and it is to be hoped that in due course it will be possible to devise psychometric and other methods to deal with them systematically and rigorously. Meanwhile they are already being taken into account in a more intuitive way by clinicians who are using reversal theory in their work.

1. First of all, we have all those questions which are to do with the different factors which induce reversal in one direction or another in each person, and the relative sensitivity which he or she has for each of these. We can look at these under the headings already introduced. Thus, under the heading 'contingency' we can ask of a given person what kinds of things they see as threats and duties, and what kinds of things they see as playful challenges. We can note here in passing a propensity which some telic-dominant people seem to have of treating their own relatively arbitrary goals, chosen at one time, as unavoidable obligations to themselves at a later time. In other words, they become *committed* to decisions they make, treating the earlier self which made the decision as an unquestionable authority. Such a person may decide on Sunday morning to go for a walk in the afternoon and then go for the walk 'come hell or high water' – it does not matter if relatives come to visit, if there is a thunderstorm, or if he hurts his ankle, he will do what he has decided. In this way, what should have been a paratelic activity becomes telic.

We can also ask, in relation to contingency, which settings tend for the individual to generate protective frames and which to break them down. Under the heading 'frustration' we can ask how quickly frustration tends to build up, and whether it is felt more in relation to certain kinds of problems and potential failures than others. And in relation to 'satiation' we can ask, in principle, how fast it builds up, and whether it builds up faster in one direction than the other – this presumably being the basic factor underlying dominance.

2. The next major question is that of how 'reversible' or 'labile' in general the individual is, quite apart from whether she is relatively more difficult to move out of one mode rather than the other (dominance) or the specific factors which tend to play a part in inducing reversals. I am here alluding to the kind of difference already referred to between the two subjects whose pattern of arousal preference choices was plotted in Figure 4: one of them reverses *more often* than the other.

In relation to this, we also have the question of how much any particular individual is in control of her own reversal processes. How far has she discovered how to do things, or to set up conditions, which will be likely to induce reversal in one direction or the other? To the extent that she is able to do this, she will be escaping in this respect from control by forces outside her own volition.

3. A major difference between people will be the types of strategies which they use in each mode in the attempt to achieve the satisfactions peculiar to that mode. Thus in the telic and arousal-avoidance modes, will a given individual tend to choose difficult and important goals, and tolerate the anxiety they are likely to bring with them, for the sake of the feelings of progress and accomplishment which he hopes to experience later? Or will he rather attempt to keep arousal down when he is in the telic mode by living in a generally low-key way and avoiding 'bother' whenever he can? What kinds of goals will he tend to see as important, other things being equal: intellectual goals, financial goals, religious goals, political goals, or yet other kinds of goals? How far will he tend to see goals as nested within each other in complex hierarchies? How far ahead, and in what detail, will he tend to plan? How flexible or rigid is he likely to be in pursuing these plans? Will he tend to pursue his goals cooperatively with others, or will he do so as a loner? These illustrate just some of the questions which could be asked about how individuals tend to be when they are in the telic mode.

In a similar way we can ask about the individual in the paratelic and arousal-seeking modes such questions as the following: Does he look for intense experiences more in relation to strong sensations (heat, noise, touch, etc.) or in relation to emotional arousal? Are the activities he chooses more likely to be mental or physical or some combination of these? How will he be likely to achieve high arousal: by doing things which are dangerous, doing things which are novel, being provocative and difficult, engaging in competition with others, empathizing with others who are aroused, or in some other way? How far will he use artificial means (especially drugs)? How much effort will he be willing to invest in the quest for, and the practice of, enjoyable activities? And which type of protective frame does he tend to make use of: the confidence frame, the safety-zone frame, or the detachment frame?

These questions about intra-mode strategies are ones which one may want, or need, to ask in building up a psychological understanding of a given individual. In particular, as we shall see in a later chapter, they are questions which the clinician may want to ask about a patient or client. But they also give rise to more general research questions. For instance, the questions already asked concern the ways the individual has of being in the mode itself, irrespective of whether he is telic-dominant or paratelic-dominant. But there is also the issue of whether individuals carry over strategies, possibly inappropriately on occasion, from their dominant to their non-dominant mode. Does the telic-dominant individual tend to choose pastimes which require a great deal of planning ahead, like gardening for example, or even try to plan ahead when this is not appropriate (for example in playing roulette)? Does the paratelic-dominant individual in the telic mode attempt to reach the goal which has been imposed on him in some dramatic and one-off way rather than by careful planning? This is in fact a research question which has yet to be addressed.

We should also not forget that all these ways in which individuals differ from each other have a developmental aspect, and a host of research questions could be asked about them. For instance, does dominance itself change? Although, as already noted, scores on the Telic Dominance Scale have reliability for periods of up to a year, meaning that not much change generally occurs over this length of time, is it possible for telic dominance to change over longer time spans? For instance, it might well be the case, from the amount of time children seem to spend playing in comparison with adults, that there is a general tendency for paratelic dominance to be the norm early in development but for telic dominance to increase during maturation (although more in some people than others). And in adulthood, the normative data on 945 Open University students does seem to show a continuation of such a hypothetical trend, the correlation between age and telic dominance being positive and significant for these adult subjects, whose ages ranged from 21 to 70 (Murgatroyd 1985b). If there is such a tendency for telic dominance to increase with age over the life span, is this biologically based, or is it the outcome of learning processes? Boekaerts (1986, 1988), in interpreting the differences between Dutch and Flemish schoolchildren on her children's version of the TDS, argues that different levels of telic dominance during childhood may well be an effect of different parental attitudes and school environments. But clearly much more research will be needed on this fundamental question.

It is also possible that significant life events may push telic dominance in one direction or the other over relatively short time periods. For instance, Girodo (1985) reported data on the training of undercover agents for the Royal Canadian Mounted Police – a dramatic and potentially traumatic procedure – which showed that these subjects (who were, as would be expected for such a job, generally paratelic-dominant) shifted significantly in the telic direction following training. (See also the case study of a 'difficult' child reported by Seldon (1980) in which certain life events seemed to trigger periods of paratelic dominance.)

From all this it can be seen that the reversal theory approach to personality is one which differs in a number of significant respects from the more conventional psychometric trait approach. From the reversal theory point of view, traits tend to be little more than labels which can be attached to people but which give in themselves very little insight into the mechanisms and dynamics at work, and which tend to imply a rather static model of people. Trait theories are also generally oriented to behavioural dispositions rather than the mental states which underlie and generate behaviour. In contrast, reversal theory focusses on the different ways in which each person experiences his or her world, and emphasizes the mutability and self-contradiction of these different styles of experiencing. If humanity is consistent in anything, it is in its inconsistency.

5

The Psychophysiology of Metamotivation

Important biological structures come in pairs.

The Double Helix
James D. Watson (1928–)

As we have seen, the telic and paratelic modes are different ways of organizing experience. Do they also give rise to different ways of organizing the body's physiological responses? If it could be shown that they do, then there would be strong objective evidence to back up the phenomenological arguments for the existence of these opposing 'ways of being'.

In the late 1970s, Professor Sven Svebak and his colleagues at the University of Bergen (Norway) set in train a continuing programme of psychophysiological research on the physiological concomitants of the telic and paratelic modes and mode dominance. In other words, they set out to examine exactly this question of the possible physiological consequences of metamotivational mode at a given time and mode dominance over time. The aim of this chapter is to review their findings.

One of the fields in which Svebak himself had been working before starting this line of research was that of the psychophysiology of humour, and he reported (Svebak 1985a) that he had long been dissatisfied with optimal arousal theory – since it seemed to him, on commonsense grounds, that humour must be a form of pleasant *high* arousal. Reversal theory appeared to make more sense, not just in relation to humour but also to a variety of other types of everyday experience (see Svebak and Stoyva 1980).

One important methodological point which Svebak has been making from the beginning of his research career is the necessity, which most psychophysiologists have ignored in their research, to connect the physiological record with subjective experience. Thus one cannot say *ab initio*, on the basis of certain kinds of psychophysiological changes, that the subject must be anxious, or mirthful, or even feeling aroused. One can only say this if one has consulted the subject, or infer it if particular psychophysiological patterns turn out, time and time again, to relate to the same reported feelings across subjects. This may seem an obvious point, but it is a rare psychophysiologist who asks her subject how he feels, and uses this evidence as part of her data base. It will be appreciated that this argument of Svebak's is thoroughly consistent with what, in the first chapter of the present book, I called the 'inside-out' approach which gave rise to reversal theory.

Throughout most of this research, to make the results from different experiments comparable, Svebak has used a carefully selected range of tasks, most of them versions of a video game representing a car race. In this task, the subject controls the position of his or her car on a television screen by means of a small joystick which is held in one hand. The subject's car runs at twice the speed of other cars in the race, these other cars appearing at random positions along the road shown on the screen. The task of the subject is to avoid running into these other cars by shifting the position of his or her own car on the road so that it overtakes them. Each 'crash' counts as an error and the error scores are accumulated over the period of the task. On each trial, the task lasts for a standard time of 2½ minutes. Although 2½ minutes may sound like a short duration, such a 'continuous perceptual-motor task paradigm', to use the technical term, is a fairly long period in psychophysiological research. (It also feels quite a long time for the subject, who has to concentrate hard throughout.) There were several ways in which the task was varied in some of the experiments. It was made more difficult by speeding up the rate at which the cars to be avoided appeared on the screen. And a threat condition was sometimes added: this was the threat of electric shock for some unspecified level of error.

While subjects performed this task, perhaps under different conditions, a number of physiological variables were recorded. The same variables were also recorded before and after the task, to provide pre- and post-baseline measures for comparative purposes. In particular, the following four aspects of physiological activity were focussed on in the course of the research: (1) skeletal muscle tension, (2) cardiovascular activity, (3) respiratory activity, and (4) cortical activity. Thus four of the major investigative areas which go to make up current psychophysiology were included in this research programme.

In many of these experiments, as we shall see, subjects (university students) were recruited to make up extreme groups in relation to telic dominance. That is, subjects were chosen with scores which were either extremely high or extremely low on telic dominance, so as to make a clear-cut comparison possible between telic-dominant (high scoring) subjects and paratelic-dominant (low scoring) subjects. (Actually,the criterion used here was the score on the serious-mindedness subscale of the Telic Dominance Scale, rather than the total score on the scale as a whole, since the serious-mindedness scale is the defining subscale.) In other experiments, subjects were simply chosen randomly. Where it was necessary to know the mode that the subject was in at any time, the Telic State Measure (TSM) was used.

This state measure consisted of four 6-point rating scales to which subjects were asked to respond by circling the point corresponding to the number which most nearly represented their feelings during the period indicated by the experimenter (typically the period of the experimental task). The scales were defined by pairs of adjectives representing the opposite end-points of each scale. These were: (1) serious–playful, (2) preferred spontaneity–preferred planning ahead, (3) felt low arousal–felt high arousal, and (4) preferred low arousal–preferred high arousal. Three of these items (1, 2, and 4) were state versions of the three subscales of the TDS (as described in the last chapter), while the fourth (item 3) measured how aroused the subject actually felt. A measure of 'tension' could be obtained by subtracting the subject's response to item 4 from his or her response to item 3 – this represented a discrepancy between preferred and actual level of arousal (in either direction). Brief descriptions of the words used in defining the scales were also used as part of the standard procedure of scale presentation; subjects read these before responding to the scales for the first time. The aim of this, of course, was to help to ensure consistency of interpretation between subjects.

The basic question in all this research is how far the recorded physiological changes over the 2½ minutes of the task, or in response to such changes as adding threats or making the task more difficult, are related to (1) telic dominance, (2) telic or paratelic mode, and (3) some other factors (e.g. felt arousal level, amount of effort). Clearly, if any relationship is found at all with either of the metamotivational variables (mode or mode dominance), this brings an entirely new factor into psychophysiological research, and must count as a discovery with unavoidable implications for future research.

Since much of the discussion in what follows will concern the metamotivational state of the organism *at a given time*, for the remainder of this chapter the word 'state' will be used rather than 'mode' because it emphasizes better the momentary rather than the enduring. (After all, a mode also has enduring characteristics, but these only manifest themselves when the *state* of the organism is characterized by the operation of the mode.)

Let us look at the results of this research in terms of each of the four areas of physiological activity listed above. But before we do so there is an important distinction which needs to be made between two types of change in physiology, since both these types of change will be referred to at different points in the discussions which follow in this chapter. These two types of change are labelled 'tonic' and 'phasic', respectively. A tonic change is a slow underlying increase or decrease in some physiological variable, whereas a phasic change is a more pronounced and short-term change which, typically, can be attributed to a specific change in the environment. This is not unlike the difference between the way in which the movement of a symphony may start softly, build up slowly to a loud climax, and die away again (these being tonic changes), with momentary increases and decreases of sound level occurring over this basic pattern (representing phasic changes). Another metaphor would be the tide coming in and going out (equivalent to tonic change), and the waves coming in (equivalent to phasic change).

SKELETAL MUSCLE TENSION

When we perform some physical task, like typing or hitting a golf ball, the muscles involved increasingly 'tense up' until the task is complete. (I am here referring to so-called skeletal muscles – the muscles we have under voluntary control, such as those in our arms and legs – rather than such involuntary muscles as those involved in the digestion of food in our stomachs.) Indeed, not only do the active muscles tense up (for example, the muscles in our fingers when we type) but also, typically, passive skeletal muscles not directly involved in the task may also become increasingly more activated. For example, the muscles in our backs and our foreheads, even though these muscles are not of direct use in typing, may also show signs of heightening tension while we type.

It is possible to record muscle tension by means of electrodes attached to the surface of the skin which pick up the neuroelectric activity of the muscles beneath. This *electromyographic* (EMG) activity can then be recorded graphically, showing how it fluctuates over time in the muscles concerned. Malmo and his colleagues (e.g. Malmo 1965) were among those who drew attention to the way in which a tonic build-up of this activity continues over the course of a task, and then falls away again the moment the task is complete. They refer to this as an *electromyographic gradient*, and it represents the way in which in carrying out some task our muscle tension (in both active and passive muscles) builds up until the task is concluded, and then rapidly subsides. This build-up over time may, however, be relatively steep or shallow.

The question now arises as to what determines the steepness of this electromyographic gradient. And this is a matter of more than theoretical importance since steep gradients may produce performance decrements for some types of tasks and, if experienced frequently or maintained at high levels, cause great fatigue. Indeed they may even lead to muscle-tension problems like backache and headache. In reversal theory terms the question naturally arises as to whether the steepness of the gradient may relate to the telic–paratelic distinction, either at the level of dominance or of state. And everyday observation certainly seems to support, in a preliminary way, the notion that the telic state is productive of muscle tension (think of the way that one tenses up when having to do something important, or dangerous, or serious) and that telic-dominant people are the ones at risk of such muscle tension problems (e.g. people who experience frequent headaches seem to be chronic worriers). But which is it, if either? Is it that the telic state is what counts, and the dominance effect occurs, if it does through the frequency of the state? Or is it that telic dominance is what counts, leading both to long periods in the telic state and high muscle tension? Or does it depend on some further factor like arousal level or expenditure of effort? The experiments now to be described constitute a kind of detective story aimed at tracking down the real culprit. And the focus of attention is on passive rather than on active musculature, because the tonic effects investigated are not overlaid and obscured by phasic effects as they are in active muscles.

The first approach to the problem taken by Svebak and his colleagues (Svebak, Storfjell, and Dalen 1982) was to attempt to manipulate whether subjects were in the telic state or not by asking them to play the video game under two conditions: with the threat of electric shock for poor performance, and without such a threat. In fact, as already noted, shock was never given (for technical reasons, among others, since it would interfere with the recording). Unpleasant, but not painful shocks were given before the task proper and this had the effect of demonstrating to subjects the seriousness of the experimenter in threatening shock. The number of errors (car 'crashes') which subjects would have to make to become subject to shock was not specified, so that it remained a threat in this condition irrespective of how well in fact the subject was performing. Electromyographic activity was recorded from the forearm flexor muscle of the subject's passive arm (i.e. the arm not used to manipulate the joystick).

Over the group taken as a whole (14 male students) this manipulation certainly worked in that subjects rated themselves on the Telic State Measure as significantly more serious-minded and planning-oriented in the threat than the non-threat condition. So what effect did this have on the electromyographic gradients? In fact, the gradients were, as predicted, significantly steeper under the threat than under the non-threat treatment. Unfortunately, felt arousal was also significantly higher (as measured by the TSM) under the threat condition, and so it was in principle perfectly possible that the steeper gradients were a reflection of higher felt arousal rather than the telic state. For this reason, while the experiment was a success in showing that EMG gradient could be manipulated by threat, the data did not show unambiguously that the steepness of the gradient was due to the advent of the telic state as a result of this threat.

In the next experiment (Svebak 1984), therefore, a different strategy was used to obtain telic and paratelic states. Instead of using threat, which not only tended to induce the telic state but also to raise arousal, subjects were chosen who were extremely telic- and paratelic-dominant. The idea of this was that subjects displaying extreme dominance would be likely, other things being equal and without any special manipulation, to be in the state corresponding to their dominance during the experimental session. In fact, the ten highest and ten lowest scorers on the serious-mindedness subscale of the TDS were recruited for the experiment from a sample of 180 students who took the TDS. And this strategy worked, since TSMs completed by subjects after each 'run' of the task showed that the telic-dominant subjects were significantly more serious-minded during the task than the paratelic-dominant subjects; that is dominance successfully predicted state during the experiment in this respect. Fortunately, it also turned out that there was *no* significant difference between the two groups on their felt levels of arousal during the experimental task (again as measured by means of the TSM), so that while state varied, in this experiment arousal remained constant between the two groups.

In the earlier experiment, subjects performed the task (i.e. with and without a threat). In the present experiment they played the video game five times in sequence, and then once more at a high speed, making it more difficult for them to avoid crashes. For the reasons given, the threat condition could now be dispensed with, so each 2½-minute run took place

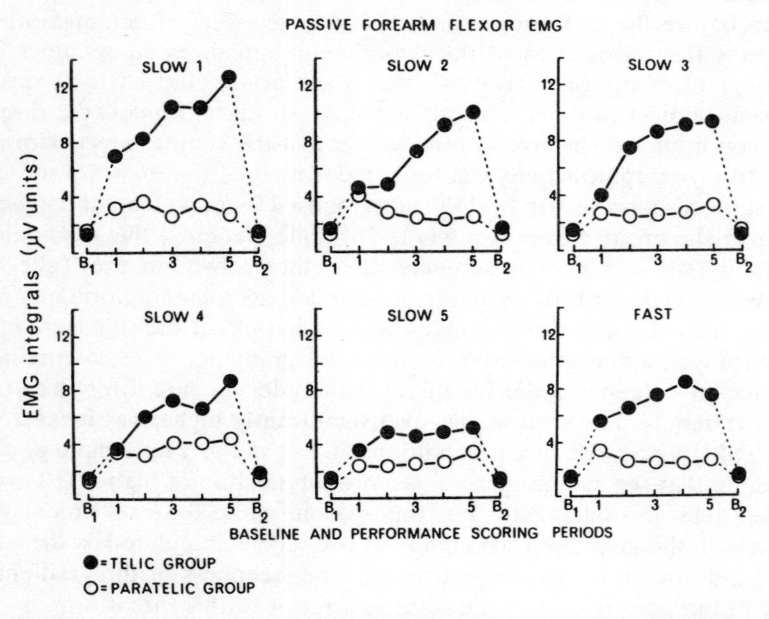

Fig. 10 The mean group-scores of telic- and paratelic-dominant subjects for EMG activity recorded from the forearm flexor of the passive arm over a 2½-minute task. Measurements were taken at half-minute intervals, and pre-and post-task baseline levels are also shown. The task was performed five times at a relatively slow speed and once relatively fast. (After Svebak 1984.)

with no threat of electric shock. As before, EMG recordings were taken from the forearm flexor muscle of the passive arm.

The results are displayed in Figure 10, which shows the mean group scores on each of the five 'runs' or games. It will be noted that for each run there is a pre- and post-baseline measure, and between these there are five measures sampled at equal intervals of time across the 2½ minutes of the task. In the case of each run for the telic group the EMG gradient can be clearly seen, rising over the period of the task itself and then falling away on completion of the task. For the paratelic group, however, this gradient can hardly be said to exist at all. Not surprisingly, and despite the fact that this difference between the two groups diminishes on each run (presumably due to a practice effect) the differences between the groups are statistically significant. Clearly, then, the build-up of muscle tension is a telic phenomenon. (It will be noticed, incidentally, that for the sixth run, when the task is made more difficult again, the difference between the gradients of the two groups re-emerges more strongly.) The fact that a comparison of felt arousal levels between the two groups shows them to have been roughly the same throughout also implies that it is the telic/paratelic distinction which is crucial in the genesis of steep EMG gradients. However, we must be a little cautious here since felt arousal levels were fairly high, and it would still be possible to argue that some minimal arousal level may be necessary in combination with the telic state or dominance, for the gradient phenomenon to occur. It is also possible that the effect was due to effort by the subject and that this happened to be higher in the telic state.

In this same experiment (Svebak 1984) not only were recordings taken from the forearm flexor in the passive arm but also from this same musculature in the active arm, that is the one controlling the joystick. In this case the measurement concerned *phasic* rather than tonic EMG response amplitudes, these phasic amplitudes indicating the vigour of the movements involved in the execution of the task. The paratelic group produced higher averaged phasic amplitudes throughout than the telic group, although this difference was not significant on the five main runs of the task. However, on the sixth run, in which the task was made especially difficult through the increased speed of the cars, something particularly interesting happened. Here the averaged amplitudes for the paratelic subjects increased throughout the 2½ minutes, whereas those of the telic subjects regularly decreased over the same period (this interaction effect was statistically significant). This is shown in Figure 11. What this means is that the two groups of subjects were using opposite strategies in order to attempt to cope with an impossibly difficult task. The paratelic subjects were responding with increased vigour, making wild and rather uncontrolled movements. The telic subjects, in contrast, were making increasingly careful and precise movements. In fact, neither strategy worked better

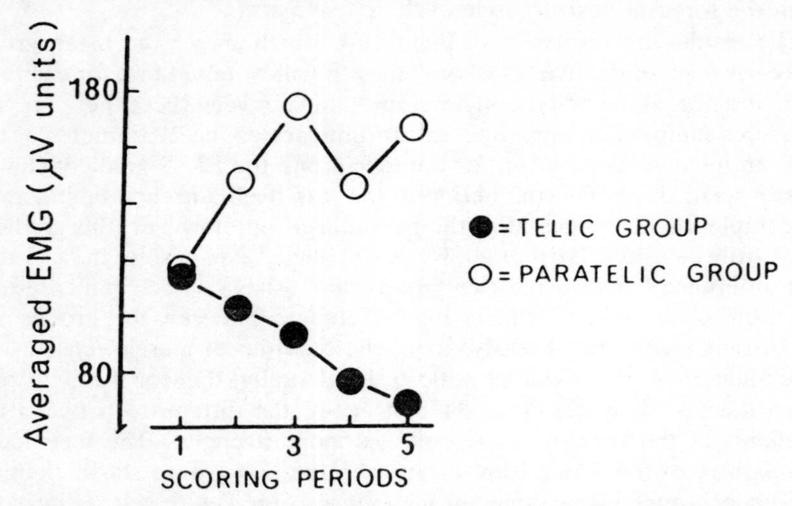

Fig. 11 The mean group-scores of telic- and paratelic-dominant subjects for EMG activity recorded from the forearm flexor of the active arm over the same 2½-minute task as that shown in Figure 10; but here only the results from the 'fast' version of the task are shown. (After Svebak 1984.)

than the other, and the error scores of the two groups were not significantly different. But it is interesting as a response style that, under pressure of a hopelessly difficult task, the paratelic subjects put emphasis on intensity of action while the telic subjects put it on tightness of control, the one group acting more and more expansively and the other becoming increasingly inhibited and narrow in its range of responses.

Returning to the main theme of the tonic build-up of muscle tension in passive 'task-irrelevant' musculature, we have seen how this experiment implicates the telic/paratelic dimension. The same is true of another experiment (Svebak and Murgatroyd 1985) which looked at EMG activity as well as other physiological variables. In this case the extreme groups (students) consisted of ten subjects each drawn from a larger sample of 110. Essentially the same results were achieved.

The problem with both these extreme group experiments is that telic-dominant subjects tended to be in the telic state during the experiment and paratelic-dominant subjects in the paratelic-state. While this was an essential and deliberate part of the experimental design in each case, it did mean that it was not possible to tell whether the critical factor in the generation of steep EMG gradients was telic dominance or telic state.

To resolve this problem, clearly a kind of experimental design would be needed in which a substantial proportion of subjects would be induced to 'cross over' in the sense that they would be in a state different from their dominance. Svebak (1986a) used both (relatively) extreme groups of telic- and paratelic-dominant subjects *and* threat manipulation, in the hope that some paratelic-dominant subjects would cross over to the telic state in the threat condition. In the event, the threat did not prove strong enough to produce a substantial transition of this kind, and so it was not possible to draw any conclusions about the relative roles of state and dominance. However, the results did replicate once again the findings of the two other experiments based on the use of extreme groups, making the robustness of these results concerning EMG activity even stronger.

In order to increase the probability of 'cross-overs' between dominance and state, Apter and Svebak (1986) recruited two groups of subjects, one telic- and one paratelic-dominant, which were far less extreme than those used in previous experiments. This meant that in principle the subjects (six in each group drawn from a sample of 222 students) should be more vulnerable to factors liable to induce reversals than those more extremely dominant subjects used earlier. At the same time, two different manipulations were used in the attempt to induce reversals: a threat of shock condition for inadequate performance and a monetary reward for good performance. In all, subjects performed the video game task four times: under threat conditions, under monetary reward conditions, and twice under neutral conditions with no threat or reward. (The order of these 'runs' was of course varied in a systematic way.) As before, recordings were made from the flexor muscle of the passive forearm.

On this occasion, rather than use the Telic State Measure, subjects were assessed for state by means of a structured interview given after the experiment by an interviewer blind to both their TDS scores and their physiological records from the experiment. This time, a number of 'cross-overs' did occur so that it was possible to disentangle and examine meaningfully the relative effects of dominance and state. In fact, in each group four of the six subjects performed the experiment in a state opposite from that of their dominance.

The results can be summarized as shown in Figure 12, where scores represent the means of the groups over all four runs. It can be seen from this quite clearly that the critical factor in determining a steep EMG gradient is that of state rather than dominance, and this conclusion is supported by statistical analysis.

Rimehaug and Svebak (1987) sought to generalize this finding with an experiment in which the task was changed to a cognitive one, so that *both* arms were passive. This allowed them to make recordings from passive musculature on both sides of the body simultaneously, and in this case recordings were taken from the biceps and triceps of the upper arms rather than from the forearm flexor. Nineteen subjects were selected from a sample of 99 students to represent a stratified sample from across the whole

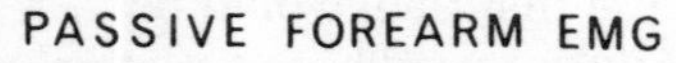

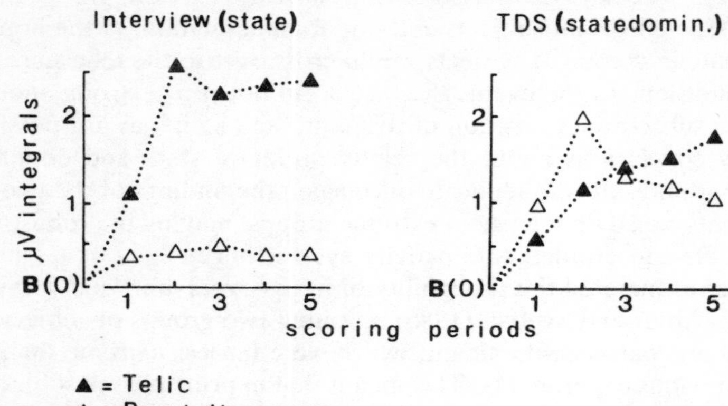

Fig. 12 Mean group-scores of telic and paratelic subjects for EMG activity recorded from the forearm flexor of the passive arm over a 2½-minute task. These scores are the averages of four trials and are relative to the pre-task baseline score (B). In the graph on the left 'telic' and 'paratelic' refer to the states of the subjects at the time of the task; in the graph on the right these terms refer to state dominance, i.e. one group was telic-dominant and the other paratelic-dominant. (After Apter and Svebak, 1986.)

telic dominance range (measured, as before, by the serious-mindedness subscale of the TDS). Each subject was given two runs on the task (each lasting five minutes), once with the possibility of monetary reward, and once without. Telic and paratelic states were determined by a post-task interview. The verbal behaviour of subjects during the task was also recorded on tape and scored for utterances which indicated distress or irritation.

As in the Apter and Svebak (1986) study, telic state turned out to be a better predictor of EMG gradient than dominance, thus showing that this effect was not restricted to the type of task used in the earlier experiments or to the forearm flexor muscle. The results were more pronounced in the right than the left upper arm, although in both cases the relation to telic state was statistically significant. Of particular additional interest was the fact that scores reflecting distress (based on evidence from the tape recordings) were also positively related to EMG activity, and the best predictor of EMG scores was an index comprising both telic state and distress scores. If we may assume that distress in the telic state is associated with high arousal (experienced as anxiety), then a tentative conclusion might be that while the telic state is necessary for steep EMG gradients, the effect is enhanced as arousal increases (Svebak 1988b). However, alternative interpretations are possible here, and it may be the case – and this is the preferred explanation of Svebak – that it is the subject's effort in responding to the task rather than arousal which acts to amplify gradient steepness. Clearly, this issue will be a focus for future research. (The nature of effort and the relationship between arousal and effort will be considered further in Chapter 10.)

CARDIOVASCULAR ACTIVITY

If muscle tension problems are regarded as one of the banes of modern life and its stresses, heart attacks are one of the major killers. Psychophysiological research on cardiovascular activity is therefore, from this point of view, one of the most important areas of investigation in the whole field.

The most widely used variable in the psychophysiological study of cardiovascular activity is the obvious one: that of heart rate. From the reversal theory point of view the question is then that of whether the degree of heart rate increase which one would expect to occur during the experimental task depends on whether the telic or paratelic state is in operation (or, alternatively, whether the individual is telic- or paratelic-dominant).

In the initial experiment by Svebak et al. (1982), already referred to in relation to skeletal muscle activity, heart rate as well as EMG activity were recorded when the experimental task was performed under the threat and no-threat conditions. Although the pattern of tonic heart rate increase is somewhat different from that of the typical EMG gradient in that it peaks early rather than at the end of the 2½-minute task period, there was, as there had been for the EMG gradient, a significant difference between the responses in the two conditions, heart rate being considerably higher in the threat condition. This is shown in Figure 13, which shows the average heart rates under the two conditions for each of the five sampling periods and the pre- and post-baselines. As before, unequivocal inferences cannot be drawn because, although the threat condition tended to induce the telic state, seeming to implicate this state in the raised heart rate, it also increased felt arousal. (And although the workload remained the same in the two conditions, this does not preclude greater effort having been expended in the threat condition.)

Heart rate was also studied in the Svebak (1986a) experiment referred to above in which subjects who were relatively high in telic dominance and relatively high in paratelic dominance were both subjected to the threat and no-threat conditions. The results in relation to heart rate are summarized in Figure 14, in which it can be seen that in the no-threat condition both groups show moderate heart rate increases, while under threat the acceleration in heart rate for the telic group is considerable –

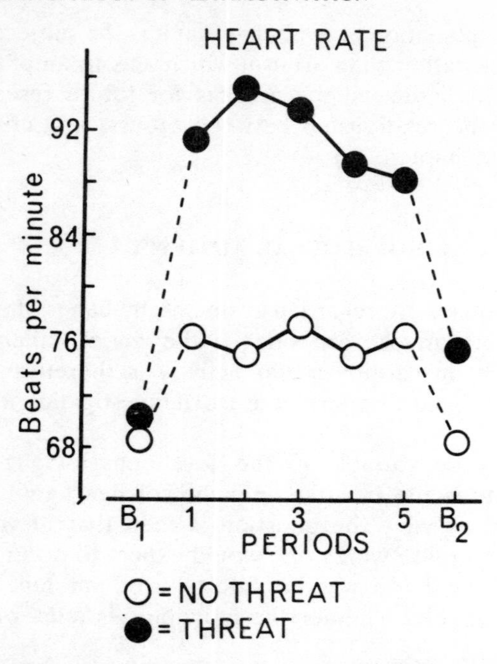

Fig. 13 The effect of threat on heart rate, averaged over all subjects in the study, and measured at half-minute intervals throughout the 2½-minute task. Pre- and post-task baseline levels are also shown. (After Svebak, Storfjell, and Dalen 1982.)

and, in fact, significantly different from the change in rate displayed by the paratelic group in response to threat. The felt arousal levels of the two groups as measured by the TSM were relatively similar, and the implication is that the critical difference related to the telic/paratelic distinction. What remains unclear from this data, however, is whether the difference is one of state or of dominance (since there were relatively few 'cross-overs', so that the results can be interpreted equally well in either way). This is obviously a matter for future research, although the state change relationship to increased heart rate observed in Svebak et al. (1982) would appear at this stage to be more consistent with a state interpretation. Meanwhile it seems reasonable to conclude that the telic–paratelic factor is an important determinant of heart rate acceleration under conditions of threat, and that this is a discovery which should be taken seriously in research on cardiovascular psychophysiology in the future.

In the last chapter, evidence was presented that the distinction between Type A and Type B behaviour patterns is unrelated to telic/paratelic dominance. People who display the Type A behaviour pattern are supposed to be vulnerable to coronary heart disease, the behaviour pattern being characterized in particular by an awareness of time pressure

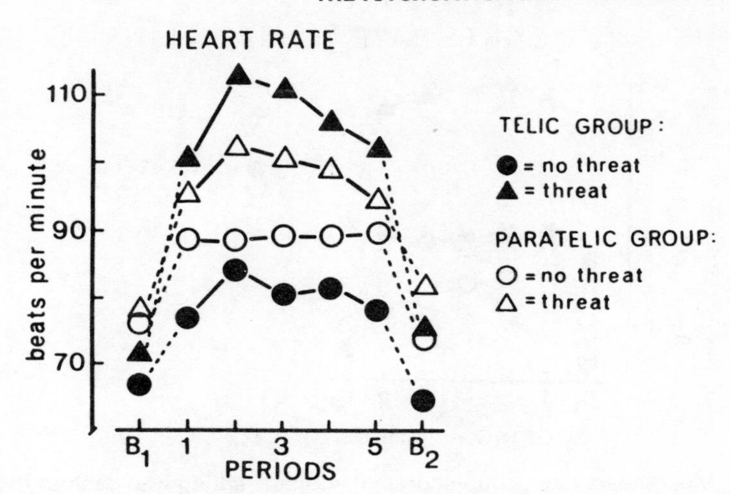

Fig. 14 Mean group-scores of telic- and paratelic-dominant subjects for heart rate over a 2½-minute task with and without threat of shock for inadequate performance. Measurements were taken at half-minute intervals, and pre- and post-task baseline levels are also shown. (After Svebak and Murgatroyd, 1985.)

(working fast, being impatient, setting deadlines, etc.) and by competitiveness (driving oneself hard, displaying irritation and hostility, etc.). These contrast with Type B patterns which display opposite characteristics. Certainly Type A behaviour has not proved itself, despite enormous research, to be more than moderately good at predicting heart disease, and other risk factors must therefore be at work too. Now since the telic/paratelic distinction has been shown to affect heart rate under the stress of threat, it is natural to ask whether it might not also be another psychological factor which plays a part in the development of this disease. This is a question which will take a great deal of time to answer, since prospective studies will be needed. But meanwhile it is possible to look at the way in which Type A/B behaviour and telic/paratelic dominance interact in relation to heart rate.

Svebak, Nordby, and Ohman (1987) recruited forty subjects into the four combinations: telic/Type A, telic/Type B, paratelic/Type A, and paratelic/Type B. Their heart rates, recorded during the course of task performance, showed that those individuals who fell into the group defined by the combination of Type A and telic dominance were particularly high in heart rate reactivity, whereas those who were characterized by the combination of Type B and paratelic dominance were the least reactive. The other two combinations fell between these two (see Figure 15). This seems to imply that there is a cardiovascular 'responder' type which can be characterized as telic/Type A, and since Type A already predicts

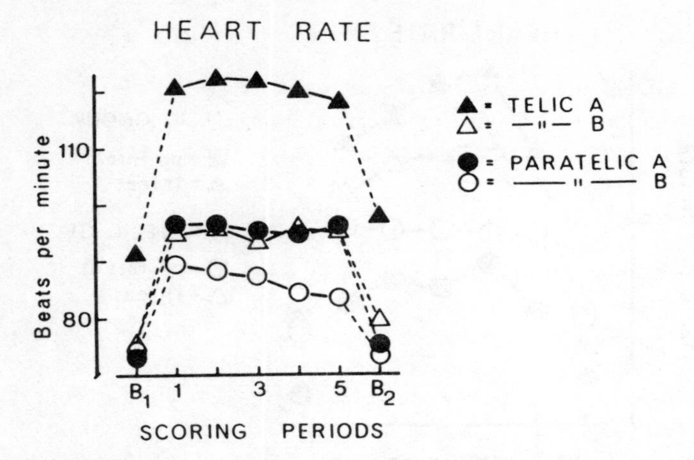

Fig. 15 Mean heart rate group-scores of subjects falling into each of the four groups made up by combining telic and paratelic dominance with type A or type B behaviour. Measurements were taken at half-minute intervals over the 2½ minutes of the task and pre- and post-task baseline levels are also shown. (After Svebak, Nordby and Ohman, 1987.)

cardiovascular disease in some measure, it would seem a reasonable hypothesis that telic/Type A may be an even better predictor.

Incidentally, in this same experiment blood pressure was also measured (by means of pulse transit time – the time it takes for a pulse to move from one part of the vascular system to another). Again, this indicated that telic/ Type A individuals were subject to the highest systolic pressure, thus providing further support for the notion of telic/Type A individuals as high cardiovascular 'responders'.

So far I have only referred to tonic heart rate changes, but shorter-term phasic responses can also be discerned. Thus, Svebak and Apter (in press) in a study of the psychophysiological effects of comedy (using a comedy film), found that such phasic responses occurred in close proximity to laughter, laughter only occurring in the paratelic state. In some instances of intense laughter, heart rate accelerated by more than 40 beats, and then returned to the pre-laughter level within a couple of beats of the end of the laughter response. The records were essentially the same for both telic-dominant subjects in the paratelic state and paratelic-dominant subjects in this state. This emphasized once again the strength of reversal theory in drawing attention to the importance of state as well as more enduring characteristics, and supported the insistence of the theory that when telic-dominant individuals are in the paratelic state they are as fully in that state as paratelic-dominant individuals (and vice-versa for paratelic-dominant people in the telic state).

RESPIRATORY ACTIVITY

If heart rate is one major function controlled by the autonomic nervous system, respiration is another. Various aspects of respiration can be recorded, especially respiration rate (the rate of breathing) and inspiratory amplitude (roughly, how much is breathed in with each breath). Both of these can be recorded by means of a narrow tube containing mercury which is strapped around the subject's trunk. This ingenious device is sensitive to changes in the circumference of the body, since these change the diameter of the tube and in turn this changes the electrical resistance of the mercury at each point, thus allowing a polygraph record to be made of these changes as the subject breathes in and out.

In Svebak et al. (1982) – the experiment described earlier in which subjects play the video game under a threat and a no-threat condition – it was found that respiration rate was significantly higher in the threat condition (i.e. subjects breathed more rapidly). In fact, respiration rate was on average twice as high as that for the baseline condition after no more than 30 seconds of task performance with threat. It was also found that threat caused higher inspiratory amplitudes (subjects breathed more deeply) in this condition. In other words, the combination of increased arousal and the telic state, brought about by the threat condition, was associated with breathing which was relatively deep and fast.

In the extreme-group experiment reported in Svebak and Murgatroyd (1985) telic-dominant subjects showed significantly greater inspiratory amplitudes than paratelic-dominant subjects (this time the measurement being taken from the thorax rather than the abdomen as occurred in the Svebak et al. (1982) study). The pattern of these differences over the 2½ minutes is shown in Figure 16.

Svebak (1986b), using both relatively extreme groups and a threat versus no-threat manipulation, adduced further data to support a relationship between respiratory activity and the telic-paratelic distinction. This time he took measurements from both the thorax and the abdomen, and found overall high scores for the inspiratory amplitude of the thorax in telic-dominant subjects (thus replicating Svebak and Murgatroyd (1985)). This was true in both conditions. However, under the threat condition several other differences emerged. First of all, the abdominal breathing of telic-dominant subjects also became greater than that of paratelic-dominant subjects. Second, their respiration rate became significantly greater. In other words, under threat the telic-dominant subjects breathed both more rapidly and (since abdominal breathing is deeper than thoracic breathing) more deeply.

Taken together these experiments show that the telic/paratelic distinction is one which enters into respiration as well as other physiological functions, although the relative contribution of telic state as against telic

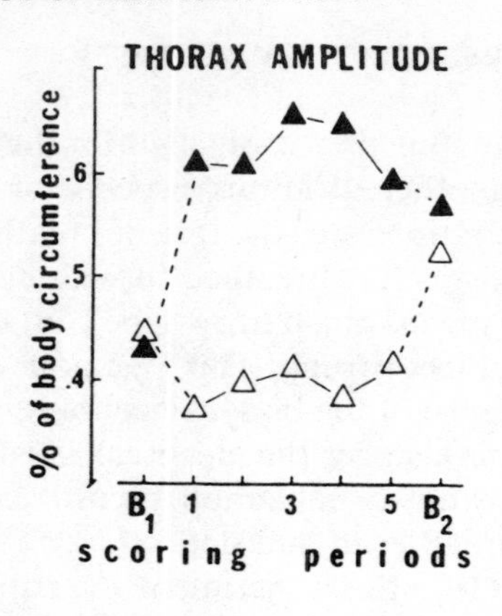

Fig. 16 Mean group-scores of telic- and paratelic-dominant subjects for thorax amplitude over a 2½-minute task. Measurements were taken at half-minute intervals, and pre- and post-task baseline levels are also shown.

dominance, and the way in which these interact with such other factors as felt arousal and effort, remains to be investigated more fully. Meanwhile the evidence is perhaps strong enough to make a cautious prediction that in everyday life hyperventilation (overbreathing) and the psychosomatic complaints that go with this (dizziness, nausea, pounding heart, tingling feelings, etc.) are likely to occur more frequently in telic-dominant than paratelic-dominant people. In this context it is interesting that Svebak and Grossman (1985) reported a positive association between the state of serious-mindedness as measured on the Telic State Measure and number of hyperventilation-related psychosomatic complaints reported when subjects were required to hyperventilate.

In discussing cardiovascular activity, reference was made to an experiment on the effects of a comedy film (Svebak and Apter, 1987). It was noted that in the paratelic state which this 'manipulation' tended to induce in both extremely telic- and paratelic-dominant subjects (ten in each group), *phasic* heart rate changes were observed. The same is true of respiratory activity, laughter itself being a phasic response in which a substantial exhalation ends in an inhalation (the opposite of the gasping for breath which goes with panic). One matter of interest here is the close relationship of the phasic respiratory and heart responses: the sudden jump in heart rate noted earlier is initiated with the exhalation and dies down following the inhalation.

Incidentally, this same experiment lends support to the reversal theory view (Apter 1982: Chapter 8) that the experience of humour is a pleasant paratelic high-arousal experience, since the amount of laughter was positively associated with felt levels of arousal. Certainly this data does not accord well with the more prevalent optimal arousal view that the pleasure of laughter is associated with a return to a moderate level of arousal from a higher level.

CORTICAL ACTIVITY

So far we have looked at research which has investigated the relationship of the telic/paratelic dimension to somatic arousal (in the form of skeletal muscle activity), and autonomic arousal (in the form of cardiovascular and respiratory activity). Let us turn our attention now to the third major type of physiological arousal, and the one which is 'nearest home' for the psychologist: cortical arousal.

Svebak (1982) recorded electroencephalographic (EEG) activity from electrodes placed on the parietal area of the cortex (both right and left hemisphere) while subjects performed the standard video game for the normal 2½-minute period. (The parietal area is, roughly speaking, on top of the head towards the back.) Subjects were selected so as to form extreme telic- and paratelic-dominant groups, and there was a threat-of-shock manipulation so that the game was performed twice, once with and once without the threat of shock. Power-spectrum scores were computed on-line (i.e. while linked up to subjects) for the theta, alpha, and beta frequency bands. (Power-spectrum analysis is a standard technique for getting an overall 'picture' of the relative power found in different frequency bands.)

In general terms what Svebak found was that the paratelic-dominant subjects consistently produced significantly higher power-spectrum scores in the theta and beta bands, and this was true for both the threat and no-threat conditions. Indeed, the conditions had rather little effect in these results, implying that questions of arousal, effort, and the like were playing little part in determining the cortical activation patterns. It was also the case that the paratelic group on average produced higher power-spectrum scores in the alpha band, but this was only true in the baseline scores (i.e. before and after the task, while resting) and for the left hemisphere. By and large, however, and contrary to the current fashion for attributing a variety of psychological effects to the differences between hemispheres, the hemisphere differences in the present data were relatively unimportant, and the higher amplitudes shown by paratelic subjects in the theta and beta bands occurred in both hemispheres.

Since the threat manipulation in this experiment did not seem to have had much observable effect on EEG power-spectrum activity, Svebak (1985b) decided to carry out another experiment using a manipulation known to exert marked changes in cortical activation, to see if this would make any difference to the pattern of results found in the earlier experiment. This manipulation involved the use of self-induced respiratory changes of the kind known as *hyperpnea* and *hypopnea*. In hyperpnea the subject is instructed to breathe 'in and out as fast and as deep as possible from now until you are told to stop'. For hypopnea the subject is told to 'stop breathing and continue to hold your breath until you are allowed to go back to normal breathing again'. In the present experiment each of these periods lasted for 30 seconds. As before, power-spectrum scores were computed on-line for the theta, alpha, and beta frequency bands respectively, the recordings coming from the parietal area. The subjects consisted of a group of ten extremely telic-dominant and ten extremely paratelic-dominant subjects drawn from a group of 110 university students.

As expected, the hyperpnea (the overbreathing condition) generally increased power scores from their baseline levels for both groups of subjects in the theta and beta bands, and the hypopnea (the underbreathing condition) generally lowered them. (However, the alpha scores were depressed for both groups in both conditions in comparison with baseline. This was probably an artefact of the very high baseline alpha levels due to instructions to subjects to keep their eyes closed before the breathing task and open them during it – alpha scores are always high with eyes closed and low with eyes open.)

How did the increased and decreased levels interact with the telic/paratelic subject grouping? Overall, in both conditions, and over all three bands, the paratelic-dominant subjects scored more highly than the telic-dominant subjects. And the difference was especially marked in the theta band, as shown in Figure 17. In other words, despite the changes induced by the different conditions, the main result of this experiment is essentially the same as the previous one. It is therefore possible to conclude that the higher power scores in paratelic-dominant subjects are independent of different levels of cortical arousal, and that the main conclusion of the previous experiment can be generalized across cortical arousal levels.

There would seem, therefore, to be a characteristic difference in what one might think of as 'cortical information-processing style' between the telic- and paratelic-dominant subjects. As Svebak points out, since it is not the case that the paratelic-dominant subjects are producing high activity in one band rather than another, but are rather displaying the same pattern in *all* bands, it would seem that relatively high amplitudes are a general characteristic of the paratelic-dominant person and relatively low amplitudes of the telic-dominant individual. He goes on to argue, consistent with current theory (e.g. Cooper, Osselton, and Shaw 1980), that high amplitudes reflect a large cortical area in synchrony 'driven' by a common source, whereas small amplitudes, in contrast, represent numerous small areas independently in synchrony. In other words, the cortical activation in

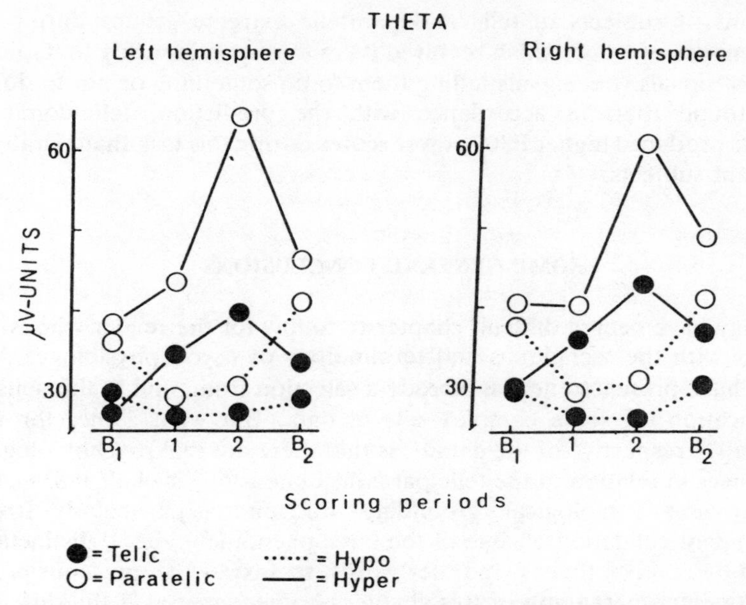

Fig. 17 Mean theta band power-spectrum scores for telic- and paratelic-dominant subjects, from right and left hemispheres respectively, during hyperpnea (deep and rapid breathing) and hypopnea (breath holding). In each case the breathing instructions were followed for 30 secs, and measurements taken after 5 secs and 20 secs. Pre- and post-task baseline levels are also shown. (After Svebak 1985b).

the paratelic-dominant subject is rather global and diffuse, whereas in the telic-dominant subject it tends to be more focal and localized at a number of particular points. Intriguingly, then, the phenomenological distinctions made by reversal theory seem to be reflected in the very workings of the brain itself as displayed in EEG power-spectrum recordings.

Another kind of measure of cortical activity is that of event-related cortical potentials, which are averaged EEG responses to particular repeated sensory inputs. One of the most widely studied of these has been the P300, so-called because it has a peak which occurs around 300 milliseconds after stimulus onset. The P300 is generally held to be a manifestation of an individual's ability to attend to stimuli that are 'task relevant'. This type of potential is usually discussed in cognitive terms, but ability to attend to task-relevant information will presumably also depend on motivational factors. For reasons discussed in an earlier chapter, we would expect the telic state to provide a more favourable metamotivational setting for such goal-oriented attention than the paratelic state, and if this is the case then the P300 power score should be higher in the telic state. Svebak, Howard, and Rimehaug (1987) tested this by comparing the reactions of subjects in telic and paratelic extreme groups during the performance of a task which required them to respond quickly to 'Go' and 'No Go' signals (i.e. signals telling them to do something or not to do it). They found that, in accordance with the prediction, telic-dominant subjects produced higher P300 power scores during this task than paratelic-dominant subjects.

SOME GENERAL CONCLUSIONS

This may have been a difficult chapter to follow for the reader who is not familiar with the techniques and terminology of psychophysiology. And what I have presented here is already a selection from, and in this sense a simplification of, some complex sets of data. But what comes through above all, irrespective of the details, is that there are real psychobiological differences in relation to the telic/paratelic dimension (Svebak 1983). And this provides a biological 'grounding' for, and a particularly strong independent validation of, one of the basic phenomenological distinctions offered by reversal theory. In other words, to answer the questions posed in the opening paragraph of this chapter, it *does* seem as if the different ways of organizing subjective experience suggested in the theory are related to different ways of organizing physiological and neurophysiological processes in the body.

Looking at the data as a whole, Svebak (1985a) has attempted a first tentative patterning of the results by means of a table (Table 2). Laying things out in this way brings out, among other things, an emerging relationship between the telic state and strong tonic changes on the one hand, and the paratelic state and strong phasic changes on the other. And this seems to be pleasingly consistent with the phenomenological description of the telic state as involving movement towards long-term and preferably planned goals, and the paratelic state as concerned with the present moment, preferably in intense, vigorous and spontaneous ways.

Another very general point to emerge is that measures of physiological arousal, be they somatic, autonomic, or cortical, cannot necessarily be equated with, or used as indices for, subjective arousal. For example, the felt arousal of telic and paratelic subjects may be high, but this will only be reflected in a rising EMG gradient in the case of telic subjects, the gradient tending to remain flat in the paratelic case (Svebak 1984). Or again, similar levels of felt arousal may be related to very different heart rate increases in telic- and paratelic-dominant subjects (Svebak 1986a). In both these cases, looking at the objective measures alone, erroneous conclusions could be drawn, at least in some subjects, about arousal as experienced.

This lends support to the general reversal theory approach which, as we have seen in earlier chapters, argues that it is necessary to start from

Table 2 A tentative pattern of relationships between metamotivational mode and activation patterns in different physiological response systems, as suggested by current findings.

	Metamotivational state	
	Telic	Paratelic
1. Skeletal muscles		
a) Tonic changes (passive)	High	Low
b) Phasic changes (active)	Low	High
2. Heart rate		
a) Tonic changes (threat)	High	Low
b) Phasic changes (comedy)	Low	High
3. Pulse transit time	Short	Long
4. Respiration rate (threat)	High	Low
5. Respiration amplitude		
a) Tonic changes (threat)	High	Low
b) Phasic changes (comedy)	Low	High
6. Cortical activity		
a) Area in synchrony	Small	Large
b) P300 amplitude	Large	Small

mental life and work outward into behaviour and physiology rather than, as is customary in psychophysiology, to remain at the level of objective measurements alone or to make unsubstantiated and simplistic inferences from objective physiological measurements to features of mental life. In the research described in this chapter, sense could *only* be made of the data by reference to the actual subjective metamotivational characteristics reported by the subjects. And once such reference was made, then certain patterns began to emerge. To put this another way (*viz*. Svebak 1983: 71) there were qualitative as well as quantitative differences in motivation, and the qualitative differences necessarily related to subjective mental states.

At the very least this implies that experimenters in psychophysiology should take some account of the subjective feelings of their subjects and carry out *post hoc* testing of some kind to this end. It is no good assuming that subjects will have no emotions (especially in situations which involve intrusive interference with the subjects' bodies by means of needles and the use of fearsome-looking forms of instrumentation). Neither can one assume that a manipulation intended to produce some desired state will have done so without checking this in some way by means of ratings scales, structured interviews, or the like.

This conclusion may sound rather negative. But the positive side is that psychophysiological research which does take subjective feelings into account may help to make sense of the notorious lack of correlation between different measures of physiological arousal which has characterized the field, and the inconsistencies which often seem to occur when researchers attempt to replicate each other's experiments. In particular, reversal theory implies, and Svebak's results tend to support, the notion that subjects may produce different physiological records if different experimental procedures have tended to produce contrasting metamotivational states in their subjects.

In any case, there is much to be gained from 'playing off' different types of data against each other in reference to the same experimental situation. Thus objective physiological data may help to validate the judgements of the interviewer, while the interviewer's evidence and insights may add depth of interpretation to the physiological record, making it more psychologically meaningful. An excellent example of such 'playing off' is provided in the experiment by Svebak and Murgatroyd (1985) in which there was a kind of 'triangulation' between psychometric data (the TDS), psychophysiological data (as described earlier in this chapter), and interviews about subject's lifestyles (examples of which were quoted in the last chapter). The psychophysiological and interview data helped to tie the interview material into systematic and rigorous psychometric and experimental evidence; and the psychophysiological data were given meaning in terms of the personality inventory and the interview material derived from subjects about their everyday lives. In this way the three different methods supported each other in building up a coherent and multifaceted picture of telic dominance.

6

The Experience of Social Pressures

I am not more sure that my soul lives, than I am that perverseness is one of the primitive impulses of the human heart – one of the indivisible primary faculties, or sentiments, which give direction to the character of Man.

The Black Cat
Edgar Allan Poe (1809–44)

NEGATIVISTIC AND CONFORMIST MODES

It is easy to become so involved in trying to make sense of one aspect of the experience of motivation that one forgets that there are others. Another important component of the experience of motivation which we have not yet examined, and which we shall turn to in this chapter, concerns whether one sees what one is trying to do as in accordance with, or contrary to, some social pressure to conform. Is one being compliant or defiant, docile or rebellious, malleable or stubborn, easy or awkward? Is one following the rules or breaking them, being 'good' or being 'bad'?

As before, let us consider some concrete situations, and the way in which you would normally expect to experience them:

1. You are about to meet someone important and you are dressed up and on your best behaviour.
2. You are at a boring dinner party and, to stir things up a bit, you make some provocative remarks.
3. You are at a committee meeting and feel a strong urge to walk out, but you resist it.
4. You go to a party in a lounge suit, only to find that everyone else is in evening dress.

Here we have four types of experience of social pressures of different kinds. In two of them one wants to go along with social expectations and etiquette. In the first such case one succeeds (in meeting someone important), and in the other (case 4) one fails (being dressed incorrectly for the party). In the remaining two situations, one wants to react *against* certain pressures. Again, in one case one succeeds (by not observing the niceties of good behaviour at dinner) and in the other one fails (by being unable to summon the courage to leave the meeting). To put this another way, in two cases one behaves 'badly' – although this was only intended in one of the cases, the other happening by mistake. In the other two cases, one behaves 'well' in the sense that one submits to pressures of expectation – although, again, this was only desired in one of the two cases, occurring in the other through a failure of nerve.

The alert reader will probably already have discerned the way that the argument is going, and that the pattern bears some resemblance to the different ways of experiencing arousal. Just as high arousal can be experienced as pleasant or unpleasant, and likewise low arousal, so reacting in a negative way to social forces of different kinds can be experienced as pleasant or unpleasant, and likewise behaving in a conforming way. And, as before in the case or arousal, this leads to the suggestion that there are two states of mind which are opposite to each other. In this case they are opposite ways of experiencing something about one's behaviour rather than simply one's internal bodily states. This 'something' is the degree to which one perceives one's behaviour to be in accordance with, or contrary to, salient expectations. Let us call this *felt negativism* (although we could equally invert the dimension and call it *felt conformism*). What this means is that when felt negativism is high, one sees oneself to be defying the pressures; when it is low one sees oneself to be going along with them, to be conforming to them. These pressures are not restricted to social conventions, but may be any kind of expectation, norm, rule, regulation, constraint, or requirement. That is, anything which sets limits on what may be done, from the mildest custom to the strongest taboo, or which points or pushes in certain directions, constitutes such a pressure. (The word 'pressure' may be a little strong for some of these limitations, but it is a reasonable word to depict such social forces taken as a whole.)

Having defined the dimension, it is now necessary to define the two opposite ways of experiencing it, that is the new pair of metamotivational modes which have been introduced. Let us call one the negativistic mode and the other the conformist mode. The negativistic mode can be defined as a mode in which one enjoys behaving in a way which one perceives to be in opposition to some external pressure to behave in a particular way, and in which one finds it unpleasant to see oneself to be conforming to such a pressure. The conformist mode can be defined as the inverse of this: it is a mode in which one enjoys behaving in a way which one perceives to be in conformity with some external pressure to behave in a particular way, and in which one finds it unpleasant to see oneself as not conforming to such a pressure. So both modes operate in opposite ways over the whole felt negativism dimension.

Note that, as in the case of arousal-seeking, the negativistic mode defines what one *wants*, and not necessarily what one actually experiences. Just as arousal may be high or low in the arousal-seeking mode, so felt negativism can be high or low in the negativistic mode. For example, the constraints can be such that, although an individual is negativistic in mode, it is not possible for some reason for him or her to express this negativism in behaviour. An obvious example would be a convict whose possibilities for negativism are, in the prison environment, highly restricted. In exactly the same way, because one is in the conformist mode, this does not mean that one will necessarily be able to conform – just as, if one is in the arousal-avoidance mode one will not necessarily experience only low arousal. Thus, one may want to conform to the behaviour of some social group, but not have enough money, or ability, or 'background' to be able to do so. It is therefore important to distinguish 'felt negativism' from 'being in the negativistic mode', just as it was previously essential to distinguish 'felt arousal' from 'being in the arousal-seeking mode'.

Another point to notice is that the kind of pressure being referred to in the definition of the negativistic and conformist states is not any kind of pressure, but social pressure to behave in a *certain kind of way*: to behave in a way that is 'acceptable' in the given situation, to follow the explicit or implicit rules that govern the situation, and so on. For example, in playing a game of tennis one will be aware of pressure from one's opponent to lose; but in opposing this, one is not being negativistic since this is normal and expected in this situation. (We will look at the experience of this kind of pressure of competition in the next chapter.) If, however, one decided to flout convention by taking one's shoes off to play, or break the rules of the game by serving from the wrong place, or be unsportsmanlike by calling a ball hit by one's opponent out when it was in, then, provided one were aware of the significance of what one was doing in this respect, one would be behaving negativistically.

It must be emphasized in all this that which state of mind the individual is in depends on how *he or she* sees the situation and what they are doing in it, not how it is seen, or defined, by others. Thus, a teenager may seem to be dressing in a way which is defiant to his parents or other adult authority. But he may see what he is doing, at least at a given moment, as conforming to the expectations of his own social group; since it is this conformity which is desirable to him, he would be in the conformist mode.

There is a further point here too. It will not always be the case that a social pressure of any kind will be in the focus of attention, although there will always be a variety of such pressures on the fringes of the phenomenal field. For example, in driving one is at least dimly aware of all kinds of rules and regulations governing one's activity, but one is not necessarily thinking about them at a given time or concentrating on them in some way. It seems reasonable to see this kind of situation as essentially conformist: one is happy to go along with the rules without questioning or confronting them. So we see a certain asymmetry here between the two modes. In the negativistic mode there must be some requirement to challenge, and this must therefore be in the focus of the phenomenal field. In the conformist mode there may also be a focal requirement – in this case one that one really wants to go along with – but it may also be the case that there is no salient requirement at all and one is conformist, as it were, by default.

In the light of all this, let us look back at the four situations listed at the beginning of this chapter. In the first, that of meeting someone important (an extreme example would be royalty) the point is that it is not just the meeting itself which is enjoyed; rather, it is the whole paraphernalia which makes the event an occasion, and the business of going along with it and becoming part of it, which is relished. Here we have conformist behaviour enjoyed for itself in the conformist mode. In the next situation, the boring dinner party, there can be a kind of malicious glee in stirring things up and causing consternation by needling someone, or by being *risqué*, or even outrageous. Of course, part of the enjoyment, if one happens to be in the paratelic mode at the same time, will be the excitement caused; but the point being made here is that the expression of the negativism itself, quite apart from any exciting effects which it may have, will be a source of personal pleasure in the negativistic mode. The third example was that of resisting the desire to walk out of a committee meeting. Here one's failure to defy the situation will produce a certain disgruntlement in itself, quite apart from the displeasure of what is becoming a tedious occasion. Finally, going to a party in the wrong clothes, thus committing a social solecism, exemplifies the distressing experience of acting negativistically although one's intention had been to conform. (In this case, as one must presume is fairly typical, whether one sees one's action as high or low in negativism will depend on how one supposes that others will be viewing this action.)

Since one's actions (unlike felt level of arousal) are normally under voluntary control, it would appear that, unless one makes mistakes or is inadequate to the situation in some way – as in two of the examples just given – there will be little need to experience low felt negativism in the negativistic mode or high felt negativism in the conformist mode. However, this overlooks something important, which is that there will very often be more than one salient pressure at a given time, and that sometimes these pressures will work in opposite directions. In conforming to one pressure in such circumstances, you will necessarily be acting against the other. For instance, in everyday life one will frequently have to suppress one's negativistic behaviour because the consequences of expressing it are such that it would not be worthwhile – which is another way of saying that the pressure to 'be sensible' is too great. We have already seen this in the example of the failure to leave a committee meeting. In the same way, one will probably not be rude to one's boss in case one loses one's job, even though it would give one great pleasure at the time to be thoroughly impolite. Similarly, one may behave negativistically because, even though one is in the conformist mode, the pressure is too strong to resist. For example, you are having dinner out and your companion asks you to call the waiter over and complain about the quality of the food. You are in conformist mode, and conform to this pressure to behave in a certain way, but in doing so, in causing a fuss, you will inevitably also see yourself as acting to this extent negativistically. You create a scene, because the pressure to conform to the demand to do so is greater than the counter-pressure not to do so. Since you are in the conformist mode, you submit, while hating that degree of negativism which you see to be forced on you.

The negativistic and conformist modes, as conceived in this way, might each seem to be implicated in a hodge-podge of diverse actions. After all, the external pressure that is responded to can be any kind of social convention or expectation or norm. And between them, responses in the negativistic and conformist modes cover pretty much the whole gamut of human activity: there is, after all, nothing we can do which we cannot experience as in some way for or against some external social pressure, from giving a research seminar to putting the cat out. But it is exactly this generality, this fact that the two states of mind between them appear to be applicable to every situation that one finds oneself in, which makes it appropriate to think of them as different ways of interpreting a general and omnipresent aspect of motivation ('omnipresent' in the sense that there are always social pressures in the phenomenal field, whether or not at the focus of attention). In other words, it is precisely this which makes it appropriate to think of them as a pair of metamotivational modes, on a par with other pairs of modes we have looked at in earlier chapters.

BEING JEKYLL AND BEING HYDE

At base, the two modes are directional: they are about whether one is willing to go along in the same direction as the principal pressure which one perceives to be acting on one, or whether one feels the need to turn around and move against it. Put in this way, it is obviously related to the deep-rooted biological distinction between flight and attack as alternative ways of dealing with threat; but in the human case they have become a part of the whole fabric of social consciousness and inform all our actions in some way, and not just our responses to potential danger. Do we 'go with the flow', or do we 'say no'? Indeed, the negativistic mode, defined in this general way, would seem to be an essential ingredient in what makes us human: our ability to say no, to rebel, to refuse to conform to a pressure or expectation once we have identified it, even to be simply 'bloody minded' on occasion. And it is a part of human nature which, on the whole, psychologists have been unwilling or unable to assimilate into their theories – so that, generally speaking, it has tended simply to be ignored in psychology.

Since *both* modes are part of human experience, and it is possible to switch from one to the other, it means that each of us in some measure lives a Jekyll-and-Hyde existence. Indeed, it is perhaps the recognition of both these characteristics in ourselves that made Stevenson's novel such a classic. This is not to say that Jekyll and Hyde play equal parts in our everyday lives. Most of us are presumably strongly conformist-dominant: most of the time we are not like nice Dr Jekyll. But the negativistic mode is always waiting in the wings, and from time to time its is called on stage.

What are the factors which induce reversals between the negativistic and conformist modes? They can be seen to fall under the same three headings as those which govern reversal in the pairs we have already looked at.

First of all, there are the factors which induce contingent reversals. For example, it would seem to be the case that situations which are interpreted as *unfair* in some way will induce the negativistic mode: one will certainly feel defiant towards a colleague who behaves in a manner which is less than even-handed; one will be furious if one catches an opponent cheating in some game one is playing; and so on. In other words, negativistic behaviour on the part of someone else is likely to induce the negativistic mode in oneself. Again, situations that seem to impose *limitations* on one's movements or actions seem to call forth the negativistic state, especially if one sees them as arbitrary – one chafes at such restrictions and challenges them at every turn. On the other hand, being a member of a large crowd, for example at a political meeting, seems to induce the conformist mode, and with it a desire to become part of, and go along with, the feelings and expectations of the crowd, whatever these might be.

Second, frustration can obviously call forth the negativistic mode. If one is unable to keep up to certain expectations in a group that one belongs to, then one may reach a point at which one says 'bugger them' and does something defiant. Less obviously, perhaps, frustration can also act in the other direction. An inability to defy the expectations of a group of people may eventually produce a kind of relieved feeling of 'if one can't beat them, join them'. In other words, one gives up resisting and conforms.

Finally, it is not unreasonable to suppose that if there are satiation effects at work in the other pairs of modes, then this will be the case here too. And indeed, it does help to explain those sudden and apparently inexplicable feelings of 'irrational' rebelliousness which many of us experience from time to time, especially when we have been on our best behaviour for a long time – for example, at a business meeting, at a funeral, in hospital, at a prize-giving. Here, indeed, there may be no obvious pressure to resist so that we have to cast around to find something to object to or cause a fuss about.

Sometimes the reversal will have immediate behavioural effects, which will make it evident to observers, especially since negativistic behaviour can be dramatic and shocking. In other cases it will not be obvious to others which mode one is in, and whether one has changed modes. Thus on some social occasions one may suddenly find oneself totally out of sympathy with the whole affair and wanting to do something outrageous, but keep one's impulses in check – for example because one is also in the telic state and aware of the long-term damage which could be caused by such behaviour. The result is that one keeps smiling and the negativism one is experiencing is not made manifest.

MODE COMBINATIONS

A question which you will, no doubt, have had at the back of your mind, and which may have been brought to the forefront by the last point, is that of the relationship between negativism and conformity on the one hand and the telic and paratelic (including arousal-avoidance and arousal-seeking) modes on the other. In principle, it would seem that both the negativistic and the conformist modes can be combined with either the telic or the paratelic mode and that it is possible to experience each of these possible combinations in experience. This does not mean that one mode may not be more likely to be associated with another in a given individual, so that these two modes tend to occur together, but that phenomenologically the negativistic and conformist pairs are independent of the other mode pairs and qualitatively distinct. So let us consider each of the possible pairings in turn.

First of all, in the telic-conformist mode combination, one would be trying to conform to all salient requirements during the pursuit of a goal which one saw to be important. For example, while taking an examination one would be likely to see passing the examination as an important goal, and conforming to the rules (not cheating) as essential to the achievement of the goal. Second, in the paratelic-conformist combination, one might be attempting to enjoy oneself, and feel excitement, by conforming to some current fashion (for example dressing in essentially the same way as others and dancing to the same beat at the disco), or by becoming part of some larger group activity, like a parade or a political rally, which 'sweeps you off your feet'. Third, we have telic-negativism. Here the individual will see himself or herself to be acting against some social pressure in order to reach a seemingly essential goal. An example might be an artist defying convention in order to achieve a particular aesthetic effect, or a politician refusing to go along with other members of his party on some important issue. Fourth, we have the combination of paratelic mode with negativistic mode. A typical type of action here would be that of behaving badly in order to produce exciting effects: swearing, writing graffiti in public places, starting rows, gossiping in a malicious way, speeding, and so on. We can note here that an activity which is exciting in itself may often be enhanced through an awareness that it is immoral or involves breaking a law, from reading pornography to taking cannabis.

When modes are combined in this way, it seems that one mode can be used 'in the service of' the other. Thus, behaving in a negativistic way, while itself pleasurable in the negativistic mode, can also be used, as in the examples just given, *in order to* achieve excitement, that is to achieve one of the satisfactions of the paratelic (including arousal-seeking) modes. Or, to take one of the other examples just given, in conforming to the rules in the examination room one can be seen as behaving in this way *in order to* have a chance of achieving the goal of passing the examination. In both these cases a member of the negativistic-conformist mode pair is being used in the service of a member of the telic–paratelic pair. But in principle matters could be the other way round. Thus, one could enter a situation likely to induce the paratelic mode in order to defy pressures to be serious: thus a schoolchild could go out to play with his friends primarily in order to defy the pressure of his parents to do his homework. Alternatively, a child could enter a situation likely to induce the telic mode (for example, going to church) in order to conform to expectations and pressures of parents and others. Now it may well be the case that in a given person one mode tends, when it occurs with another mode, to be used in the service of that mode. For example, a particular person may well tend to use the negativistic mode in the service of the paratelic mode, when these two occur together. Another person (or, indeed, the same person) may tend to use the telic mode in the service of the conformist mode. If future research shows that such couplings are characteristic of different individuals, then we would be faced with another important aspect of personality – and one which, since it deals with meaningful structures and relationships *within* a personality, will inevitably tend to be missed in trait formulations. The implication for reversal theory would be that a knowledge of the dominance of each pair of metamotivational modes in a given person would need to be supplemented by a knowledge of the typical hierarchical arrangement of modes across pairs for that individual.

THE POWER OF NEGATIVE THINKING

On the face of it, negativism is liable to cause nothing but disruption, destruction, and distress. So where did it come from? Why do human beings appear to be programmed with the capacity to spend periods of time in the negativistic state and to display such behaviour? Presumably it must serve some personal and social functions, otherwise it would not have survived the exigencies of natural selection during evolution.

In fact, if one considers the matter, one can discern a number of invaluable advantages which flow from the ability to be negativistic. One of these is the continual dissatisfaction – the 'divine discontent' – which appears to be part of human nature. The unwillingness to accept old ways of doing things without regularly re-examining them, the eventual defiance of any dogma, the restless quest for improvement, the intolerance of unnecessary rules, indeed, all those psychological qualities which lead to progress, both social and material, appear to be tied up with the rebellious spirit of negativism. No society is likely to continue for long, leave alone evolve, without the internal dynamic for change which negativism provides. And it would seem that those in the forefront of change – the scientists, artists, engineers, architects, and pioneers of all kinds – particularly need to spend periods in the negativistic state of mind if they are to overcome the inertia of old ideas and ways of doing things. As Picasso once said: 'Every act of creation is first of all an act of destruction.' It is no surprise, therefore, if time and again one finds that the most creative and inventive people are also among those who are the most awkward, 'impossible', boorish, eccentric, and anti-social.

At a more personal level, negativism allows us quickly to test the limits of the situations in which we find ourselves so that we can learn just what is and is not possible and allowable – in the home and the classroom as children, and later as adults in the office, the club, and elsewhere. Furthermore, as we shall see, it enters into anger, and anger also has its function, including warning people when they have tested one's own limits of toleration too far.

There would appear to be one other major function of negativism, and this is interesting enough for us to consider it at a little more length. It relates to an area in which the concept of 'negativism' will already be found; that of developmental psychology. In particular, there are two ages at which children display defiant and difficult behaviour, and to which the concept of negativism has been applied: first, the age between about one and a half and three and a half, and second, the years of mid-adolescence. The first of these two periods has been called by some writers the 'negativistic period' or 'period of resistance'. In it, the child will frequently display episodes of refusing to do anything asked, and even doing exactly the opposite. Psychologists first became aware of it professionally when attempting to test children during this period of persistent 'naughtiness'. One of the earliest accounts is given by Binet and Simon (1905) in relation to their work on the development of their classic intelligence test. The second period, that of the 'storm and stress' of adolescence, is well known to parents and teachers as one of rebelliousness and defiance – manifesting itself in outlandish dress, rudeness, unpunctuality, and a host of other characteristics which in some cases may go so far as to include vandalism and hooliganism.

These two phases of what one might term 'negativistic dominance' would appear to be a normal and preprogrammed part of healthy development and we are therefore led to ask what the function of such negativism might be. The clue is given by the way in which the two periods are similar: they are both major periods of psychological *transition*. In the earlier period, the transition is from babyhood to childhood, and in the second from childhood to adulthood. In other words, the developing individual is, in each case, moving from a certain kind of dependence to a certain kind of independence.

Clearly this will require a struggle if the transition is to be successfully accomplished, and the developing individual must win such independence in the face of a world which, at least at times, is oversolicitous, unable to recognize increased maturity, or even just unwilling to grant the necessary freedom. And this is another way of saying that negativism is needed to establish the new set of personal and other relationships which go with and define increased independence. Thus, the young child can now walk without help, but must demonstrate his or her ability to decide when to walk, and how to walk, and where to walk. The adolescent is sexually mature and able to form intimate relationships with those outside the family, and must demonstrate that he or she is able to decide when to form such relationships, how to form such relationships, and who to form such relationships with. In both these examples, the ability does not in itself necessarily lead to the freedom to use this ability, this freedom having to be won for itself.

But if we look at things phenomenologically rather than behaviourally, we can discern a deeper aspect of all this. The two major life changes we have been referring to would appear to be not only about gaining increased independence, but also about developing enhanced feelings of personal identity. The child is in each case discovering *who* he or she is, and doing this despite the threat to feelings of selfhood that inevitably come with the momentous transformations involved in each of these stages. Erikson has referred to the transformations of adolescence as constituting an 'identity crisis', and the same must be true, albeit in a different way, of the transition from babyhood.

Now the suggestion here will be that negativism helps to maintain identity and to enhance it during these periods. How might it do this? To answer this we first need to look at identity itself. (The following argument is spelled out more fully in Apter (1983)). Identity would appear to have at least the following three components: a sense of personal autonomy, personal distinctiveness, and personal continuity. In other words, to have a feeling of identity one must feel that one is in control of one's own life, that one is different from other people (even unique), and that one remains the same person despite outward changes. Without these qualities one's sense of selfhood will be impoverished and inadequate; indeed, in the extreme case, a lack of these qualities will be associated with psychotic breakdown. Negativism, the tendency to be in the negativistic mode for prolonged periods and to produce behaviour that one will feel to be negativistic, would seem to help in different ways in relation to the development of each of these aspects of identity during the two transition periods we have been talking about.

First of all, negativism can aid the development of a feeling of *autonomy* (the phenomenological counterpart of increased independence) because through negativistic acts the individual can demonstrate to himself (as well as others) his independence, and do so in the clearest possible way. The young child discovers that if he can say no to someone, and resist that person's pressures, then he must have a will of his own. He is now a law unto himself. If the adolescent can decide for himself what to do despite the arguments, cajoling, and sanctions of his parents, then he knows that he can make up his own mind and that the mind to be made up is truly his own. Indeed, he may provoke such parental concern deliberately through his mode of dress, accent, expression of views, and so on in order to provoke pressures which can then be defied.

Second, negativism helps to preserve and develop a sense of *distinctiveness*. Knowing what something is means knowing what it is *not*. (The fish does not know it lives in water, because it has nothing to contrast water with.) As Lowen (1975) has put it, knowing is 'no-ing'. To know what one *is*, therefore, one must see clearly what one is *not*. And what better way of demonstrating to oneself what one is not than by acting out one's opposition? So the young child demonstrates his distinctiveness by deciding he does not like a particular food and will not eat it, even though his brothers and sisters do. The adolescent will adopt an extreme position on some political issue and take to the streets on it. The process is the same: what I am is defined by what I am opposed to. What I am is what I am not.

Third, the sense of *continuity* can be maintained by stubbornly defending whatever is felt to be essential about oneself. There is a reactionary quality about this, which can bring the youngster into conflict with those forces for change thrusting him towards a new level of autonomy. The child may now refuse to get out of the pram, preferring to feel cosseted; and the adolescent may refuse the responsibility of making a career decision, preferring to return to the security of childhood, where others make the decisions. But brakes are needed as well as accelerators in psychological development, and there may be times when the child or the adolescent will need to feel the underlying sameness which also defines him or her before gathering the strength to throw himself or herself once more into the headlong pursuit of change.

In such ways as these, then, negativism can be seen to be a positive rather than negative psychological characteristic. Our conclusion must be that it is essential to psychological health and development, and on the whole more beneficial than detrimental to society – however uncomfortable its consequence may be at times, or however damaging its effects may be on those occasions when it leads to extreme forms of mindless destruction.

ANGER

When we were discussing the basic emotions of anxiety, excitement, relaxation, and boredom, it may have occurred to the reader to wonder what had happened to the presumably equally basic emotion of anger. Now that the conformist and negativistic modes have been introduced it is at last possible to see where anger fits into the picture. It is obviously a negativistic mode emotion. That is, the angry feeling of wanting to hurt, harm, or destroy is a clear expression in consciousness of opposition towards some person or situation and of an urgent intention to move against the pressures that emanate from this source – be they expectations, presumptions, threats, orders, or whatever. In other words, the normal expression of anger is to do something which one is not expected to do or which is not normally allowed – such as swearing, breaking something, or hitting someone.

Putting it this way reminds us that anger is not only a negativistic emotion, but also a high-arousal emotion. Indeed, the more angry one feels, the higher the arousal which is experienced, and, it would seem, the more unpleasant the experience. In this sense, anger is just like anxiety. It must therefore be the case that, like anxiety, it is a telic arousal-avoidance emotion. How, then, does it relate to anxiety? Why do we sometimes feel anxiety in the telic mode and sometimes anger? The answer is that when, in the telic mode, the negativistic mode is also operating, high arousal will be felt as anger, but when the negativistic mode is not operating (i.e. when the conformist mode prevails), then high arousal will be felt as anxiety. In other words, it is precisely the presence of the negativistic mode at a given time which *converts the anxiety of the telic mode into anger*. (As with anxiety, we can take anger here to represent a set of emotions which are essentially the same but differ in terms of intensity, duration, context, etc. In the case of anger, these would include irritation, annoyance, temper, fury, and rage.)

If negativism converts anxiety to anger, what effect does it have on each of the other basic emotions of excitement, relaxation, and boredom? Let us take relaxation first. If arousal is low when the telic mode is combined with the negativistic mode, then the arousal level will be felt as pleasant. The word 'relaxation' would still be fitting for such a state of unemotional antagonism, but another word which is a better antonym for anger in this respect would probably be 'placidity'.

When we come to excitement and boredom, we are dealing with the combination of the negativistic with the paratelic, rather than the telic, mode. That is, we are talking about the experience of hostility and opposition which occurs within a protective frame of some kind – for example while playing sport or watching a film. This means that high arousal will now be enjoyed and that the anger will be experienced as *parapathic* anger (which, you will recall, means an emotion which is unpleasant in the telic mode but pleasant in the paratelic). Hence, it is now the kind of devilish glee one might experience while being objectionable in some social setting, or the joyous hate one experiences towards the villain in a cowboy film. Following a useful convention for parapathic emotions, we can put this parapathic anger in inverted commas and refer to it as 'anger'. As to low arousal in the negativistic-paratelic mode combination, the paratelic word 'boredom' would be quite suitable, but again there is a word in the English language which more exactly expresses this negatavistic low arousal looking for high arousal, and the word is 'sullen'.

We now have two versions of the arousal-seeking and arousal-avoidance curves: a conformist version, which is the version we were in fact dealing with in Chapter 2, and a negativistic version. The negativistic version is shown in Figure 18.

The effect of all this is that we now have eight different kinds of emotions in the new, larger schema, rather than the original four. The upshot is that there are two alternative forms of pleasant high arousal, two of unpleasant high arousal, two of pleasant low arousal, and two of unpleasant low arousal. And the analysis implies that only *one* or the other of each of these two forms, negativistic and conformist, can be experienced at a given time. For instance, one would not be able to experience both anger and anxiety at the same instant, although of course it would be possible to oscillate between them if there were rapid alterations between the negativistic and conformist modes while arousal remained high. Another way of putting this is to say that either the graph shown in Figure 3 applies, or the graph in Figure 18, but it is possible to *reverse* from one graph to the other just as previously, in the graph in Figure 3, it was possible to reverse from one curve to another. In doing so one's position in the space defined by the axes of these graphs (felt arousal and hedonic tone) remains the same, but the emotion associated with that position in the space is transformed into another emotion, for example, it is transformed from excitement to 'anger'.

If the emotion of anger is defined in terms of high felt arousal in the presence of the negativistic mode, where does this leave felt negativism? The answer is that while felt negativism plays no part in the definition of anger, it is an important determinant of the hedonic tone associated with anger. Remember that felt negativism is the degree to which one sees oneself to be actually behaving in a negative way, and that when this is high in the negativistic mode, the action is enjoyed. Thus, if one expresses one's

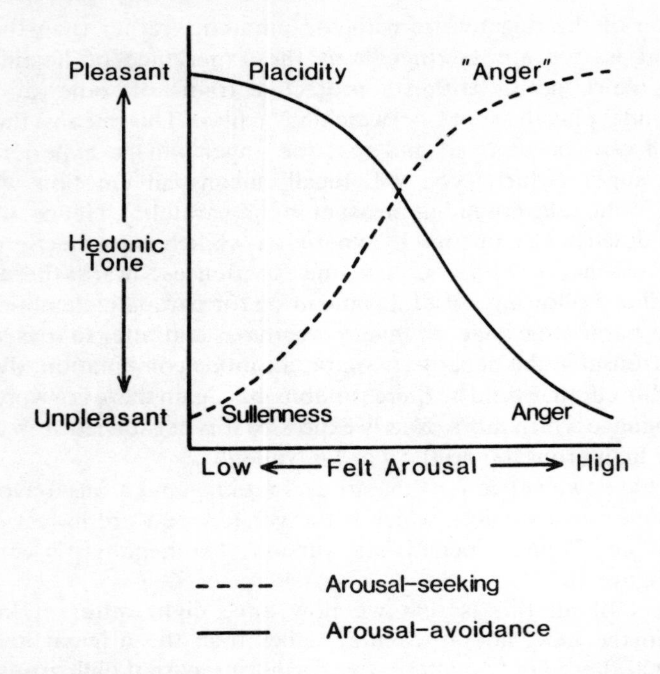

Fig. 18 The hypothetical relationship between arousal and hedonic tone for the negativistic mode. One curve shows the arousal-seeking version of this relationship (represented by the dashed line) and the other the arousal-avoidance version (represented by the continuous line).

anger effectively, by overcoming opposition, causing damage, being hurtful, and so on, these actions will be experienced as pleasant. If, on the other hand, one is unable to express one's anger then the resulting low felt negativism will be distinctly unpleasant. (Conversely, as we have seen, being appeasing, conforming, staying in line, etc. will be pleasant in the conformist mode in which 'making waves' will be experienced as embarrassing and unfortunate.) If one gets into a rage and breaks a vase, therefore, the moment of breaking the vase, and immediately afterwards, will be enjoyable – or at least that component of the experience which is to do with felt negativism will be enjoyable.

Consequently, there are always two potential sources of satisfaction, or dissatisfaction, in the negativistic mode. One is to do with whether the preferred level of arousal has been achieved through a negativistic act, this preferred level of course being high or low depending on whether the arousal-seeking or arousal-avoidance mode is operative at the time. The other, as we have just seen, concerns whether the preferred high level of felt negativism itself has been achieved, this high level remaining the preferred level in the negativistic mode whether or not it is the arousal-seeking or the arousal-avoidance mode which is operating at the same time. It is therefore possible to experience mixtures of pleasure and displeasure in relation to anger or angry acts. For example, if one says something spiteful in the negativistic mode, this may give pleasure, but if one is concomitantly in the telic mode the increased arousal that goes along with this will be unpleasant. Whether the overall result is more pleasant than unpleasant will then depend on just how high one perceives one's negativism to have been, and how high one's arousal level is actually experienced as being. All the same considerations apply to the conformist mode, except that now pleasure will be associated with low felt negativism and displeasure with high felt negativism. If all this is becoming confusing, Table 3 may help you to see the pattern. This table shows which combinations will be wholly pleasant (in some degree or another, depending on just how high or low the two variables are); if the combination in each cell of this table is not that shown, then the experience will be partly or wholly unpleasant rather than pleasant.

Table 3 The outcome, in terms of hedonic tone, of different combinations of felt arousal and felt negativism. For simplicity, only pleasant outcomes are shown; it is to be understood that unpleasant outcomes will arise if the opposite modes to those shown in each cell are operative.

		LOW	HIGH
FELT AROUSAL	HIGH	Pleasant in the Conformist and Arousal-seeking mode.	Pleasant in the Negativistic and Arousal-seeking mode.
	LOW	Pleasant in the Conformist and Arousal-avoidance mode.	Pleasant in the Negativistic and Arousal-avoidance mode.

To try to bring these abstract relationships to life, consider the following scenario. You are having a row with your girlfriend or wife, and as a consequence you are in the negativistic mode and arousal is mounting. You take the row to be serious, and therefore you are also in the telic, arousal-avoidance mode. The anger, as it mounts, therefore becomes increasingly unpleasant, and your bottling it up makes it more intense (and therefore more unpleasant) and denies you the pleasure of felt negativism. At last you reach breaking point and say something hurtful. The sudden surge of arousal at this instant is highly unpleasant, but mixed with this is the momentarily equally intense pleasure of the felt negativism. She starts to cry, and this induces the conformist mode in you, in which the felt negativism now feels bad. So instead, you start to apologize and to appease, and this feels good. Your arousal starts to subside and this feels better too. She makes a joke, and this induces the paratelic mode, and with it the need for higher arousal. You now start to argue in a playful way which you both recognize is not serious, but which induces the negativistic mode again. The 'anger' you now experience becomes increasingly pleasant as it builds up in the paratelic mode, and you egg each other on; but the low felt negativism, the lack of real impact in what you are saying, becomes galling. You therefore 'needle' even more and produce an angry effect in her. This felt negativism feels good, but her reaction switches you back into the telic mode in which the increased arousal now feels bad and . . . One could continue this little 'drama' indefinitely; the point is that there is always a potential conflict between the two sources of satisfaction and dissatisfaction in each mode and this can help to generate sequences of different combinations of mode, felt arousal level and level of felt negativism.

THE NEGATIVISM DOMINANCE SCALE

Just as there appear to be innate biases towards the telic or paratelic mode, the degree of such bias in one direction or the other being a personality characteristic, so we may assume that there are innate biases to be in the negativistic or conformist mode. As already implied in discussing the use of negativism, we can think of this personality characteristic as 'negativism dominance' (although we could of course equally well invert the characteristic and conceive of it as 'conformity dominance').

It may well be the case that the amount of time which most people spend in the negativistic mode is relatively small in comparison with the conformist mode, except in those stages of developmental transition discussed above which appear to be more or less universally characterized by negativism dominance. In this the relationship between the two modes may be unlike that between the telic and paratelic modes, which appear to be more evenly balanced in most people. But the principle remains the same for alternative modes between which different individuals will display differing degrees of bias.

To measure this characteristic, a Negativism Dominance Scale (NDS) has been developed by McDermott along lines similar to the Telic Dominance Scale. Copies of the scale itself, however, bear the innocuous title Social Reactivity Scale in order not to imply anything which might bias a subject's responses through a social desirability effect. The items in the scale, like those in the Telic Dominance Scale, are forced choice, with a 'not sure' option. They are scored, consonant with the name of the scale, in the negativistic direction.

The scale was constructed by subjecting an initial pool of items to a process of rating by 100 students at a US university, followed by a first tryout on another 100 American students, followed by item analysis. The resulting scale, consisting of 30 items which were not excluded at either of these steps (together with four 'filler items' used to prevent response set from occurring) was then administered to 130 sixteen- to seventeen-year-old pupils at a US high school and 136 seventeen-year-olds from five schools in Cardiff, Wales. These two sets of data were factor-analysed independently, and in both cases a two-factor solution was found to be most appropriate and produced similar patterns of item loadings. Further statistical analysis showed that the similarity between the two sets of data from different cultures was great enough for them to be treated together. So a final factor analysis was carried out on both sets of data combined. The seven items which loaded highest on each of these two factors on this final analysis were then selected to make up two subscales. Together with four 'filler' items, the final Negativism Dominance Scale therefore consisted of 18 items in all (see McDermott and Apter 1988).

What were these two factors which gave rise to the two subscales? Inspection of the items disclosed that one of the factors involved a kind of negativism which is directed towards obtaining pleasure, especially in the form of fun and excitement, in an actively provocative way. The second factor was more to do with reaction to disappointment and frustration, and displayed a tone of vengefulness, bitterness, and vindictiveness. It was decided, therefore, to call the first factor 'proactive negativism' and the second 'reactive negativism', which brings out the way in which the first is about 'going out and looking for trouble', whereas the second is about 'causing trouble when things do not go right'. It would appear that the proactive form of negativism, therefore, is one which is likely to be experienced in the paratelic state, and that the reactive may be associated with frustration in the telic state, although undoubtedly matters are more complicated than this and will require further research. (The two factors are also not orthogonally related, which means that they correlate with each other to some extent.)

The nature of these two factors can best be exemplified by means of items from the scale itself. Here are several examples of items from the proactive negativism subscale:

> Do you tease people unnecessarily just so as to have some fun at their expense?
>
> (a) yes, often, or (b) no, hardly ever, or (c) not sure.

Do you find it exciting to do something 'shocking'?
(a) yes, often, or (b) no, hardly ever, or (c) not sure.

In contrast, here are a couple of examples from the reactive negativism subscale:

If you ask a person at a party to dance with you who says 'no' without offering any explanation, would you
(a) get annoyed, or (b) accept it, or (c) not sure.

If you get yelled at by someone in authority, would you
(a) get angry and argue back or
(b) try hard to avoid an argument, or
(c) not sure.

In order to validate this final version of the scale, McDermott examined the scores of 72 American high school students (drawn from the group of 130 originally used in scale development) against three criteria. These criteria were the number of non-excused absences from school, the number of referrals (for misbehaviour) by the teachers to the headmaster, and academic achievement as measured by grade point averages. All of these applied to the semester in which the scales were taken. Excused (as against non-excused) absences were used as a check on this data, the assumption being that these absences (accompanied by medical certificates, or letters from parents) would be unlikely to be related to negativism, in contrast to the other three criteria where one would expect a relationship to be found. In fact, significant correlations were found in the directions expected for the group as a whole in relation to all three criteria (i.e. positively for the first two and negatively for grade point average) for both the proactive and the reactive subscales and for the total score. Indeed, for the total scale score all the correlations were significant at the 0.0005 level. (At the same time, correlations with excused absences for the group were nonsignificant in relation to either of the subscales, or scale total.) It could be concluded that the more negativistic the child, as measured by the scale, the more he or she would be likely to truant from school, get into trouble with teachers, and do badly in terms of academic achievement. The data therefore clearly provided support for the validity of the scale.

As another type of validation, McDermott (1987, 1988b) carried out interviews with a group of high-scoring and a group of low-scoring subjects (three males and three females in each group) selected from a sample of British students. His aim was to repeat the kind of interview study carried out by Svebak and Murgatroyd (1985) on telic dominance (as described in Chapter 4), this time focussing on negativism dominance. In this way he hoped both to provide evidence for what has been called 'ecological validity' (the extent to which a construct relates meaningfully to everyday life) and to explore further the lifestyle and other differences between negativistic- and conformist-dominant subjects. (By 'conformist-dominant', of course, one means subjects who are low in negativistic dominance in the sense that they produce low scores on the scale.)

As in the Svebak and Murgatroyd study, subjects were asked, 'What did you do yesterday?' But this was followed by questions which focussed on reactions to external pressure: 'Which of these things did you do because you had to do them?' 'How did you feel about that?' 'Which of these things you did yesterday did you do even though you should *not* have done them?' 'How did you feel about that?' 'Why *did* you do them?'

To provide something of the flavour of these two types of dominance, I shall reproduce some brief extracts from the transcripts of the interviews. First of all, here is a subject (female), who was negativistic-dominant on the total scale score, answering the question, 'What did you do yesterday?'

> Oh . . . fuck it. (Laughs) What day was it yesterday? Monday. I had an eleven o'clock lecture in psychology and then I went around town with Cathy and then I met some people for lunch and after that I was sorting out some things, like a house for next year. And then it was towards dinner time. And ten in the evening I was just with some friends and then I went to bed and then I went to sleep.

Contrast this with a conformist-dominant subject (male) answering the same question. Here is the beginning of the answer.

> I probably got up fairly late. I can't remember the exact time. Probably about half ten. Got washed. Got changed. Had breakfast. Had a read and a pray. I remember my Mum asked me to give her a lift to town 'cause the bus drivers were on strike. So I said I'd take her in about twelve o'clock 'cause I had to go into college anyway to drop a letter off to you . . . to tell you the time I was coming in. So I took Mum in about twelve o'clock.

Quite apart from the content – the conformist-dominant subject referring to obligations and generally 'being a good boy' – there is a stylistic difference between the two. As McDermott (1987) points out, the negativistic respondent does not sympathize with the tacit requirement to provide a detailed description of the day, and gives only a generalized and minimal account. Furthermore, her swearing at the beginning, and her parodying of her own response by concluding 'and then I went to bed and then I went to sleep' imply that she is unwilling to take the interview entirely seriously or to conform to expectations. The conformist-dominant subject is quite different in these respects: he sets out to satisfy what he sees to be the requirements of the situation by giving a detailed and systematic account of his day. In fact, his response is considerably longer than that of the negativistic-dominant subject, and it is for this reason that only the beginning of it has been quoted here.

The difference between the answers to questions about why they did things which they should not have done, is also instructive. Here are two more extracts to contrast with each other, from two new subjects (male). Both subjects had failed to work during the evening when they should have been preparing for examinations. (All the interviews took place during the examination period.) First the negativistic-dominant interviewee:

> Well, because I was ill I shouldn't have gone out. That was one thing. But everyone had gone out the night before because they had got their exam results and I had sat in with this girl who was really ill as well. She had a really bad throat infection. We got a bit cheesed off sitting around watching the telly all night and then everybody saying what a wonderful time they had. So I thought, 'Well, I'm going out', but I did feel better anyway. It did help me to sleep [laughs] . . . drinking rather a lot.

And now the conformist-dominant subject:

> Oh yeah. Watching telly all evening. You know I hadn't done any revision all day and I had planned to spend the evening, you know two or three hours, revising and I ended up not being able to concentrate for about three-quarters of an hour in front of my books and then watching television all evening so I felt as though I had wasted that time. . . . They were quite informative programmes as well, most of them. So I felt as though I was learning something . . . two of them were on psychology . . . so that was a bit helpful.

The negativistic-dominant subject not only fails to do what he should have done (revise), but does something totally different which might even make things worse: he stays up late and gets drunk. Neither does he show any remorse, but seems rather pleased with himself about it. The conformist-dominant subject by his own account does his best to do what he must do, but finds that he is too tired to concentrate. He therefore chooses a rather mild and relaxing form of distraction (watching television), and even here watches two programmes which, because they are related to the subject he is studying, may help him. Despite this, he is, unlike the negativistic-dominant subject, feeling rather unhappy that he 'had wasted that time'.

In answer to the question 'How did you feel about that?' (referring to failures to do things that should have been done), a conformist-dominant subject (female), who also watched television during the revision period, said:

> I don't think I should have watched as much television. I think I should have done a bit more revision. I feel I should have done a bit more. I wasted some time I shouldn't have done. I had friends around. I could have told them to leave, you know, asked them to leave a bit earlier but I kept on chatting to them. I shouldn't really have done any washing yesterday. I suppose I should have just left it.

Again, we see the feeling that the time was 'wasted' even though some of it was used for the practical purpose of doing some washing.

Let us finally look at two different negativistic answers to this question about feelings connected with failing to do something which should have been done, because they will enable us to contrast proactive and reactive negativism. Both of these subjects (who were negativistic-dominant on total scale scores) went out for the evening when they should have been studying. The first subject's feelings clearly display his proactive negativism:

> Actually it gave me great pleasure going out. I suppose I enjoy doing things I know I shouldn't do. Also, if I can't afford to do something I'll do it. Well, I think I spoil myself sometimes and just go out. I enjoy things better though if I'm not supposed to do them than if I am supposed to do them, or if it's O.K. to do them, because I get more excitement out of doing them then. 'Course you're a bit guilty about it but that was O.K. that was. I wasn't bothered at all.

The second negativistic dominant subject described feelings that were more bitter and angry, and appeared to be reacting to earlier disappointments and disillusionment. She volunteered that she was not bothering to revise 'Because I don't give a shit about exams' (this said vehemently). When the interviewer prompted her to say more she continued:

> I don't know. I've always thought that way. I just don't have any respect for some reason. I've always walked out of exams. I've always done it. I don't know why. I just think there are better things I should be worrying about and better things to be doing.

These are, of course, only brief extracts from longer interviews but they do give a good impression of what it means to be a highly negativistic-dominant or conformist-dominant sort of person, and what episodes of proactive and reactive negativism are like. Taken together, the complete interviews do also show something of the ecological validity of the Negativism Dominance Scale.

7

The Experience of Personal Relationships

> I'll give thrice so much land
> To any well-deserving friend;
> But in the way of a bargain, mark ye me,
> I'll cavil on the ninth part of a hair.
>
> Harry Hotspur in Shakespeare's *King Henry IV*, Part I

Consider what it is like to have just won a game or to have lost it. Imagine, for example, that you have just come off the tennis court, tired and sweating, having finally beaten someone you have been trying to defeat for a long time – or alternatively that you have just lost to someone you considered to be less skillful than you. Certainly you may experience one or another of the emotions we have already discussed, such as excitement or anger. But you will also be likely to experience some other emotion, such as triumph or humiliation.

The account of the emotions which has been given so far is therefore not a complete one; there are other emotions, which we all recognize in our everyday lives, but which have not so far been assimilated to the theory. And a little reflection reveals that these emotions are all ones which arise particularly out of transactions with other people or situations: they are essentially emotions which are to do with relationships, especially interpersonal relationships – emotions like gratitude, hate, and pride.

The relationship between these emotions is particularly difficult to make sense of immediately. Nevertheless there *are* underlying structures which it is possible to discern (Apter and Smith 1985, Apter 1988b, in press). The attempt here will be to show as clearly as possible, and in a step-by-step way, how they can be teased out. Let us start, as we have done before, by considering a set of contrasting situations. (In fact, we shall need to consider several such sets in the course of the chapter in order to give a complete account.)

AUTOCENTRIC AND ALLOCENTRIC MODES

This time, instead of attending to the arousal that might be experienced in the situations to be listed, think of the way in which you might experience the outcome. In other words, the variable in question will be what one might term (albeit a little pompously) 'felt transactional outcome', extending from high loss to high gain. This can refer to many different particular kinds of outcome, but they are all subjectively equivalent in that they are to do with such feelings as those of winning or losing, succeeding or failing, doing well or doing badly. Thus, if you lose at tennis you will be somewhere on the loss side of the dimension and if you win you will be on the gain side – exactly where in each case depending on such subjective factors as how hard you conceive the opposition to have been, what outcome you expected, and so on. Just as for felt arousal, the variable is subjective – it is to do with the way you yourself see the situation, not the way in which it is judged from the outside by someone else (except to the extent that this influences your own way of seeing things).

So here is the first set of situations, again centred on tennis. In the manner to which you will now be becoming accustomed, we shall see two opposite forms of outcome associated with pleasure and two with displeasure:

1. Winning at tennis against a player of comparable ability.
2. Losing at tennis against a player of comparable ability.
3. Winning too easily at tennis against a child who is learning.
4. Deliberately only just winning, or even losing, against a child who is learning.

It goes without saying that, in the normal way of things, winning at tennis against someone of comparable ability (situation 1) is pleasant, and losing against such an opponent is unpleasant (situation 2). But if we assume, for the sake of the argument, that we want the child we are playing against to grow in confidence and ability, and that this is the primary consideration, then we shall want him or her to do well, which is the same as saying that we shall want to do comparatively badly against him or her. So, in this case, the desirable and pleasurable outcome will be that depicted as situation 4 – only just winning, or even losing. In contrast, the situation depicted in situation 3 – winning too easily – will be undesirable and unpleasant. So the two pleasant outcomes are those listed as 1 and 4, and the undesirable outcomes are listed as 2 and 3.

This might at first sight seem to be a rather contrived way of showing that here too we have opposite ways of experiencing the values of a given motivational variable – in this case the variable of felt transactional outcome. But if one reflects on personal relationships, one of the most salient characteristics that one can observe is that in interacting with another person one either puts oneself first at a given moment or one puts the other first. In other words, one does or does not empathize or identify with the other at a given time; it is either what happens to oneself *or* what happens to the other which is one's primary concern and which constitutes the principal source of one's satisfaction or dissatisfaction. In this way one's motivational and emotional centre is able to jump to and fro between self and other. It is this ability to put oneself in the place of the other, to treat him or her as more important than oneself, and to experience his or her pleasures and pains vicariously, at least for a period of time, which makes human interaction so peculiarly human. And it is what goes to make human relationships so subjectively absorbing, and often so objectively paradoxical. And it is the movement between these self-centred and other-centred orientations which makes people's relationships over time as complex as they are.

Again we see that there is a pair of states of mind which interpret a given variable – in this case 'felt transactional outcome' – in opposite ways. This means that the same value of the variable (i.e. degree of gain or loss) will be pleasant or unpleasant depending on which state is operative. Since the variable is another kind of motivational variable, we are again therefore confronted with a pair of metamotivational modes (although in this case we could equally describe them as 'metarelational').

Let us call the first of these two modes, the one which is self-centred, the autocentric mode, from the Greek *auto* meaning 'self', and *kentron* meaning a 'spike' – from which the English word *centre* is derived. (The spike referred to in the Greek is the spike of a pair of compasses, which is placed at the centre of any circle which is to be drawn). We can then call the other mode the allocentric mode, from the Greek *allos* meaning 'other'. To be sure, we could have referred to the first mode as an identificational mode and the second as a non-identificational mode, but the term *identification* carries a great deal of psychoanalytic baggage, and this could have caused confusion in a non-psychoanalytic theory.

As with felt arousal, we can now attach some emotion labels to the pleasant and unpleasant outcomes in each of the relevant metamotivational modes. If one is in the autocentric mode, then gain will be felt as *pride* at having done well, whereas loss will be experienced as some degree of *humiliation*. If one is in the allocentric mode, then gain at the expense of the other will be felt as some degree of *shame*, and loss will be felt as *modesty*. In other words, there are two dimensions, one running from humiliation to pride and the other from modesty to shame. These are shown in the hypothetical curves shown in Figure 19.

Thus, if you attempt to impose your sexual needs on another, depending on whether you succeed or not, you will feel some degree of pride in your prowess and irresistibility, or humiliation at your impotence and unattractiveness. If, on the other hand, you put the needs of the other first, then any feeling that you have taken advantage of him or her will be associated with shame, while self-discipline will be associated with modesty. Or, to take another situation, suppose that you are at a party. If you show off in a self-centred way, then you will feel pride or humiliation to the degree that

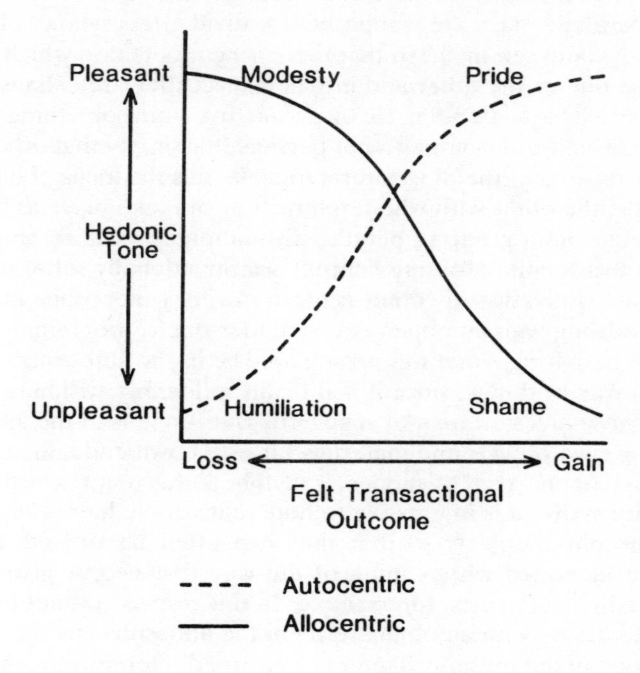

Fig. 19 The hypothetical relationship between felt transactional outcome and hedonic tone when these are experienced in the mastery mode. One curve shows the autocentric version of this relationship (represented by a dashed line) and the other the allocentric version (represented by a continuous line).

others do or do not pay admiring attention to you. But if you identify with the others then the realization that you may have been showing off will produce feelings of shame, whereas reticence and an interest in others rather than yourself will provide feelings of worthy modesty.

As before, in discussing felt arousal, each of the four contrasting emotion words used to make up the basic set is really a label on a box of essentially similar words, varying in respect of intensity, duration, and other factors. For example, in the pride 'box' we would also find such words as 'triumph' and 'dominance', and in the humiliation 'box' words like 'embarrassment' and 'foolishness'. But the words chosen here can act to represent the essence of the emotion concerned in each case.

Since we are not always interacting with other people during our waking lives, can these two modes be seen as truly constituting a pair of metamotivational modes in the sense used earlier? After all, modes like the telic–paratelic pair are supposed to divide the whole of waking consciousness between them, so that there is no moment in which a person is not in the one or the other and in this respect they are exhaustive. We *are*, however, always attending to, or interacting with, something while we are awake, even if this is not another person. It is simply that other people are so important to us that it is natural to make this the focus of discussion. But if we see the other with whom interaction can take place as being not only a person, but a group of people, a situation or even an object, then this makes the definition of autocentric as motivationally self-centred and allocentric as motivationally other-centred, a very general one indeed. Of course, in dealing with an object – a computer one is programming or the meal one is preparing – one will presumably be in the autocentric mode in the normal way of things, since it is difficult to identify with a screen and keyboard, or with a saucepan of spaghetti. But if one is in the autocentric mode, using such objects and materials for one's own ends, then one *is* in one member of the pair of modes, and this is the point which is being made. Incidentally, it is interesting to note that people have a tendency to anthropomorphize objects so that they can often be treated almost as human and identified with – think of the way that people give cars and airplanes individual names, for example. In this respect it is not impossible even in interacting with an object to be in the allocentric mode. As far as the discussion in the present chapter is concerned, therefore, we can for all practical purposes treat these two modes as exhaustive. To be strict, however, we must recognize that there are times when there is *no* direct interaction between self and other – for instance when one is merely observing others, or when one is attending entirely to oneself. There is a way in which the definitions of the autocentric and allocentric modes can be generalized to cover these situations too, as I have done elsewhere (Apter 1988a) (these totally exhaustive forms of the autocentric and allocentric modes are labelled autic and alloic). But the issues involved in this final step of generalization need not detain us here.

MASTERY AND SYMPATHY MODES

We seem to have assumed so far that interpersonal (and other kinds of) interactions always involve some sort of contest, or trial of strength, and that transactions are about either taking by force or yielding up in the face of superior force. But there is another kind of interaction. Consider the following four situations, and how you would be likely to feel in them:

1. You are given an unexpected present.
2. A friend fails to turn up to meet you for a drink.
3. You listen sympathetically to a colleague's problems and give advice.
4. You forget to send a close relative a birthday card.

We are now in a completely different psychological domain: a domain of care and nurturing rather than power and control. As before, the key variable involved is still that of felt transactional outcome, and as before it runs from loss to gain. But now transactions are experienced as being about giving or being given rather than about taking or 'giving up'. In the four situations listed we see: (1) being given; (2) not being given; (3) giving; and (4) not giving. The 'giving' of course is, as these examples testify, not only about material goods, but also about attention and concern and help – indeed anything which represents to the person being given that he or she is sympathized with and liked. In terms of the dimension of felt transactional outcome, being given an unexpected present (situation 1 in the list) represents pleasant gain. Not being given what one expected and counted on – in the example, not being met by a friend (situation 2) – represents unpleasant loss. (As always, we are talking about the way the individual sees things, and if something is counted on, then its absence represents loss.) Listening sympathetically to a colleague's problems and giving advice (situation 3) represents loss (of time and effort, in this case) – but the loss of giving is a pleasant loss. And finally, the gain represented by failing to give something expected – as in failing to send a birthday card (situation 4) – is an unpleasant gain.

As in the earlier examples, the reason why there are two types of gain outcome, one pleasant and one unpleasant, and similarly two types of loss outcome, is that there are two modes involved: as before, these are the autocentric and the allocentric. In the autocentric mode, which centres on oneself, pleasure comes from being given and displeasure from not being given, or being deprived of something. In contrast, in the allocentric mode, in which the emotional centre is the person one is interacting with, pleasure comes from altruistic giving and displeasure from failing to give or even 'making on' the person one intended to give to.

We are now in a position to characterize these four contrasting types of outcome in terms of the emotions which are likely to be associated with them. In the autocentric mode, gain will be associated with *gratitude* (e.g. on being given a present) and loss with *resentment* (e.g. when one's friend does not turn up). In the allocentric mode, loss will be associated with feelings of *virtue* (e.g. when listening to a colleague's problems) and gain with feelings of *guilt* (e.g. when forgetting to send a birthday card). Other words could have been chosen for these four emotions, for example 'self-righteousness' for virtue, and 'bitterness' for resentment, but we can take the four words chosen as representative of four basic and contrasting types of emotion. In this way, we now have two new dimensions representing opposite ways of experiencing felt transactional outcome: one runs from resentment to gratitude, and the other from virtue to guilt. These are shown in the hypothetical curves of Figure 20.

What differentiates these two new versions of the autocentric and allocentric states from the ones discussed earlier is that the felt transactional outcome variable is interpreted in an entirely different way. And this is another way of saying that there is a metamotivational difference between these two ways of experiencing personal relationships. To put it simply: we have another pair of metamotivational modes, a pair which cuts across the autocentric and allocentric modes, so that either member of one pair can be combined with either of the other. The situation is exactly the same as it was in relation to felt arousal where the negativistic and conformist modes

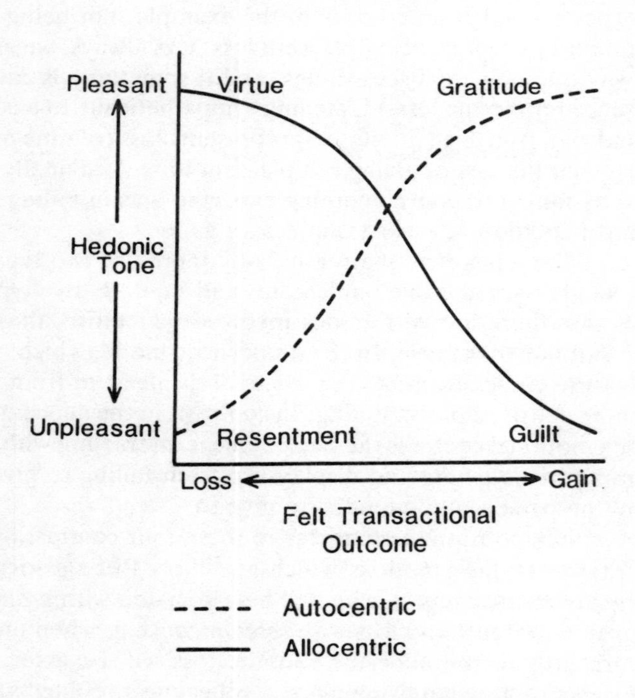

Fig. 20 The hypothetical relationship between felt transactional outcome and hedonic tone when these are experienced in the sympathy mode. One curve shows the autocentric version of this relationship (represented by a dashed line) and the other the allocentric version (represented by a continuous line).

cut across the arousal-seeking and arousal-avoidance modes, producing four different mode combinations, each with its own dimensional version of the felt arousal variable. Now we have a new set of four different mode combinations, this time each combination being associated, as we have seen, with its own dimension in relation to the felt transactional outcome variable: (1) humiliation to pride, (2) modesty to shame, (3) resentment to gratitude, and (4) virtue to guilt.

Like the other pairs of metamotivational modes introduced in this book, the pair being considered here must be supposed to be exhaustive in the sense that one or the other will be operative throughout waking life. Since one is not always interacting with other individual people, we must also therefore suppose that the modes are general ways of interacting with any aspect of the world, including groups of people, situations, and objects. And this should continue to be borne in mind even though the focus of discussion in this chapter is that of interpersonal relationships.

Let us call the first of these two modes, the one oriented to feelings of strength, the 'mastery mode'. This is a suitable term because it is general enough to cover not only interactions with people but also with objects and situations. One can master a person, master a problem, master a situation, master a skill, master the way a piece of equipment works, and so on. Thus, mastery implies any way of 'being on top of things', of more than matching the requirements needed to do something or be something. This does not , of course, mean that in the mastery mode one *is* being successful in this way. One may be floundering around, vulnerable, inadequate, dominated, and so on. But the point is that in the mastery mode this is a focal issue. Is one weak or strong, dominant or subservient, controlling or being controlled?

The other mode is to do with whether people are sympathizing with you or not: are you attractive, do you feel liked, do people care for you, are they affectionate towards you? Let us call this the 'sympathy mode'. As with the mastery mode, being in the sympathy mode does not in itself imply that you are sympathized with, but only that whether you are is the central issue. In this case, it seems reasonable to suppose that the 'other' must normally be another person rather than an object or situation, but even here it is possible to feel, however irrationally, that an object is 'in favour' of you or not – that, for example, a house is friendly, a car that breaks down does not care about you – or that a situation is propitious or not (hence the avidity with which some people consult horoscopes).

Now, of course, it is possible to feel both strong and liked (or weak and disliked), but what determines which mode you are in is which is the important and salient thing at the time. And often one will have to be traded off against the other: to be strong one may have to do things which make one disliked, and one way of being sympathized with is to appear weak and vulnerable. But whether or not such a tradeoff is needed, these are two different ways of 'being in the world' which are mutually exclusive, in the sense that only one can be at the focus of attention. And each has its own priorities and ways of seeing things. In one case the person one is interacting with is seen as, in a sense, object-like, something to be manipulated and coerced for one's own ends, while in the other mode the other person is seen to be a subject, able freely to impart human feelings and warmth. (In the allocentric version of these, of course, the need is to perceive that the *other* feels either strong or sympathized with.)

In summary, then, in the mastery mode the overriding aim is to feel strong, and transactions are seen as evidence of one's strength or weakness. In the sympathy mode the overriding aim is to feel liked or sympathized with, and transactions are seen as evidence that others care for you or that they do not. A perfect image of the contrast between the two is that of students during the campus unrest in the 1960s decorating the muzzles of soldiers' rifles by putting flowers into them.

MODE COMBINATIONS

We are now in a position to compare the characteristics of each of the combinations of the mastery/sympathy and autocentric/allocentric pairs of modes. This is done in Table 4.

Table 4 Four basic relationship needs which arise in relation to each combination of the mastery/sympathy and autocentric/allocentric modes.

	AUTOCENTRIC	ALLOCENTRIC
MASTERY	TO MASTER	TO BE MASTERED
SYMPATHY	TO BE SYMPATHIZED WITH	TO SYMPATHIZE

To help to bring out more the flavour and generality of each of the combinations, here are some examples of situations which might be expected, in most people, to be experienced within each of the four different mode combinations. To keep things manageable, let us just consider situations where things are 'working out' so that the potential satisfactions of the combination concerned are actually being achieved:

1. *Autocentric mastery*. Making a successful business deal, winning a game, giving orders to an employee, building a piece of apparatus, controlling an elaborate piece of equipment, solving an intellectual problem, being promoted at work.

2. *Allocentric mastery*. Enthusiastically submitting to discipline in the army, displaying solidarity in a trade union, undergoing a demeaning ritual to join a prestigious club, conforming to the decisions of a political party you are proud to belong to, submitting to the demands of a religious leader.

3. *Autocentric sympathy*. Being given a present, having your personal anecdote listened to, accepting someone's advice on a problem, being helped by a relative when in trouble, being cared for when ill, being invited out to dinner.

4. *Allocentric sympathy*. Donating money to a charity, giving a present to a child, taking an interest in someone in conversation, buying a friend a drink, giving a colleague encouragement, tending a garden with loving care, feeding a pet.

A problem which the reader may be experiencing, in trying to understand these relationships, is that of the difference between the allocentric mode and the sympathy mode. After all, if you are putting the other first, as is the case by definition in the allocentric mode, does this not necessarily imply that you are caring for the other, and being sympathetic? The point is, however, that it is possible to be in the allocentric mode but to be mastery-oriented rather than sympathy-oriented. Here, in identifying with the other, one will get vicarious pleasure from the other's strength, not from the sympathy which the other receives from you. To help to make this clear, think back to the example of playing tennis against a child and allowing him or her to do well against you. Here, you are in the allocentric mode – your satisfaction and dissatisfaction come more from what happens to the child than what happens to you – but the 'what happens' here is about the child feeling strong, not about him or her feeling liked or sympathized with by you. Indeed, if the child felt that you had *given* him or her the game out of sympathy, that you had 'thrown it' so to speak, he or she would have none of the pleasure of mastery which would come from wresting success from your opposition. Consequently, in empathizing with the child, you would have none of the pleasure of mastery either.

There is a kind of paradox in this combination of mastery and allocentric modes, and this is that the weaker you are, the stronger you feel – because you are identifying with another whose strength is at least in part drawn from your own weakness. This comes out particularly clearly where the other is some powerful social group, or even a mass movement like a political movement. Indeed, this may be part of the secret of fascism and totalitarianism of all kinds: if people want to feel strong they can be helped to do so by abasing themselves, provided they abase themselves before someone or something they identify with or feel part of. In this way, weakness breeds strength.

This difference between the allocentric and sympathy modes is conceptually difficult to grasp – it is perhaps the trickiest part of the whole of reversal theory. But what it comes to is that we cannot equate the sympathy of the sympathy mode with the identification of the allocentric mode. Sometimes the two modes will occur together, but there is no necessary connection between them, and the allocentric mode can be experienced in conjunction with the mastery mode, just as the sympathy mode can be experienced along with the autocentric mode. And the submission and yielding up which one looks for in oneself when one is mastery-oriented in the allocentric mode is phenomenologically quite different from the affectionate care one looks to give in the allocentric-sympathy mode combination.

NURSING: A CASE STUDY

Rhys (1988) reported on a study of the way in which nurses experienced different aspects of their work, this being based on detailed interviews which were structured around the ideas which have been presented here. The evidence from these interviews provides real-life concrete illustration of the metamotivational modes which have been introduced in this chapter, and shows how the concepts involved can be used to disentangle some of the threads of everyday experience as this touches on personal relationships.

The nurses involved were working in a hospice which was part of a large National Health Service hospital in Britain. All 41 nurses in the unit took part in the interviews. We can look at the different experiences which they described in terms of each of the four mode combinations discussed earlier.

First, we have autocentric mastery, the experience of personal strength or weakness. Clearly, much of a nurse's job entails controlling patients and equipment: giving drugs and injections, taking temperatures, washing patients, treating bedsores, helping patients to get dressed, and so on. We should therefore not be surprised to learn that much of their experience of nursing involved the mastery state, and specifically the attempt to be efficient, skillful, effective and 'professional'. Where this was achieved, the nurses expressed great pride in their work, whereas many of the feelings of unhappiness which they described related to mastery frustrations. These included the frustrations of lack of time to carry out routines properly, having to give treatments which they considered inappropriate, and feeling helpless to do anything about certain kinds of irreversible medical conditions. Some nurses also said that they felt humiliated when patients ordered them around, since they felt that they, the nurses, should be in charge, and the patients should accept this.

Second, we have allocentric sympathy, the vicarious experience of being cared for and nurtured. Since nursing is also traditionally supposed to be about looking after others, we should again not be surprised to learn that many of the reported experiences of the nurses referred to the feelings of happiness and unhappiness, virtue and guilt, which came with their perceptions of how patients were experiencing their care and concern, or lack of it. Nurses often felt good when they perceived that their patients were feeling liked and supported by them and bad when they perceived that patients were feeling disliked by them or neglected. In order to show that they were caring for people as people, rather than just as bodies, nurses reported that they would do such things as cook special things for particular patients to replace institutionalized meals, and sit on their beds to talk to them, even though they should have been doing other things at the time.

From the nurses' descriptions of their feelings during the working day, it was clear that these two combinations of mode – the autocentric–mastery combination and the allocentric–sympathy combination – were those in which they spent most of their time. But they also experienced the other two combinations as well. There were periods, for example, when some nurses wanted their patients to take control of them, rather than being in control of their patients at all times. In other words, at these times they wanted their patients not to feel totally helpless but to begin to regain feelings of personal strength and responsibility, and they wanted to experience this growing strength empathically by identifying with the patients. For example, as one nurse said: 'I wait for patients to talk and ask them what they mean. . . . Perhaps the other person decides what they think is very important, but it may not be to me.' At such times the nurses were obviously in the allocentric mastery mode combination, wanting the other to feel strong at their expense, and willing to play a more modest role than that seemingly thrust on them by hospital organization.

The final mode combination – that of autocentric sympathy – also appeared in many accounts. Here the nurses wanted to feel sympathized with and liked by the patient, rather than the other way round. And when they did so, they sometimes experienced overwhelming gratitude. For example, one nurse said, 'The patients make you feel you have done wonders. I go home feeling terribly tall, especially if I had been feeling down, and the patient holds my hand and says something, and it lifts you out of yourself. It's a really fantastic feeling. Sometimes I think, "I get paid for this as well".'

Several points emerge from these interviews, taken together. One is that successful nursing requires both the mastery and the sympathy modes at different times: sometimes patients must be treated as bodies and sometimes as people, so that sometimes nurses must act as technicians and sometimes as carers. If one or the other of these elements is missing, then the nursing that results will be inadequate. A nurse in the mastery mode must have the emotional detachment necessary to perform some unpleasant function efficiently, like giving an injection, but if she remains in this mode she will be unable to provide the sympathy and solace which the patient requires afterwards. Conversely, a nurse in the sympathy mode may be able to improve a patient's morale, but if she remains in this mode she may have emotional difficulty in aiding the surgeon during an operation. Detachment and involvement, hardness and tenderness are both needed, but at the right times and in the right places. The good nurse will therefore be able to reverse between the sympathy and mastery modes at appropriate points in the working day. An example of such a point mentioned by a number of the nurses interviewed was that of washing the patient. Whether because of the childlike position the patient is placed in, the privacy from the rest of the ward together with the personal physical exposure to the nurse, or for some other reason, nurses reported that patients tend to confide in them at this time and that therefore it is appropriate for them to switch from a professional to a more caring and personal role – in our terms to reverse from the autocentric mastery to the allocentric sympathy mode combination.

For most nurses, reversals between the autocentric and allocentric modes take place from time to time throughout the hours of duty. In particular, it is difficult in the sympathy mode, unless one is a saint, to put the other first at all times, and there will be periods where the nurse herself will be looking for solace, support, and even gratitude. We have already seen that patients sometimes provide this. Rhys argues that there is nothing wrong here, and suggests that the good nurse will recognize that it is helpful both to her and the patient that these periods should occur: helpful for her because she is, after all, human too, and helpful for the patient because it is good that he or she should sometimes be allocentric rather than continually selfish and dwelling on his or her own problems.

The general picture which derives from these interviews is one of complexity and change: the nurse must be a different kind of person at different moments, and a variety of contrasting relationships develop, and need to develop, between her and a given patient over time. The same is, incidentally, true of her relationships with other nurses and with her superiors and the hospital administration.

In reversal theory terms, the hospital ward provides a microcosm of personal relationships and allows us to see a changing kaleidoscope of modes and mode combinations. It would also seem to demonstrate how reversal between modes is an integral part of human relationships over time. This suggests that we should now look further at the process of reversal itself in relation to the autocentric/allocentric and mastery/sympathy pairs of modes.

REVERSALS AND THEIR INDUCTION

Just as was the case for metamotivational reversals looked at in earlier chapters of this book, reversals between the mastery and sympathy modes and between the autocentric and allocentric modes appear to be brought about the three factors of external events, frustration, and satiation, or some combination of these. Let us look at each in turn.

First of all, events and situations of a variety of types are likely to induce reversals of the kind being considered here, and these can all be included under the general heading of contingency. For example, someone pleading for help may induce the allocentric–sympathy mode combination, as may any signs of vulnerability or weakness, such as those of children, cripples, and pets. Going into a pub or a bar seems to induce the autocentric–sympathy combination in some people, and with it the need to be listened to, counselled, and generally sympathized with. Sports necessarily induce the autocentric–mastery combination in players – the need to dominate the opposition and master the skills necessary to do so. While reversal into the allocentric–mastery mode combination seems to be facilitated in many people by displays of strength and invitations to join or support some masterful group – such displays typically making use of music, banners, processions, inflammatory speeches, and the like. (For simplicity, I have talked about mode combinations here, but obviously some events will tend to induce particular modes rather than mode combinations: for example, going to a party may induce the sympathy mode in some people and be in itself, as it were, neutral with respect to the autocentric/allocentric dichotomy.)

Second, frustration in achieving the satisfaction of one or another of these modes also seems, if sufficiently prolonged, to lead to reversal. For example, if one's expressions of sympathy to another are continually rejected, one may well start to look for sympathy for oneself instead, thus reversing from the allocentric to the autocentric mode. If one is frustrated in some game one is playing in the autocentric mastery mode, this may induce the sympathy mode in which, while remaining in the autocentric mode, one looks for sympathy for one's poor performance – or tries to be liked (e.g. by means of sardonic jokes against oneself) rather than admired for one's sporting abilities. If one is frustrated in the autocentric sympathy mode in being liked – for example, a person one is talking to at a party shows no inclination to be friendly or even interested – then one is likely to switch to the autocentric mastery mode and attempt to prove one's superiority over the other instead, or take advantage of him or her in some way. This is not to say that reversal will necessarily take place in these examples – there will no doubt be individual differences in this respect, and how far some particular kind of dissatisfaction is felt as frustrating will also be expected to vary from person to person. But these examples do point to frustration as one potential factor among others in bringing about reversals between these modes.

Finally, we come once more to satiation. As before, the suggestion is that there is an internal dynamic for change which builds up over time, so that it makes a reversal increasingly likely in combination with other factors, and eventually triggers a reversal on its own account if nothing else does so. Once a reversal has taken place, the satiation process then starts all over again increasingly to facilitate, and finally to actuate, a reversal back to the original mode. In this way there is an underlying pattern of alternations which may be interrupted and overridden by external factors or frustration. The reason why this postulate is needed is to explain why it is that people confront others, even the same 'others' in the same situations, in different moods on different occasions.

We may also suppose that an imbalance in the satiation process, such that it builds up more rapidly in one direction than the other, will lead to people being more or less autocentric- or allocentric-dominant, and more or less mastery- or sympathy-dominant (using the term 'dominance' in the way defined in earlier chapters). Thus we might expect the businessperson to be mastery-dominant and autocentric-dominant, the priest to be sympathy-dominant and allocentric-dominant, and so on. This also raises questions about whether such dominance is related to biological characteristics. For example, are women more sympathy-dominant than men? Are children more autocentric-dominant than adults? Such questions, however, are matters for future research.

Looking back at Figures 19 and 20, we see that reversals can produce a variety of emotional transformations. Here are a few examples. If you switch from the autocentric to the allocentric while in the sympathy mode and experiencing gain, then your feeling of gratitude will be changed into one of guilt (see Figure 20). Thus, if you have just been given a present, but then identify with the person who has given it to you and empathize with his or her money problems, you will feel guilty at having accepted the present. If, again in the sympathy mode, you feel virtuous at having bought someone lunch, but then switch from the allocentric to the autocentric mode, you will feel resentful that you have unnecessarily spent so much money. In the mastery mode (see Figure 19) you may feel proud at having made a brilliant joke at someone else's expense, but then in switching from the autocentric to the allocentric mode feel shame at what you have done. These are all examples of switching *within* each of the graphs, that is reversing between autocentric and allocentric modes. This has involved jumping from one curve to a point vertically above or below on the other curve. But it is also possible to switch from one graph to the other, this representing reversal between the sympathy and mastery modes. In this case, the position, as it were, remains the same, but the nature of the space changes. For example, if you feel pride at having won a ballot of some kind (i.e. you are in the top right quadrant of the mastery graph) and you reverse into the sympathy state, you will instead feel gratitude to those who voted for you (i.e. you will now be in the top right quadrant of the sympathy graph) Or, if you feel humiliation at having lost face on some social occasion and you reverse from the mastery graph (lower left quadrant) to the sympathy graph (also lower left quadrant), then you will now feel resentment against those who might have been more charitable, helpful, or understanding.

LOVE AND HATE

In dealing with emotions that are essentially to do with human relationships, we appear to have lost sight of the two most important interpersonal emotions of all: love and hate. The first thing we can observe here is that these are both obviously sympathy mode emotions: they are to do with transactions that are about giving and being given (or not giving and not being given), they both involve seeing the other as a subject rather than an object, and they are both concerned with liking, caring, and nurturing – or their absence.

If we are thinking of love in sexual terms, the difference between the mastery and sympathy modes exactly reflects the difference between love and lust, since the latter is clearly a manifestation of the mastery, rather than the sympathy, mode. That is, lust is to do with dominance and taking – or in its allocentric form with submission and yielding. Indeed, putting things in this way helps us to see that sexual perversions are all mastery mode phenomena. Those perversions involving dominance – rape, bondage, and sadism of different kinds – involve autocentric mastery, while those involving submission – masochism of one kind or another – involve allocentric mastery. Among other things, then, this analysis discloses the common origins of masochism and sadism in the mastery mode.

If love and hate are sympathy emotions, what kind of sympathy emotions are they? One thing to notice is that they are not restricted to either the autocentric or allocentric mode. Love can involve the good feelings which come out of either sympathizing and giving (allocentric) or being sympathized with and given to (autocentric). Similarly, hate can involve the bad feelings which come out of either not being sympathized with or given to (autocentric) or not being allowed to sympathize and give (allocentric). This implies that hate only arises in situations where one expects to give or receive sympathy, not in relationships where there are no such expectations. So one can hate lovers, relatives, and friends, but never strangers. For strangers one can only feel such negative emotions as fear, antipathy, or distrust.

Love, then, would appear to be an emotion felt towards someone who provides strong satisfaction in the sympathy mode, and from interacting with whom one derives, at different times, feelings of both gratitude (autocentric) and virtue (allocentric). Hate, in contrast, would appear to be an emotion felt towards someone who causes, or has just caused, strong dissatisfaction in the sympathy mode, either in the form of resentment (autocentric) or guilt (allocentric). Either way, people tend to reserve the terms 'love' and 'hate' for those who produce unusually strong sympathy emotions – and, as we all know, it is often the very same people who elicit both the emotions of love and hate at different times. In any case, it can now be seen that love and hate both involve the two mode combinations of autocentric sympathy and allocentric sympathy, and in this respect are more complex than such 'simpler' emotions as gratitude or guilt – which are simple in the sense that they only arise within a single mode combination. (There is a further complication in the case of hate, which is that the perceived unfairness and frustration involved may concomitantly induce the negativistic state, and with it anger.)

This general way of looking at things also helps us to understand the relationship between jealousy and envy, and why two such apparently similar words are needed in the English language. Both of these emotions involve a third party to the relationship between self and other, and in both it is the third party which receives the benefit of some transaction with the other rather than oneself. So one's expectation, or desire, is disappointed. The difference is that in one case – that of envy – one is in the mastery mode, and the third party has won or *taken* what one wanted. In the other case – that of jealousy – one is in the sympathy mode, and the third party has been *given* what one wanted. So one is envious of someone who has the power, money, status, or privileges that one wants for oneself in the mastery mode, and jealous of someone who has the love and affection that one craves in the sympathy mode.

In this, the difference between envy and jealousy is not unlike that between some other pairs of emotions which appear similar but which are associated with different metamotivational modes. Shame and guilt, for example, are clearly similar in that they both involve some regretted transactional gain. But according to the analysis given earlier, shame is a mastery mode emotion while guilt is an emotion which is experienced in the sympathy mode. Similarly, humiliation and humility would appear to be similar in some respects, but if humility is the same as modesty, then these are alternative autocentric and allocentric versions of loss in the mastery mode. What the reversal theory analysis does is to show why pairs of words like these are needed – words which are difficult to differentiate systematically without the distinctions drawn by the reversal theory analysis.

RELATIONSHIP TO SOMATIC MODES

Another question which arises concerns the relationship between the metamotivational modes discussed in this chapter and the telic/paratelic, arousal-seeking/arousal-avoiding and negativistic/conformist modes which were discussed earlier. This is a complex matter, and for present purposes it will be enough to make some general points. Some others will be made in the final chapter.

First of all, we have seen how those modes which bear on felt arousal – let us call them somatic modes – give rise, depending on which mode is in fact operative, and the felt arousal level at the time, to a particular (somatic) emotion such as anger or boredom. Similarly, in the present chapter we have seen how the modes which bear on felt transactional outcome also give rise, depending on the level of that variable and the operative mode, to a particular emotion such as gratitude or pride. We must conclude, therefore, that at any given time two types of emotion will be felt in conjunction: a 'somatic' emotion and a 'transactional' emotion. For example, one might experience some degree of anxiety and humiliation, or excitement and gratitude. (This is not to be taken to imply that one is always experiencing *strong* emotions; but unless one is exactly on the neutral point of a given dimension like boredom-to-excitement, at least some emotion will colour experience in however mild a way.)

Second, the hedonic quality of these two types of emotions seems to be different – which is hardly surprising since the somatic emotions centre on immediate feelings which arise from within the body, while the transactional emotions are more to do with how one experiences one's self, or the perceived self of the person one is identifying with. (Apter and Smith (1985) have suggested that the term 'self tone' might be used for the hedonic tone experienced in relation to transactional emotions.) Now, if there are, as there seem to be, two types of negative and positive hedonic tone, one which tends to be described by people in terms of how much pleasure or displeasure they are experiencing and the other in terms of how happy or unhappy they feel themselves to be, then it seems not unreasonable to associate pleasure/displeasure with the somatic emotions and happiness/unhappiness with the transactional emotions. After all, most people would probably agree that happiness is a matter of feeling good about oneself – feeling pleased with oneself, loved, and so on. Pleasure and displeasure, on the other hand, seem to be more to do with immediate feelings such as those of excitement and anger. If this is the case, then it should be possible to feel any combination of these, including both displeasure-and-happiness and pleasure-and-unhappiness. An example of the former might be pride at winning a game combined with anger at the opponent who cheated. An illustration of the latter might be humiliation combined with excitement – for example in sexual masochism.

These examples lead naturally to a third point which is that it is possible to use one mode in the service of another. We have already discussed this in the previous chapter in relation to the way in which negativism or conformity can be used in the service of other modes (or vice versa), and now we are confronted with it again. Thus, one person may often put himself in anxiety-provoking situations in order to feel the pride which comes with handling these situations successfully. Here the arousal-avoidance mode would be in the service of the mastery mode. Another person might frequently engineer situations of resentment in order to experience the parapathic 'anger' which results. In this case, the sympathy mode would be being used in the service of the excitement-seeking mode. Examples could be multiplied.

And this brings us to a fourth point. This is that we may expect people to differ from each other, not only in mode dominance across all the modes we have looked at, but also in terms of the mode hierarchies which are typical of them, that is which modes tend to serve which other modes. (Again this is a point made in the previous chapter, but its generality can now be extended to cover the transactional emotions.) At the very least, people may focus on one type of hedonic quality rather than the other, so that for some pleasure is more important than happiness and for others matters are the reverse: this would imply that for some people, somatic modes are likely to be used in the service of transactional modes, and for others matters will be the other way round. In any case, we would expect such hierarchies to be recognizable phenomenologically in the different degrees of *salience* which the different pairs have for different people. For example, in one person attention may tend to be focussed mostly on the telic/paratelic pair, while for another mastery/sympathy may more often be at the centre of awareness.

The system introduced in this chapter for describing contrasting ways of relating to others, and one's needs in these different relationships, might seem to be a long-winded and jargon-ridden way of saying what people already know. Why not say that someone wants to be kind, rather than that he is in the allocentric sympathy mode? Or why not say that someone wants to dominate rather than saying that she is in the autocentric mastery mode? But the point is that this set of terms brings out the abstract structure of contrasts which underlies personal and other types of relationships. This descriptive system gains whatever theoretical force it has from its usefulness in disclosing the similarities underlying a huge range of apparent differences, and the way it helps us to discern a certain simplicity of pattern beneath a complexity of appearance. There is no implication that this terminology should be substituted for everyday speech! It also helps to emphasize one of the main themes of reversal theory: that each of us is a different kind of person at different times, but that there are a small number of universal basic aspects of personality which we all share and which come together in different combinations to constitute these 'different kinds of person'.

8

The Nature of Cognitive Synergy

in the beginning and now
creation, falling away and the marriage of opposites.

The Mask of Time
Michael Tippett (b. 1905)

SOME SYNERGIES

We now turn to another important aspect of experience.

'Is there something wrong?' she asked him. The sun was on the point of dropping over the brim of the sea, and a cool breeze was getting up as they stood on the cliff edge.

'No, not exactly wrong', he said. She could feel his warmth beside her, and clasped his hand more firmly. Since he did not continue, she turned towards him and in the dusk she could see dimly that his blue eyes were twinkling, that he was laughing gently to himself.

'Do you love me?' he said at last.

'Yes', she breathed.

'And I love you.' He turned and faced her squarely. 'You think I am the hospital porter. Now I am going to tell you the truth.'

'The truth?' she stammered.

'Yes. In reality – and I did not want you to know before – I am the Senior Consultant.'

Now we can turn back to the important aspect of experience I mentioned in the first sentence. In reading the passage which followed and which you found yourself launched into unexpectedly, you no doubt felt some puzzlement. Instead of reading something dry and academic you found yourself reading what seemed to be a lurid romantic novella. The book you thought you were reading seemed to have turned, without warning, and mercifully only momentarily, into another kind of book altogether. The result is that you have just experienced what the present chapter is about: something which is known in reversal theory as cognitive synergy.

When you were reading Chapter 2 you experienced another example. On inspecting the two reversal figures shown there (Figures 5 and 6), you will have seen them seem to switch back and forth while you watched, so that at one moment they appeared one way, at another moment another way. Here are several other examples. Suppose you have watched someone cut out a seemingly arbitrary pattern of holes in a folded newspaper: suddenly he lets it drop open, and as it concertinas outward it discloses a neat cut-out line of boys and girls holding hands. A friend points a pistol at you and pulls the trigger: out of the barrel comes a small flame which he then brings over to you so that you can light your cigarette.

What do these examples have in common? The answer is that they all involve the experience of something changing into something else *while remaining itself*. When you read the opening lines of this chapter it seemed to have turned into a different kind of book, and yet the lines were an integral part of the psychological argument, as you will now have realized. Similarly, the reversal figures seemed to change while actually, as you were also well aware, they remained constant on the page. The newspaper with holes in it which is also a clever pattern, the pistol which is really a cigarette lighter: again in these cases we are aware of both change and continuity, sameness and difference. Indeed, it is this paradox of something which changes but remains the same, this kind of phenomenological self-contradiction, which makes such experiences so interesting to us when they occur in the course of our everyday lives.

This type of 'paradoxical change' is one of the two main types of synergy. Let us look at some examples of the second type before reaching a definition which will be general enough to cover both.

Imagine a favourite view of a stretch of countryside that you know, perhaps one with hills and trees and a river running through it. Now think of a flat rectangular board. These two images are obviously of very different things. The view is of a complex scene, which has depth and distance, extends outwards from the eye in all directions, and contains movement – the river flows, clouds sweep majestically across the sky, and perhaps a horse gallops in a field. The board, in contrast, has no depth, is limited in size and motionless. Also, unlike the scene, it is possible to pick it up and take it away. And yet if the scene is painted on the board, the resulting landscape seems to have the properties of the real view – or at least enough of them to satisfy the eye.

Now, in looking at such a landscape, the observer is perfectly well aware that he is not looking at the real view – and yet he still sees the view. He also still sees the flat board, and recognizes its spatial limitations, and knows that it is moveable (and even, if it is in a gallery, buyable). The point is that we have a kind of phenomenological contradiction: a view which is not really a view, and a flat board which appears not to be a flat board. And this is exactly one of the characteristics of any figurative work of art which makes it interesting. In the case of a landscape painting one is aware of the coming together in experience of such opposites as flatness and depth, extension and limitation, movement and stillness. (For a discussion of other types of synergy which enter into aesthetic experience, see Apter (1984a).)

Next let us consider a child's toy, like a doll's house. If it is a good one, then it will be highly realistic and contain in miniature everything with which one's imagination would like to furnish it: tiny replicas of mahogany chairs and table, chaises longues, brass bedsteads, oak wardrobes and cupboards; in the bathroom a bath; in the kitchen a sink; in the parlour an upright piano. If it is a particularly splendid doll's house, like Victorian ones of the kind that one sometimes sees displayed in museums, there will even be minute but readable books, real paintings painted to scale, silver cutlery, labelled wine bottles, antimacassars on the button-back easy chairs. As with the landscape painting, the fascination is with the realism of something which cannot possibly be mistaken for what it appears to be. But, whereas in the painting the contradictions are between such features as flatness and depth, movement and stillness, in the doll's house they are all to do with scale. The doll's house seems to be a house, but cannot really be a house because it is so small. The key opposition is that of large and small, and these two characteristics are brought together to the extent that the doll's house does indeed look like a real house. If this illusion is destroyed – as it is for example in some museum pieces by including out-of-scale dolls – then the experience is to this extent immediately spoiled.

What these two examples have in common is the fact that they involve the experience of something being something else while remaining itself. Whereas our former examples were of 'paradoxical change', these are of 'paradoxical sameness'. There is still a tension of opposites, but the tension is of simultaneous rather than sequential opposition: it does not unroll in time but is there before our eyes from the beginning. The painting is always a representation, the Victorian doll's house is always a model.

THE NATURE OF COGNITIVE SYNERGY

There is a fundamental law in logic which is known as the Law of the Excluded Middle. This says that A must either be B or not-B. An animal must either be a dog or not a dog, a football team must either wear red shirts or shirts of some other colour. In other words, whatever the category which something belongs to, it cannot belong to both this and to a mutually exclusive category; or whatever characteristic something has, it cannot both have this characteristic and a contradictory characteristic.

What the two types of synergy that we have looked at share is that they apparently break this law. Thus, in the first type something is experienced as both a cigarette lighter and not a cigarette lighter (or, which is the same thing, both a pistol and not a pistol). In the second type, something is experienced as both a valley-with-a-river and as not-a-valley-with-a-river (or, which is the same thing, as both canvas-and-paint and not-canvas-and-paint). In both cases, mutually exclusive categories are brought together and seemingly made to overlap.

Of course, these are not real logical contradictions. The pistol is really a cigarette lighter all the time, the painting is really canvas-and-paint, the doll's house is really always a toy. But the analysis here is phenomenological, not logical. In experience, some kind of contradiction and paradox *is* experienced: opposite qualities are brought together in consciousness and made to cohere in relation to some identity. (By an identity we mean any person, thing, or situation.)

We can now define a cognitive synergy. It is *the experience of incompatible characteristics in relation to an identity*. In the first type, these incompatible characteristics occur one after another; in the second, they occur at the same time. We can refer to the first type as a 'reversal synergy' since the incompatibilities arise through a switch from some characteristic or category to a mutually exclusive or opposite characteristic or category. (This, of course, is not to be confused with metamotivational reversal.) We can refer to the second type as an 'identity synergy' since the incompatibilities both relate to the same identity throughout. The difference between them can be exemplified by the experience of seeing a woman remove her wig and turning out to be a transvestite man, as against seeing a male friend wearing female attire at a fancy dress ball.

Generally speaking, synergies tend to produce a feeling of puzzlement or oddness: the identity seems to be intriguingly or disconcertingly strange in some way, and to require further attention and scrutiny. This feeling may be momentary or prolonged, intense or almost unnoticed. But an important effect seems to be to increase arousal in some degree or another, as the meaning of the experience is worked on.

At the same time, synergies also appear to produce a general heightening of conscious awareness, be this a sudden 'blip' (the pistol is really a lighter) or a more gentle and suffusive effect over time (the landscape). That is, the identity appears to become more 'alive' and the characteristics which enter into it more intense and vivid. The effect is perhaps not unlike that which occurs when complementary colours – such as red and green – are placed next to each other; the red comes to look redder and the green greener. In other words, a conceptual contrast effect is occurring which is not dissimilar to this perceptual contrast effect. But since concepts cannot actually be juxtaposed in space like patches of colour, the only way in which they can be truly brought together in experience is to relate them to the same identity. In this way they can be held together while they play off each other. And the greater the contrast, the greater the effect: the more convincingly authentic the pistol, the tinier and more minutely perfect the furniture in the doll's house, the more 'painterly' the painting, the greater the impact which the synergy would appear to have in this respect.

In case the reader should think that synergy is nothing more than surprise – and it is true that they both cause increased arousal and do often go together – he or she might like to reflect on cases where each nevertheless occurs without the other. For example, the surprise of a sudden unexpected loud noise is not obviously synergic. And the synergies which enter into a landscape could hardly be said to be surprising or unexpected: they are always and necessarily there every time we look at this type of painting.

Why is the term *synergy* used to describe the effects of incompatible or incongruent qualities being brought together in experience? The word itself comes from the ancient Greek *syn* meaning 'together' and *ergon* meaning 'work'. So a synergy is something which 'works together'. In fact, over the years it has come to be used in a number of areas to refer to situations in which different processes or qualities come together to produce effects which are greater than, or different from, those which either could have produced alone. For example, an alloy could be said to be synergic in this sense since its strength is greater than that of the separate metals which enter into it. In medicine, drugs are said to produce synergic effects when, in combination, they amplify each other's powers, or produce unexpected side effects. In embryology, two tissues in a growing body are said to act synergically when they interact in such a way as to initiate essential new developmental processes in each other which would not otherwise have occurred. The way in which the word is being used in reversal theory, then, is perfectly consistent with these other uses, since the bringing of opposing qualities into the same 'conceptual space' produces special psychological effects which the qualities themselves could not have produced on their own. As I have argued, the effects of the resulting 'collisions' and the ripples of disturbance which they set up, seem to include increased arousal and an enhanced vividness of experience.

THE ENCHANTMENT OF PARADOX

If one of the main effects of synergy is to raise arousal, we can infer that synergies will be enjoyed – and even sought out and created – in the paratelic mode, and that they will be generally disliked and avoided in the telic mode. Indeed, a minimal understanding of these two modes is not possible unless the different response to synergy which occurs in each is taken fully into account. Thus, wherever we see playful paratelic activities being engaged in, there also we see synergies tending to come to the fore; wherever we see people undertaking serious telic tasks we see them tending to eschew synergies of any kind. If you think back to the opening lines of this chapter, can you remember how you experienced the puzzlement you felt on reading romantic fiction? Were you irritated or amused, concerned or entertained? Your answer will give you a good indication of whether, at that time, you were in a telic or a paratelic state of mind.

Quite apart from the arousal they generate, the reason why synergies are not favoured in the telic mode is plain to see. When one is trying to get a serious job done, the bafflement or distraction of a synergy, mild as it might be, is simply another complication to be avoided or frustration to be overcome. One is not interested in trick cigarette lighters when trying to close a business deal, or clever synergic language when drawing up a legal document. If one is a developer about to put up an estate on a tract of land, one will not want to see an impressionistic painting of the site, but will need a proper plan. On the whole, in the telic mode, one likes to know what one is dealing with and to deal with it in the most direct manner possible.

Among other things, this means that the telic mode abhors ambiguity, because ambiguity is a form of synergy. That is, when there is some ambiguity about an identity, this means that one is aware of conflicting ways of perceiving it, and these remain associated with the identity until the ambiguity is resolved. If you are a businessperson, you need to know whether the letter you have just received is actually placing an order or not: there is no pleasure to be gained in recognizing that it could be read either way. If you are a soldier you need to know if the person approaching in the swirling mist is friend or foe: at such a time you are hardly likely to ponder in a detached and amused way on the vagaries and indefiniteness of military costume.

It is interesting that so much has been made in psychology of 'intolerance of ambiguity', not to mention the discomforts of dissonance, incongruity and anomaly – which may also be produced by synergies. One suspects that in this, as in so much else, present-day psychology is only half right, and that the telic mode has been unfairly generalized to the whole of mental life. When we turn to the paratelic mode we find that, on the contrary, ambiguities in particular, and synergies in general, are relished. This is because of the very same arousing and awareness-enhancing properties of synergy which are so disliked in the telic mode, together with the delicious games which they invite us to play with appearance and reality, and the irresistible way in which they allow us to suspend logic and turn expectations on their heads.

In the course of everyday life, cognitive synergies are always liable to crop up; and if they can be experienced in the paratelic rather than the telic mode they can add significantly to life's passing pleasures. You notice a youth in the street, and you are not sure, from the outlandish dress, whether the youngster is male or female. You see a woman in a restaurant and it suddenly 'clicks' that you know her but that she has changed her hair style in a way which entirely alters her appearance. You see a child playing in the park dressed up as a policeman and acting officiously. You look up at the clouds and they seem to form the pattern of a face. Such examples of incompatible qualities being yoked together in everyday experience are typical and could be multiplied endlessly; on the basis of this handful of illustrations you should be able to identify plenty of examples of your own and spot them as they occur during the daily round.

Rather than depending on such casual occurrences, some people develop hobbies and interests which have, among other effects, that of providing regular synergic rewards. To take just one example (developed in Smith and Apter 1977), part of the enjoyment and fascination of antique collecting derives from synergies of several types. An antique object is of the present, but also of the past; it belongs to you but it has belonged to many other people before; it is a personal possession but somehow remains intriguingly alien; and it may be both ordinary in the sense that it was once commonplace (like a pewter tankard, a pot lid, or a brass candlestick) and yet it is concurrently extraordinary in that it is now rare, special, and sought after. So the antique can present us with a satisfyingly rich brew of contradictory qualities.

Not only can individuals deliberately pursue synergies in their own ways, but culture sets up institutionalized settings for the communal enjoyment of synergy. A good example is the circus, which may be regarded as a veritable moveable feast of synergy. Here practically every performer or act represents a colourful synergy of one kind or another. The ring master is someone who officiates but has little real power except to crack his whip occasionally; the clowns are adults who behave like children, not to mention experts who turn out to be incompetent and aggressors who finish up as victims; the lions and tigers are simultaneously wild and tame, ferocious and docile; the human cannonball is both object and person; the ponderous elephants are made to do things which are dainty, perhaps while wearing ballet dancers' tutus, which creates human/animal synergy; the human/animal synergy is also produced by dogs walking on their hind legs, chimpanzees having tea parties and seals playing games with balls; and the jugglers and acrobats make the seemingly impossible not only possible but actual. In all these cases something both is and is not what it appears to be: thus the dog is an animal, but appears in a certain respect to be human, the lions appear to be docile but are really ferocious (or perhaps it is the other way round).

Another representative 'celebration of synergy' is professional wrestling. This institution bristles with obvious synergies. The wrestlers are very large men behaving like very small children, taunting each other, having temper tantrums, and generally showing off. They are highly 'macho', but at the same time feminine in their vanity and fondness for self-decoration and dressing up. They are both strong (physically) and weak (intellectually). And they are abstract symbols (e.g. of the Wild West, Cossack Russia, the

Marines, comic super-heroes) while remaining particular individuals with their own individual personalities. And the wrestling contest as a whole is theatre masquerading as sport.

In fact, every form of institutionalized entertainment – the theatre, the disco, the casino, the fun fair, the parade, the beauty contest – makes use of synergies to some degree. (See if you can think of some of them.) But there are also *times* when the creation of certain kinds of synergy is allowed, and even culturally expected in the form of recognized customs. As the anthropologist LeCron Foster (1988) has pointed out, in our own culture, at Christmas, we do such things as put an evergreen tree inside the house rather than leaving it outside, and at Halloween we allow our children to beg food from strangers, something we would never normally permit them to do. Such ritual reversals of normal expectations and behaviours are well known to anthropologists, who have documented numerous examples from around the world, both in primitive tribes and more advanced communities. In all these cases, such culturally sanctioned inversions occur at special moments in the development of the individual or the group, or they mark special sacred times in the calendar. An often cited example of ritual reversal is the so-called Naven ceremony which is practised by a New Guinea tribe, the Iatmul. When an Iatmul child reaches a certain stage of maturation an uncle dresses up as a poor, widowed, and pregnant woman and humbles himself before the child in various prescribed and stylized ways (Bateson 1958).

LeCron Foster argues that, in general, such ritual reversals are probably experienced as synergic and that these cognitive synergies play a part in triggering reversals to the paratelic mode. That is, they are culturally learned cues for contingent reversal. And in the paratelic mode which results, they are themselves then much enjoyed (think of the Christmas and Halloween examples). In other words, cultures tend to recognize special periods which are sacred in the sense that they are perceived as outside the normal profane time frame, and in these periods the high arousal generated by synergies may be a source of great pleasure. Synergies therefore play two roles here, since they both instigate the paratelic mode and provide fuel for enjoyment within it. (She also argues that the ritual reversals involved are socially functional in that they play an important part in keeping in check various processes which might otherwise risk getting out of hand: thus the individual who is displaying an unbridled drive for power may be playfully reminded that he is still human and symbolically shown that his changes in status can always be reversed.)

THE COMIC AS SYNERGIC

A young and callow Catholic priest is making his way up the high street of a town when he is accosted by a prostitute: 'How would you like a quickie for ten pounds?' she says.

The priest, puzzled, shakes her off and continues on his way only to be stopped by another prostitute. 'Ten pounds for a quickie', she offers. Again he breaks free and goes on up the street.

Later in the day, he is having tea in the convent with the Mother Superior.

'Please tell me one thing', he says to her, 'What's a quickie?'

'Ten pounds, the same as it is in town', she replies.

Now obviously this is a synergy. The joke revolves around the two quite different and very incompatible meanings of the same sentence. That is, the question, 'What's a quickie?' can be interpreted as asking either 'What is a quickie?' or 'What's a quickie [worth]?' The situation is also synergic in that the question is simultaneously answered and not answered. But there is also a more subtle synergy, and one which represents the nub of the joke. This is that the Mother Superior, who we naturally take to be a holy and reverend lady, shows herself by her mistake to be no better than, and just as mercenary as, the madame of a brothel. The priest is also incidentally shown up as being even more innocent and unworldly than we thought, since he was not aware of this. Nor do the nuns come out of the whole thing particularly well.

Imagine a fashionable cocktail party by a swimming pool. A rather haughty waiter is bringing a tray full of drinks, carrying the tray above his head with one hand. He accidentally kicks over a cocktail shaker he had left on the ground, then steps on it so that he skates on it a little way, loses his footing and lurches sideways. For a moment he stands unbalanced on the edge of the pool – all eyes on him – does a little flamenco-like dance to try to regain his balance, the tray of glasses still held high above his head, and finally tumbles in. Again we have a synergy. The same identity (the waiter) is characterized by the opposite qualities of superiority and inferiority. Even on the brink he maintains something of his superior demeanour while everyone is aware that he is about to be humiliated.

Comic situations of all kinds constitute a major category of cognitive synergy. And there are many kinds within this category: human beings who behave like objects (as in slapstick), men dressed as women (pantomime dames), animals behaving like humans (Mickey Mouse and other cartoon animals), objects that seem to be alive (ventriloquists' dolls), and so on. But it is not enough just to say that comic events and situations are synergies. It is necessary to go further and find out how they differ from all those other synergies that do *not* make us laugh or produce that glorious feeling which we call humour. After all, we do not normally laugh at a landscape painting, a mistaken identity, or an antique. So what is it about comic synergies in all their forms that makes them funny? There would appear to be two essential characteristics.

First of all, although there is a sense in which all cognitive synergies involve both appearance and reality, in comic synergies the identity *purports* to be one thing whereas in reality it is another. The doll's house does not purport to be a real house, or the landscape a real view; indeed they could hardly do so. In the typical non-comic synergy we know what something really is, but add on one or more opposing qualities in our imagination, or enter into the spirit of the situation by following the signposts with which we are presented. We are happy to see the landscape *as if* it were real; we willingly enter into the illusion of the doll's house while recognizing that this is what we are doing; we perceive the Necker cube to change although we are perfectly well aware that it cannot possibly do so.

In the comic situation, however, the signposts with which we are presented are misleading, and it turns out that, through accident, or a changing perspective, what we are invited to take as real is, in reality, only appearance. We assume that the Mother Superior is holy and that her nuns are chaste, but discover that we have been mistaken and that things are quite otherwise. We are impressed by the haughtiness and professionalism of the waiter, only to find that he is capable of a grotesque piece of incompetence.

But this in itself, although essential, is still not enough to make synergies funny. We do not laugh every time we find we have made a mistake. Neither do brilliant new discoveries in science, which show the deep reality underlying superficial appearance, normally give rise to mirth and hilarity. The second special feature of the comic synergy is that the appearance which is disclosed is in some respect less than the reality – less in importance, less in status, less in monetary value, less in competence, and so on. In other words, the identity must be downgraded in some way. The scientific discovery reveals that there is more order and beauty in some aspect of nature than we had suspected. The joke discloses that there is less of some valued characteristic in relation to an identity than we thought. The Mother Superior turns out to be inferior, at least in her morals if not her street wisdom. The waiter turns out to be less competent than we were led to suppose that he was. The pistol which is no more than a cigarette lighter – to remind you of an example from early in the chapter – may also raise a laugh, especially if it is a large and dangerous looking weapon that produces a small and feeble flame.

Such comic downgrading is perhaps particularly clear in parody, where the characteristics of an identity are exaggerated in such a way as to make them negative. The parody of a romantic novel given at the beginning of this chapter is an example, especially the final line of it. But whether the deprecation is subtle or blatant, implicit or explicit, it has to be there somewhere for humour to be felt. This is why the pun, even though it is a synergy (based of course on the dual meanings of a single word) is not very funny – there is usually little or no downgrading involved.

Very often humour turns on a surprise (like the banana skin) in which appearance gives way very rapidly to reality, or a suddenly changed perspective allows us to see things as they really are – the camera moves back in the comedy film to reveal that the smart man is wearing no trousers. But the effect of comic synergy, as in earlier examples of other types of synergy in this chapter, does not depend on surprise, even if it is much enhanced by it. For example, we may continue to be amused by a comic character whose synergies are 'built in' and well known to us. Charlie Chaplin's tramp character continues to appeal to our sense of humour even though we are aware that his meticulousness – as evidenced by his walking stick and bowler hat – belie his shabbiness, and that his attempts to help in some situation will only make matters worse (or, through his mistakes, paradoxically, make things better). The point is that one thing is purported while the reality is something else – and inferior to what is purported; and this is amusing whether we discover this discrepancy at the time or are aware of it all along.

For something to be experienced as funny there are, then, five essential requirements. The first three are to do with synergy: the situation should display cognitive synergy, the synergy should be one in which an appearance which purports to be reality is 'unmasked', and the reality thus disclosed should be 'less' in some evaluative sense than the appearance.

The fourth requirement which is essential if humour is to be experienced is that the individual should be in the paratelic mode; and one of the functions of the joke or comic situation is to induce this mode. This is occasioned by the way in which the structure of the comic synergy is such that it appears to escape from the restrictive demands of logic, and do so in a clearly playful way; and since, as we have seen, the comic identity is 'less' than it seems, it removes all questions of a serious threat being posed. (Typically in a comic situation there will also be other cues which tend to induce a contingent reversal to the paratelic mode, most notable among these being the expectant smiles and the laughter of other people.) If for some reason the paratelic mode is not induced, then humour will not be felt. If, for example, the waiter injures himself on falling into the pool, the increased arousal experienced by spectators will be of concern rather than mirth. To a devout Catholic, the joke about the priest and the Mother Superior may be shocking rather than funny.

Fifth, the comic should produce a surge of increased arousal, since the feeling of humour is a form of paratelic excitement. The comic synergy, therefore, as in the reversal rituals discussed by LeCron Foster, does two things at the same time: it triggers a reversal and provides appropriate material for the new mode. In this it is not unlike the flintlock pistol which, when the trigger was pulled, both opened a gunpowder chamber and struck a spark in the same action. LeCron Foster's word 'trigger' here is therefore particularly apt.

The greater the increase in arousal, and the longer it can be sustained, the more enjoyable the effect is likely to be. In this respect, the more surprising the synergy, the more intensely pleasurable it should be. The more arousing the content the better – and hence the use of the sexual and aggressive material which is so typical of jokes. And the more numerous the synergies which can be tied into a complex knot of incompatible meanings, the funnier the result. (Apter (1982b) gives a detailed analysis of an episode from a television comedy series, 'Fawlty Towers', showing just how complex such 'multiple synergies' can be in the best comedy.)

Obviously humour is a complicated topic. More detailed discussions of some of the aspects touched on here will be found in Apter and Smith (1977) and Apter (1982a: Chapter 8). Meanwhile, the first research on humour generated by, or related to, reversal theory is encouraging. Martin (1984), using the Telic Dominance Scale, found significant negative correlations between total telic dominance score and each of four different measures of sense of humour (the tendency to respond to a variety of life situations with smiles and laughter, the tendency to use humour as a device in coping with stress, the sense of humour, and the degree to which humour device is valued). His data, therefore, show that the more likely someone is to be in a paratelic state of mind, the more likely they are to see the funny side of things in everyday life. Wicker, Thorelli, Barron, and Willis (1981) administered a measure of mood state (the Nowlis-Green Mood Adjective Check List; Nowlis 1970) to students, and asked them to rate jokes for funniness and for thirteen other attributes of humour (originality, good taste, etc.). One of their principal findings was that subjects' humour appreciation scores – the average for each subject of how funny he or she found all the jokes – was significantly correlated with three mood variables in particular, these being the variables labelled 'surgency', 'elation', and 'vigour'. It should be explained that by surgency is meant feeling carefree, playful, and witty – in our terms, paratelic. On the basis of this, and the fact that most of the mood factors that correlated with humour appreciation implied some degree of arousal (quite apart from the high arousal obviously implied by 'elation' and 'vigour'), they argued that, as predicted by reversal theory, humour appreciation is related to high arousal, but only in a playful, paratelic mood. Consistent with this are the findings of Svebak and Apter (1987), in an experiment already referred to earlier in this book (Chapter 5), that a comedy film tended to induce the paratelic mode, even in telic-dominant subjects, and that the amount of laughter was positively correlated with degree of felt arousal in this mode.

We now have a structural phenomenology of an aspect of everyday experience which enters into consciousness in many guises, and which, at the level of generality addressed here, has not been previously recognized in psychology. The analysis is 'structural phenomenological' in that it involves discerning in subjective experience a type of deep structure which may take a variety of particular surface forms – such as toys, artworks, ambiguities, and jokes – and involve many different types of concrete content. There are some more complex forms. For example, metaphor may be said to involve two incompatible identities being brought together, rather than incompatible qualities being related to a single identity. (A detailed discussion of metaphor in these terms will be found in Apter (1982c).) But every form of synergy, simple or complex, reversal or identity, single or multiple, arises from the way in which incompatible ideas may be held together in consciousness where they are converted into special mental 'alloys' of the types we have considered here.

9

Clinical Implications of Reversal Theory

The mind is its own place and in itself
can make a Heaven of Hell, a Hell of Heaven.

Paradise Lost
John Milton (1608–74)

STRUCTURAL DISTURBANCE

David, who is aged 37, has a problem which has taken control of his life. This is that he lives constantly in fear of harm, and a disproportionate part of his time is spent in protecting himself from it. Thus he fears harm from burglary, so that he repeatedly checks the locks on doors and windows. He fears accidental fire, so that he frequently checks the wiring of electric plugs. He fears being attacked, so that wherever possible he avoids contact with strangers. And above all he fears infection, so that he washes his hands up to 25 times each day, always takes two showers a day, cleans his teeth up to 12 times a day, flushes the toilet two or three times after use, and records all his feelings of ill health, however minor or transitory, so that he can make accurate reports to his doctor, whom he visits regularly. Not surprisingly, his sexual relationships with women (he is unmarried) have been infrequent and short-lived. And although his job was not one which was exactly fraught with danger – he was a clerk in an accountancy company – his fears and obsessions made life difficult for others and he now finds himself unemployed. He does not drink, because of the danger of alcoholic poisoning, smoke because of the danger of lung cancer, take snuff because of the danger of throat cancer and nasal infection, or use hair conditioner – he read in a Sunday newspaper that this can cause scalp diseases. (For more details concerning David, see Murgatroyd and Apter (1984).)

Now it need hardly be said that every normal person experiences fear and anxiety from time to time. But in the case of David his anxiety has reached neurotic extremes, so that most of his life has become subjected to the need to avoid potential harm. As a result, he is experiencing a great deal of unnecessary suffering and distress.

If we look at his case in reversal theory terms, we see that he is locked in the telic mode so that, unlike most people, he is not reversing back and forth between the telic and paratelic modes in the course of everyday life.

Instead, everything is oriented around the serious and long-term goal of remaining healthy and unharmed, his life is planned in detail in order to ensure this, and if something disturbs his routines – for example he can only clean his teeth three or four times in a day – then he becomes extremely anxious. In short, he is suffering from what one might term 'reversal inhibition' (together with an inability to achieve many of the satisfactions of the telic mode in which he is 'stuck').

Now let us compare David to Sally, who also has problems that are to do with the experience of anxiety and fear (for more details see Murgatroyd and Apter (1986). Sally, aged 30, is a housewife with a son aged four, living with her husband on a pleasant surburban estate. She has an attractive and outgoing personality, a good sense of humour, and gets on well with people. Unfortunately, from time to time she has panic attacks – often when going out shopping – and these are so severe that she prefers to remain at home, with the consequence that her ability to live a full and normal life has been seriously disrupted. The psychiatrist to whom she was referred diagnosed her as suffering from agoraphobia and prescribed minor tranquillisers, but these turned out not to be particularly helpful. She was then referred to a therapist who, on asking her to keep a diary recording situations in which her panic arose, discovered that these were far more varied than even she herself had fully realized. They included such situations as being involved in an argument with a neighbour who called, starting to make love to her husband, watching an especially exciting programme on television, telling a joke to a friend, listening to a relative's problems, and being visited by a male friend to whom she felt some sexual attraction. So, although not going out had reduced the frequency of her attacks, they were still occurring distressingly often (at least once a day).

Now Sally's problem is obviously different from that of David. She is not trapped in the telic mode, and spends much of her life in the paratelic mode; indeed, on the Telic Dominance Scale she turned out to be highly paratelic-dominant. Her problem is that, from time to time, she reverses into the telic mode, often at inappropriate moments (e.g. while watching television or starting to make love) and consequently experiences the arousal she is feeling as anxiety. She is then worried that this anxiety will lead to a panic, this worry producing even greater anxiety which in turn leads to anxiety about this new level of anxiety. The result is that the classic vicious circle of phobia is set up in which each new level of anxiety generates yet further anxiety until, in short order, a full-blown panic attack is produced.

Her problem therefore has two components. The first is a tendency to treat any sudden surge of arousal as threatening, whatever its source, be it social, sexual, synergic, or of some other type, with the result that the telic mode is induced and the arousal experienced as anxiety. This will often be entirely inappropriate – for example, when telling a joke. The second is then the tendency to overreact to the anxiety, converting it into panic. The upshot is that she can only rarely experience excitement in any of its forms, because every time she tries to do so – for example through engaging in gossip, flirting, or going out with friends – she risks inappropriately inducing the telic mode and experiencing anxiety and even panic instead. For someone who is paratelic-dominant like Sally, this is not at all a happy state of affairs, and means that she spends much of her time in a state of boredom rather than risk a panic attack. (Among other things this also means that her sexual life has become almost non-existent.) All this further produces an overlay of depression, since she finds herself in a situation in which she can seemingly never experience arousal in the way she wants. And it is hardly surprising that the tranquillisers do not help; they in fact seem to make matters worse by generally keeping arousal levels low, with the result that boredom is even more difficult for Sally to overcome. At the same time, they are not strong enough to counteract the acute anxiety which still occurs when some strongly arousing situation suddenly sets in train the sequence of events described above.

In the case of both David and Sally it can be seen that their problems are intimately bound up in difficulties with metamotivational reversal. In the case of David, the problem is that of inhibited reversal; in the case of Sally it is to do with inappropriate reversal. In this respect their problems are what one might think of as 'structural' – they are to do with the metamotivational structure of their conscious experience. Between them they illustrate both forms of such disturbance.

As it happens, both these illustrations principally involve the telic mode. But reversal inhibition and inappropriate reversals may equally involve the paratelic mode. For example, Du Plat-Taylor and Hourizi (1985) describe a 15-year-old Jamaican boy, Tom, at a day adjustment unit for adolescents. Tom's problem, as they see it, is that he is stuck in the paratelic mode. The effect is that he can never think beyond the immediate moment, plan ahead, or see the long-term effects of what he is doing, and devotes himself in a haphazard way to immediate thrills. At school he finds it impossible to sit quietly and listen to teachers, and attempts to gain excitement by talking, making jokes, mouthing faces, creating noises, standing up, asking to go to the toilet, picking quarrels, and the like. By his own admission he believes that what you do today has little effect on what happens tomorrow, and sees most of life as being dependent on luck, or dictated by the whim of some irrational force. There is, therefore, no point in working at school or thinking ahead to a future career.

A comparable example, but this time of inappropriate reversal, has been documented by Blackmore and Murgatroyd (1980). Anne is a six-year-old at an infant school. Much of the time she works well in class, but from time to time, especially when she is frustrated by what she is doing, she switches to a 'disrupt now' state which combines the paratelic and negativistic modes. For example, on one occasion, the teacher wanted the class to work at some problems associated with numbers, while Anne wanted to colour a picture in a book. When the teacher refused, Anne harangued her, telling her to 'Fuck off' and to 'Get stuffed'. Such states could be brought on by small incidents – such as breaking the point of a pencil or being handed a piece of drawing paper with a jagged edge, although occasionally they seemed to occur spontaneously (perhaps under conditions of satiation). In any event, the subsequent disruption was usually severe, Ann doing such things as shouting, charging around the classroom, tearing up other pupils' paper and even lashing out at other children. Then, as suddenly as it started it would stop, Anne returning to 'normality' and resuming her previous activities.

In all four of these cases, the 'structural disturbance' is compounded by the use of inappropriate 'strategies' within the problem mode. Both Tom and Anne achieve high arousal in the classroom in ways which disturb others, rather than making use of the intrinsic stimulation of the material and skills being learned. Both David and Sally use inappropriate strategies in handling arousal which they experience as uncomfortably high in the telic mode. David goes to irrational lengths to remove anything from his life which might cause him anxiety – but in the event all this does is to ensure that problems and threats are always at the centre of his attention. Sally worries about the anxiety which she is experiencing, but this simply has the counterproductive effect of making the anxiety even worse and converting it into panic.

In other words, these problems have two different levels: a 'higher' or structural level which is about the relationship *between* modes, and a 'lower' level which is about the psychological processes which occur *within* a mode. Although the problems in our illustrative cases involve both levels, it is perfectly possible for people to experience problems at one level alone. For example, a person might be locked in the telic mode but behave in a way which enables him to achieve the satisfactions of that mode: his problem is rather that he can never 'let himself go', or 'have fun' which means that he misses out on some of life's greatest pleasures, fails to take full psychological advantage of situations in which he unavoidably finds himself from time to time (e.g. at parties) and, which is worse, makes life something of a misery for his wife, family, and friends (if he has any). In contrast, someone else might be generally in the 'right' mode at the 'right time' – the telic mode in the office, the paratelic mode at parties, and so on – but use strategies in one or other mode which are inappropriate. For example, when he is in the telic mode he might tend to behave like David, in a compulsive and ritualistic way.

INAPPROPRIATE STRATEGIES

What *is* a psychological problem? One view, and the view which will be adopted here, is that psychological problems, at least of the clinical variety, are problems of *unnecessary distress*. That is, they arise when a person tends to react to certain kinds of situation with more prolonged or acute distress than others would, or a person brings on problems which raise distress which others would avoid. Consistent with the whole approach of reversal theory, this definition is essentially a phenomenological one: a problem may only be said to have arisen when someone *feels* distress, not when their behaviour is abnormal, unless this has contributed to the distress. (After all, much abnormal behaviour – the behaviour of the creative artist, for example – produces pleasure rather than displeasure.)

In the light of this definition, the reader will now be able to appreciate the way in which the word 'inappropriate' has been used here. An inappropriate reversal or strategy is one which leads to unnecessary distress – either on the part of the person who is indulging in it or others with whom he or she is interacting. It should be emphasized that this does not imply a moral definition of appropriateness and inappropriateness, but is simply descriptive in terms of the outcome.

Inappropriate strategies within a metamotivational mode – that is, inappropriate ways of attempting to obtain and maintain the satisfactions intrinsic to that mode and avoid the dissatisfactions – can take many and varied forms. Among other things they can be deliberate or involuntary, conscious or unconscious, rigid or flexible. And no mode is safe from them. But in terms of their pathological effects, they would appear to fall into three main categories.

The first inappropriate type of strategy is that which is simply the wrong strategy to obtain the pleasure, or diminish the distress, in the mode which is in operation at the time. This could be described as 'functionally inappropriate'. Thus, Sally's worry about her anxiety, and David's compulsive activities for avoiding anxiety, are both counterproductive and play a part in bringing on that very anxiety which they are trying to avoid. Here are a couple of other examples involving other modes, given in order to generalize the concept a little. In the negativistic mode someone may tend to express his negativism through refusal to take part in activities with others; but this limits his chance of being able to continue to behave negativistically. For example, on a given occasion he may refuse to have an argument with someone, thus depriving himself of the chance of a prolonged and pleasurably bitter debate. In the autocentric mastery mode combination a person may attempt to prove himself by taking on exactly those tasks for which he is in fact least well suited, and persevere with this despite increasing humiliation rather than switch to something which he would be likely to be good at. In the autocentric sympathy mode combination, a person may be so demanding of time, attention, and affection that he loses all his friends.

A second category consists of those strategies which are what one might call 'temporally inappropriate'. That is, they are immediately effective in reducing distress, or obtaining gratification, and in this sense they are functional, but they have unfortunate long-term consequences. What this comes to is that the distress which individuals using these strategies are currently avoiding by means of them will become even more difficult for them to avoid as time passes, or their chance of pleasure will be much diminished. In this way they are storing up problems for themselves in the future.

A good example of this is compulsive gambling. Anderson and Brown (1984) reported that regular gamblers pursue gambling for the excitement it generates rather than for the money they might win, and that the majority of gamblers in the casino bet significantly more when they are ahead. Brown (1988), in a detailed examination of gambling in reversal theory terms, suggests that gamblers are in the paratelic mode when they play and that in this mode they are not aware of the full significance of what they are doing, or what the long-term consequences of a serious loss might be. Rather, the money is just so much paper which is needed to play the game and gain the immediate 'high' of short-term excitement. He goes on to argue that, although even compulsive gamblers tend to reverse to the telic state when they lose heavily, they continue to gamble not just to recoup their money but because they know from previous experience that when they do eventually win the rush of high arousal, and the switch to the paratelic mode that accompanies this, produces a particularly intense and pleasurable 'high'. So they gamble in both the paratelic and telic mode, in the first case for the immediate excitement and in the second because of the learned expectation of a particularly strong reward in the future. The effect of all this is that the confirmed gambler sees no reason to stop gambling until he finally runs out of resources. Only then, when he can no longer sustain his search for excitement, does the distress really begin. And then it is too late. (See also Anderson and Brown, in press; Brown 1987; Brown, in press).

A similarity to the way in which gamblers downgrade the objective significance of what they are doing in the paratelic mode, and in this way cause problems for themselves later on, might be the way in which alcoholics, smokers, and other addicts who are attempting to give up their addictions downgrade the significance of 'just one little sip' or 'one little puff' – thus setting themselves off again on the slippery slope. O'Connell (1988) (following some suggestions by Miller (1985) concerning addiction from a reversal perspective) has put forward the idea that smoking relapse is most likely to take place in the paratelic mode. This is not only because the immediate sensory appeal of smoking and the stimulation it promises are more attractive in this mode, but more particularly because it is easier in this mode to disregard the long-term consequences of smoking a cigarette. In this way it is possible to downplay the felt significance of an action which, at the moment concerned, seems to be no more than trivial. She also suggests that relapse is more likely to occur in the negativistic than the conformist mode, because in the negativistic mode the smoker can gain pleasure from resisting the pressure which he sees as being exerted on him to give up. Either way, paratelic or negativistic, the immediate pleasure can have longer-term distressing consequences, not least of which is having to start the process of giving up all over again.

These examples of short-sighted strategies or actions involve the paratelic more than the telic mode. But examples can be found where the emphasis is the other way round. Braman has described a type of child who he has encountered frequently in the course of his clinical practice over many years and whom he refers to as the 'oppositional child' (Braman 1982, 1988). He interprets this kind of child's behaviour in reversal theory terms as involving telic self-negativism. What seems to happen is this: the child's parents are ambitious for him to do well, especially at school, and he comes to realize that if he displays any ability or intelligence this will only increase his parents' ambitions for him and this means that the pressure on him will be stepped up even further. Rather than get embroiled in this 'no win' situation, he therefore disguises any ability he has by refusing to work, or he makes sure that he messes up his work in one way or another. Typically, such children do actually want to succeed, and this is why they feel so anxious about the whole situation: it matters to them. Their negativism is therefore directed not only against their parents and teachers, but also against themselves and their own desires. The strategy works for the child in the short term in that it removes the immediate pressure. But in the longer term, as he moves through the school system, he comes to feel increasingly anxious about his under-achievement, as well as humiliated, guilty, and depressed. What starts out as a perhaps dimly perceived and initially successful strategem turns into a habitual and self-defeating way of life.

There is one further general way in which strategies may be adopted by an individual which are inappropriate. This is where they are inappropriate to *others* in the sense that it is other people who are caused the unnecessary distress and suffering. Such 'socially inappropriate' strategies are exemplified by the behaviour of both Anne and Tom, described earlier, which caused upset in the classroom to teachers and pupils alike. Other obvious examples would be the street-corner vandal and the soccer hooligan (Kerr 1988a). The destructive and dangerous behaviour of these youngsters may well be functional in helping them to achieve the 'kicks' of paratelic high arousal and negativistic defiance, but they generally do so at the expense of other people. Similarly, but in a stronger form, the sexual pervert, such as the sadist or rapist, may derive a number of pleasures from his actions (Apter and Smith 1987). These include the mastery mode pleasure of domination, and the negativistic mode pleasure of breaking taboos, as well as the paratelic mode pleasure of excitement. But all these actions require the suffering of someone else. (This type of sexual problem can incidentally be contrasted with sexual dysfunction which, as described in Chapter 2, involves what we can now see as inappropriate reversal into the telic mode during a sexual encounter; for a specific case discussed in reversal theory terms, see Scott (1985).)

More subtle forms of socially inappropriate strategy often emerge in the course of family therapy (Apter and Smith 1979b; Apter 1982a: Chapter 11). It often becomes apparent, for example, that a child, in the security of the home, engages in paratelic testing out behaviour to see which actions have the most exciting effect on other family members, and especially parents. If swearing is the most effective, then the child will swear regularly; if refusing to eat sets everyone into turmoil then this may become the preferred stratagem for a while; if failing to put a cap on the toothpaste tube irritates other members of the family, then the cap will not be put on the toothpaste tube. The point is that such actions as these are frequently not so much signs of carelessness, laziness, stupidity, or faulty learning; they are specifically indulged in, in the paratelic mode, in order to produce pleasant high arousal in the contemplation of their effects. In these cases, the home is used by the child as a kind of theatre. (One is reminded of Gorki's aphorism that the family row is the poor man's form of entertainment.) Of course, for this to work, the child has to be able to remain in the paratelic state, which means that he or she must avoid events occurring which they would regard as real threats to their security. One strategy for helping to ensure such security is to set up coalitions within the family so that support and protection is received from one family member while another is being provoked. A typical pattern observed in the clinic is for the child to set up a coalition with the mother while provoking rows with the father, or rows between mother and father. For example, if the father is authoritarian, the child may put on a display of dispirited submission which makes the mother angry with the father. On the other hand, if the father is too easy-going, then the child may do things which make the mother angry with the father for allowing him to get away with them. If the mother and father cannot agree about particular points of upbringing and discipline – such as when their children should go to bed, or which television programmes they should be allowed to watch – then the child can take advantage of this and use such disagreements to set his parents against each other.

An opposite type of socially inappropriate behaviour which is observed in 'problem' families is that which occurs when one, or both, parents, in the telic mode, go too far in attempting to impose their serious telic goals on their children. We have already seen the other side of the story here in connection with the 'oppositional' child who avoid success because of the increasing demands he knows parents will impose on him as a consequence. Another example would be the obsessional perfectionist mother who makes life a misery for her children – and her husband – by insisting at all times on complete cleanliness. Shoes have to be taken off in the hallway, smoking is allowed only if the ashtray used is immediately washed after each cigarette, beds may not be sat on in the day-time in case the coverings are creased, no food is ever fried because of the lingering smell. In this and other ways, such a mother may reduce her own anxiety, but at the expense of everyone else in the household.

Often, of course, these two types of socially inappropriate strategy are combined: one or more members of the family are looking for excitement while one or more of the others are desperately attempting to avoid anxiety. Such an incompatibility of mode and strategy is a formula for disaster and (if the pun is excused) under these conditions one is likely to see the nuclear family explode.

A NEW TAXONOMY FOR MENTAL DISORDER

Now the cynical reader might say, 'What is special about all these cases and problems which you have referred to in this chapter so far? They are not conditions which exactly went unrecognized before reversal theory. Obsessional men, agoraphobic women, compulsive gamblers, disruptive and underachieving children – these are all part and parcel of everyday psychiatry, psychotherapy, and counselling.' But this is exactly the point. What reversal theory does is not to identify new syndromes which no one had suspected existed. What it does is to take a wide variety of psychological problems and show how they fit into a structure which had not previously been discerned, disclosing new patterns and relationships between them in the process (Murgatroyd 1981; Apter 1982a: Chapter 11; Murgatroyd and Apter 1984, 1986; Kerr 1987b).

Summarizing the argument of this chapter so far, reversal theory specifically suggests that there are five major categories of psychological disorder (at the level of neurosis and personality disorder, if not of psychosis) and these fall into two larger groupings as shown in the following table:

1. Structural disturbance (across mode)
    a. Inhibited reversal
    b. Inappropriate reversal
2. Inappropriate strategies (within mode)
    a. Functionally inappropriate

b. Temporally inappropriate
c. Socially inappropriate

These types of disorder can be combined in any way (with the exception of inhibited and inappropriate reversal, which are mutually exclusive) to make up more complex conditions, such as those exemplified by Sally and David, whose problems were outlined in the first section of this chapter.

Let us take several major categories of psychological disorder and see how they might fit into this scheme. What about neurotic anxiety, for example? Clearly, the answer depends on what kind of neurotic anxiety one is talking about. Chronic anxiety would be an example of inhibited reversal, the individual being rather rigidly located in the telic mode and for some reason (environmental, cognitive, or metabolic) tending regularly to experience high levels of arousal which he or she has difficulty overcoming. This would contrast with acute anxiety and phobia which would seem to involve a combination of high arousal with inappropriate, rather than inhibited, reversal. Thus, the person who is phobically afraid of spiders will inappropriately reverse to the telic mode on encountering a spider and experience quite unnecessary fear.

Turning to depression: if we see this as a feeling of hopelessness in reaction to some form of distress – in other words, what Becker (1967) has called 'negative expectation' or Seligman (1975) has referred to as 'learned helplessness' – then it would follow from reversal theory that there are a number of different types of depression. Each of these would be associated with a different particular tension (in the reversal theory sense of a discrepancy between the preferred and actual level of a variable). Thus, there would be anxiety depression, in which the individual feels helpless about his chances of overcoming the tension of anxiety, or at least of doing so for long. There would be boredom depression, in which the individual despairs of ever achieving the excitement for which he craves, and the whole of his life world seems lacking in interest, flavour, or stimulation. There would be conformity depression, which would be characterized by a feeling of inability to live up to the expectations of others or the rules of certain groups which are important to the person. There would be negativistic depression, which would be the feeling of an inability to express hostility, so that pent-up anger is experienced instead. There would also be humiliation depression, shame depression, guilt depression, and resentment depression. All of these different forms of depression would tend to be associated with a combination of inhibited reversal and an inability, through strategies which are inadequate in some way or another, to move the variable concerned (felt arousal or felt transactional outcome) to a preferred level in that mode. Anxiety depression, for instance, would be likely to occur in someone who is unable, generally speaking, either to reduce levels of felt arousal sufficiently to feel relaxed, or to reverse to the paratelic mode and experience excitement instead. Humiliation depression, to give another example, would be likely to be the outcome of a prolonged period in the autocentric mastery mode combination, associated with regular losses on the felt transactional outcome variable.

In deciding how obsessional-compulsive problems fit into this structure, the first and obvious point is that compulsive actions – such as ritualistic washing – involve an inappropriate strategy being used. In some cases this will be functionally inappropriate, but even where it does help to reduce immediate anxiety, when taken to an extreme it so interferes with the individual's life that he causes other problems for himself and consequently greater anxiety in the long term: for example, he might lose his job because his rituals make him late for work.

But there is a second point here, which brings out a 'structural disturbance' aspect of this type of problem. It arises if we recognize the distinction, originally made by Freud, between the obsessional personality, characterized by obsessional *traits* such as orderliness, and the obsessional neurotic, whose behaviour is characterized by *symptoms* such as those of ambivalence and oscillation between different ways of feeling and behaving. Fontana (1981a) has suggested that the person with an obsessional personality is someone who, among other things, is unable to escape from the telic mode (and therefore, in the terms introduced here, suffers from inhibited reversal). The obsessional neurotic, on the other hand, suffers from an over-labile reversal system so that he reverses frequently between the telic and paratelic modes, often finding himself in the wrong mode at the wrong moment, and never quite catching up with himself. (In the terms introduced here, his problem is one of inappropriate reversal). Using the inventory of obsessionality developed by Sandler and Hazari (1960) with a sample of 84 college lecturers of both sexes, his results were consistent with this distinction: he found significant correlations between the telic dominance and obsessional traits, but not between telic dominance and obsessional symptoms.

The delinquent – to turn to another conventional diagnostic category – can be seen as a youngster who is caught in the paratelic mode and in this respect is mode-inhibited. As a result, he tends to treat everything – even things which others would take seriously, like the risk of physical danger or of arrest – as a kind of game. In this, he is the mirror-image of the adult who displays chronic anxiety, the latter treating everything – even things which others would treat playfully – with deadly seriousness. If the person suffering from chronic anxiety sees threats everywhere and is frequently worried, the delinquent would seem to see threats nowhere and respond to very little with worry or concern. Or rather, such concern as he does show is for immediate excitement, sensations, and gratifications, such as through loud rock music, drug-taking, and acts of gratuitous aggression. And his lifestyle is generally one of spontaneity and a lack of planning or thought for the future. Consistent with this view of delinquency is some evidence presented by Bowers (1985, 1988). In this study, a group of delinquent boys with records for committing various offences which included theft and physical assault were compared on the Telic Dominance Scale with a group of 'disruptive' boys identified by teachers as having behaviour problems in school and also with a control group of 'normal' children. The delinquent boys were significantly more paratelic-dominant (i.e. lower in telic dominance on total scale scores) than both the disruptive and the normal children. (As would also be expected, the disruptive children were also significantly more paratelic-dominant than the normals.)

It may be the case, especially since so much of delinquency involves acts of defiance and aggression – such as those involved in vandalism, hooliganism, and petty crime – that the delinquent is also negativistic-dominant, and perhaps in some cases effectively trapped in the negativistic mode. And the strategies used by the delinquent are also typically of the temporally and socially inappropriate type: they unnecessarily lay up problems for themselves in the future and cause distress to others.

A similar analysis can be made of the adult psychopath (Apter 1982a; Apter and Smith 1987), but here the situation becomes more complicated because there are various types of psychopath: for example, a distinction is often made between so-called primary and secondary psychopaths. However, Thomas-Peter and McDonagh (1988) and Thomas-Peter (1988) have published evidence throwing doubt on a connection between psychopathy and paratelic dominance. In their study, neither primary nor secondary psychopaths (in a hospital for mentally abnormal offenders) were significantly different in their total TDS scores from a normal control group. It may, therefore, be the case that to understand psychopathy we will have to look more closely at negativism dominance than telic dominance and at the types of strategies which psychopathic individuals use. It is also possible, as Thomas-Peter (1988) has suggested, that in relation to the telic–paratelic dimension the psychopath's problem may be more one of inappropriate than of inhibited reversal – presumably the individual tending to switch to the paratelic mode in response to certain particularly serious kinds of situations, which are then treated with levity and impulsiveness.

Looking at these examples of psychopathology, including anxiety and depression, which are probably the two most widely occurring neurotic disorders of our time – it will be seen that the structure of types of disturbance suggested by reversal theory cuts across the more conventional classification system in two ways. First, it breaks down the rather rigid distinction between neurosis and personality disorder. For example, it sees both chronic anxiety and delinquency as involving inhibited reversal (so that the latter could just as easily be called 'chronic boredom'). Second, it takes some seemingly unitary conditions, like depression, and breaks them down into not just different, but *opposite* types. For example, anxiety depression and boredom depression are seen as mirror-image forms of depression. In this respect the term 'depression' on its own, and unqualified in any way, is seen from the reversal theory perspective as unhelpfully, and even misleadingly, indiscriminate.

A FRAMEWORK FOR ECLECTIC PSYCHOTHERAPY

Now we come to the key question: can reversal theory help the practitioner in dealing with psychological problems? Clearly it does not provide any particular novel techniques that would allow one to talk about a 'reversal therapy' in the way that one could talk, for example, about behaviour modification or Gestalt therapy. But what it can do is something which may, in the long run, prove more important. This is, as Murgatroyd has emphasized, to provide a systematic framework for carrying out eclectic psychotherapy (Murgatroyd and Apter 1984, 1986; Murgatroyd 1987c).

What this framework does is to provide a rational structure within which the therapist or counsellor can make considered decisions about what type of intervention to use, and even how techniques from different types of therapy may be combined. In doing this, it makes no *a priori* distinction between 'acceptable' and 'unacceptable' techniques. It neither excludes nor requires the use of drugs, conditioning, dream analysis, relaxation, or anything else. What it does do is to encourage the therapist to try to understand what she is doing in relation to the problem categories introduced here. For example, is she trying to unblock inhibited reversal, stop reversal occurring at particular kinds of moments, bring the patient or client more into effective control of their own reversal patterns, make the person being treated aware of the long-term or the social consequences of his or her actions, or substitute appropriate for inappropriate strategies?

For example, if the therapist decides she is trying to overcome inhibited reversal and find ways of switching the client into the paratelic mode, she might use Albert Ellis's Rational-Emotive techniques for helping people to relabel their bodily states (Ellis 1962); the Gestalt therapy teaching of correct breathing which therapists in this tradition interpret as allowing the 'blocked excitement' of anxiety to be unblocked (Perls, Hefferline, and Goodman, 1973); Frankl's technique of paradoxical intention (Frankl 1973) in which patients deliberately exaggerated their symptoms (which method could be seen as requiring a form of play-acting likely to induce the paratelic mode); the techniques involved in encounter groups (which groups seem in effect to involve a kind of paratelic mode-inducing game in which interpersonal relations are bracketed off from the real pressures of everyday life); not to mention such techniques as humour which, as we have seen, is a paratelic experience (see Murgatroyd 1987b); and the imaging of particularly safe and unthreatening situations (like lying on the beach in the sun). If, on the other hand, the aim is to change some inappropriate strategy within a mode, such as the socially inappropriate behaviour of the young vandal, then counter-conditioning might be used, or behaviour modification, or some way might be sought for the youngster to achieve his craving for excitement in a more socially acceptable way – for example on the sports field.

In order to illustrate in a more concrete manner how this eclectic framework can be used to guide the therapeutic process, let us return to the case of Sally. Initially, the therapist used a number of techniques to try to understand more fully the nature of Sally's problem and the experience lying behind it. One of these, as we have seen, was the request that Sally keep a diary of her panic attacks, noting what she was doing at the time of onset on each occasion. Other techniques included the 'third-chair' technique (in which she was asked to describe herself in detail as if she were someone else sitting on a third chair in the room), and an examination of her dreams over several weeks. The latter displayed a frequent theme of fear of being overwhelmed – a typical (and in this case repeated) dream was of being caught on the seashore by a rising tide. As we saw earlier in the chapter, this and other information led the therapist to the view that any sudden surge of arousal, from whatever source, was experienced by her as overwhelming and therefore threatening, leading her to switch, frequently inappropriately, to the telic mode if she were not already in it, and experience anxiety rather than excitement. The anxiety then tended to turn into panic because of her spiralling fear of fear. Since she was paratelic-dominant, but had learned to avoid situations that might cause arousal, she was spending much of the time bored. Boredom depression had therefore become added to the problem of the panic attacks.

The therapist decided to concentrate on the panic attacks, since if these could be overcome there would be no need for Sally to avoid arousing situations, and the boredom depression would then disappear of its own accord. At this point, there appeared to be three alternative treatment options: first, finding ways of breaking into the vicious circle which was turning anxiety into panic, and hopefully lowering the arousal down to relaxing levels; second, attempting to overcome the feelings of threat associated with arousal in order to prevent inappropriate reversal in the first place; or, third, looking for techniques of helping Sally to re-reverse after an inappropriate reversal, so that she could then experience excitement rather than anxiety. The first of these was excluded on the grounds that where reversal was inappropriate this was because some level of excitement, mild or strong, should be experienced, not relaxation. For example, she should be able to enjoy the excitement of both social intercourse and sexual intercourse; experiencing low arousal here would be to miss the point, and would not be a fully healthy reaction.

Over the next eighteen months, and having explained to Sally the nature of her problem as he saw it, the therapist pursued a number of tactics along the lines of the second two treatment options, and he carefully monitored the effects of each. Without going into details, the techniques included the use of humour (Murgatroyd 1987b), role-reversal, paradoxical intention, play-acting and cognitive-reappraisal. (The interested reader will find more details in Murgatroyd and Apter 1986.)

The technique which turned out to be most successful in Sally's case, and which became the mainstay of her treatment, was the induction of parapathic anger. (It will be recalled that a parapathic emotion is one which, although supposedly unpleasant, is actually enjoyed in the paratelic mode because of the high arousal associated with it.) This first emerged in a therapy session in which, in order to test this possibility, the therapist playfully feigned a lack of sympathy and made a number of provocative remarks, as a result of which Sally responded in kind, so that a 'row' developed. Afterwards, he explained what he had been doing, and Sally said that she recognized the play-acting that had been going on and had enjoyed it for much of the time. At the end of the session she seemed euphoric and said she felt 'on top of the world'. For the following week she had no panic attacks at all. Although the attacks began to return later, the therapist felt that there had been something of a breakthrough, and over the following months the 'anger' approach was developed in a number of ways. During therapy sessions, more playful arguments were engineered, and guided daydreams involving anger were also made use of. Role-play anger was advised on a daily basis as a homework assignment: when she was on her own in the house she was to think of everything that made her angry for about 20 minutes and act out the anger – for example by 'punching hell' out of the pillows on her bed. Later the tactic was explained to her husband, who was asked for his support, and he reacted magnificently by volunteering to have regular role-playing arguments with his wife. When she felt a panic attack actually coming on, she was to attempt to experience anger instead. If she was at home she should go into the 'anger routine'; if in a public place, she was to 'think angry' (by summoning up anger-inducing images, or even by being angry about the attack itself) and do such things as furiously clench and unclench her fists.

Over these few months, Sally's condition improved considerably so that, instead of experiencing panic on a daily basis, she was now suffering from her panic attacks only rarely, and when they started she was usually able to bring them under control fairly quickly. Over the next couple of years, she found that she was experiencing a little flurry of attacks only once every three or four months, her depression had largely lifted, and she was able to lead a full life, doing such normal things as going shopping and visiting neighbours without any problems. An important bonus was that her sexual life had also improved enormously.

Why, in terms of the two tactics which the therapist was pursuing, did this use of parapathic anger work? The first tactic, it will be recalled, was that of trying to avoid inappropriate reversal. The problem here was that Sally was feeling out of control and threatened every time that she experienced a sudden increase of arousal, whatever its source, and consequently felt anxious. The regular induction of anger helped to break up this habitual pattern by showing that high-arousal emotions other than anxiety could be felt. (In Chapter 6 it was explained that anger and anxiety are alternative ways, negativistic and conformist respectively, of experiencing high arousal.) And by giving Sally practice in inducing this emotion herself, as she did with her 'anger routine', she was able to see that she could be in control of her own arousal rather than always being controlled by it. Arousal in itself, therefore, became less threatening. Furthermore, since the anger was play-acted, it was occurring as parapathic 'anger' in the paratelic mode, so that it was actually being enjoyed; in this way, Sally was able to experience for herself again the fact that arousal could be pleasant, even high arousal, and in this respect was not to be feared. (Other parapathic emotions were tried from time to time, but for some reason Sally found that this negativistic high-arousal emotion was the one she could most easily induce, through the appropriate thoughts and actions, without concomitantly inducing the telic mode, and it was the one she most enjoyed.) We should also notice one final way in which 'anger' was helping: by being angry she was breaking out of the vicious circle of feeling anxious about anxiety, and therefore avoiding 'stoking the flames'. In this way, too, she was learning that she had less to fear from increased arousal.

This new-found confidence about her ability to control and enjoy her high-arousal emotions meant that, should an inappropriate reversal actually occur, she could more easily re-induce the paratelic mode; and over the months, each time a panic attack started, she had practice in doing just this. As we have seen, to do so she would use essentially the same methods as those of her 'anger routine', except that now she was doing so in response to the start of a panic attack rather than under more auspicious conditions. She found this difficult at first, but it became easier. In this way, the second therapeutic tactic – that of helping her to re-reverse should inappropriate reversals still occur – was also implemented successfully. And as she found that she was no longer at the mercy of her anxiety, even these incipient panics started to disappear from her life.

It is often the case that the word 'eclecticism' is a euphemism for 'unsystematic' and 'uncritical' and that in therapy it represents a kind of 'anything goes' philosophy. It should, however, be evident that the structure provided by the reversal theory analysis which has been presented here is far from unsystematic and uncritical and is certainly not compatible with any old mish-mash of therapeutic techniques. (Another detailed case history of eclectic therapy based on reversal theory will be found in Murgatroyd (1987a) with critiques of it by Sollod (1987) and Hart (1987).)

In particular, reversal theory not only implies that certain sets of techniques are essentially similar and can therefore be used as tactical alternatives, but it also indicates which are likely to be counter-productive in relation to different types of problem, and should therefore be avoided. For instance, the use of any kind of method for reducing arousal in someone already suffering from boredom depression (like Sally) will only make matters worse, whatever the method. (In Sally's case we saw how prescribed tranquillizers turned out to be unhelpful.) In treating truancy, to return to an illustration from the very first pages of this book, it is necessary to discover whether the child is frightened of school or bored with school. Emphasizing how important school is may make the frightened child even more anxious, while emphasizing its security may make the bored child even less likely to want to return (*viz*. Murgatroyd, in press).

In general terms, for every condition there will be forms of intervention which will exacerbate it and forms which will ameliorate it, and deciding which are which in a particular case will require ascertaining something of the person's way of experiencing his or her problems. Without this, the wrong approach may very well be used. Jones (1981) gives the nice illustration of the earnest exhortations and goal-setting of those dealing with juvenile delinquents. As he points out, the counsellors and staff of approved schools, such as those he observed in his research, tended to assume that the youngsters were in the same serious state of mind as themselves. For this reason, they not only had difficulty in understanding why they had engaged in such 'senseless and stupid' activities as they had, but why they often did not seem to respond to their well-intentioned help. From his interviews with the delinquents themselves, he found that, as far as they were concerned, the only problem they had was that of getting helpers off their backs. As one said: 'In supervision you sit down in a boring old chair and talk about how we're getting on and things.' To them, their delinquency was fun; it was the treatment which was the problem. Jones suggests that intervention programmes should be based more on a recognition of the paratelic dominance of these teenagers. For example, ways could be found of showing how fun can be created other than by messing around on the street. This would not mean that reversal into the telic mode would not be encouraged, and serious long-term advice given to the youngsters during the periods they were in that mode, but such advice would be avoided as counter-productive during paratelic periods.

Not only does reversal theory point to techniques which may be counter-productive in certain conditions, it also highlights the way in which some forms of intervention, when used together, may be contradictory. Thus, providing medication which reduces arousal and psychotherapy which increases it (e.g. through challenge, humour, guided daydream, abreaction) would be contradictory. But more subtly, contradictions may arise where one tactic acts on the level of reversal and the other on the level of the variable on which the metamotivational modes involved also act. For example, there would be no point in treating anxiety by using a technique which tended to induce the arousal-seeking mode while at the same time using a method for reducing arousal; if both these techniques worked, the outcome would still be unsatisfactory since it would result in boredom.

The reversal theory framework not only helps to provide a decision structure within which choices of tactic can be made, it also emphasizes something which is often lost sight of by psychotherapists, psychiatrists, and others working within fixed traditions: this is that there are strategic decisions to be made as well as tactical decisions. Suppose the problem to be treated is one of chronic anxiety. The strategy which is usually adopted implicitly here is that of reducing arousal. Whatever the tactic which is used in attempting to achieve this end, be it the prescription of tranquillizers or sedatives, relaxation training, systematic desensitization, autogenic training, transcendental meditation, biofeedback, or any one of a number of other techniques, the unexamined assumption in these cases is that the only way of treating anxiety is by operating to lower arousal. But reversal theory draws attention to the fact that there is an equally viable strategy which could be pursued. This would be to leave the high arousal

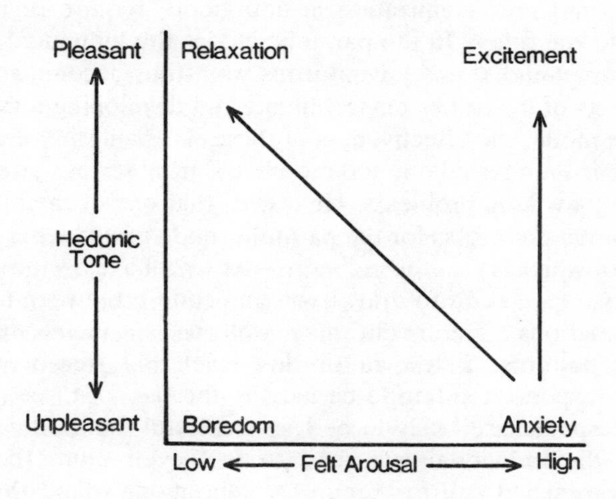

Fig. 21 Two alternative strategies for dealing with anxiety.

levels where they are, but instead to concentrate on helping the individual to reverse regularly into the paratelic mode and in this way experience the vivid pleasure of excitement. There is therefore always a strategic choice to be made: in this case between aiming for relaxation or aiming for excitement. The nature of this choice is illustrated in Figure 21.

Hence, reversal theory helps to bring out the full range of choices which confront the therapist by emphasizing that there are always alternatives – not just in the weak sense of alternatives between means to a given therapeutic end, but in the strong sense of alternatives between the ends themselves. A particularly positive aspect of this is the way in which reversal theory shows how, if one tactic fails, there is always another tactic available, and, more importantly, if one strategy fails there is always a second strategy which can be tried. In therapy it is always possible to have at least 'two bites of the cherry'.

STABILITY AND MENTAL HEALTH

One theme which has been running through this chapter is probably worth highlighting at this final stage. This is the need for the mentally healthy individual to experience metamotivational reversal on a reasonably regular basis, for each pair of metamotivational modes. This does not mean that there is anything wrong with being dominant with respect to one mode in each pair, but the other mode should be experienced at least occasionally.

Van der Molen (1985, 1986b) has argued in relation to the telic and paratelic pair of modes that healthy psychological development throughout childhood, and self-actualization in adulthood, require regular reversals from one to the other. In the paratelic mode, the individual explores in a relatively open-ended and adventurous way, thus becoming familiar with many aspects of his or her environment, and developing a range of skills. In the telic mode, the effectiveness of these skills and the relevance of this knowledge is then tested out and modified during serious attempts to cope with anxiety-evoking problems. He argues that one of the major forms of developmental 'failure' is for the paratelic mode to occur too infrequently, the effect of which is that the individual does not have a wide enough range of fully developed skills to draw upon and choose between in confronting serious situations. The result may well be an increasing rigidity of behaviour patterns, a few rather low-level and stereotyped kinds of avoidance response tending to be used in the face of threats. Since these forms of response are likely to be less successful than more sophisticated reactions, the individual will tend to feel even more threatened and become entrenched still further in the telic mode – and thus have even fewer opportunities for new open-ended learning experiences. In other words, what van der Molen calls a 'negative learning spiral' will be set up.

If, on the other hand, parents and others provide sufficient emotional support and security, thus encouraging the paratelic mode, then there is no reason why this spiral should be allowed to get started in the first place. (And in these terms what the therapist is doing can often be seen as breaking into such a spiral by providing a degree of emotional warmth and security that was lacking in childhood.)

Likewise, I argued earlier (Chapter 6) that, at least during transitional periods of life, time spent in the negativistic mode is essential to the attainment of a healthy sense of identity, as well as, throughout development, allowing the growing individual to learn the limits of action in different spheres. At the same time, conformity is also necessary if one is to take advantage of the kinds of learning experience which require discipline – such as conventional classroom instruction. In this way, an alternation between the conformist and negativistic modes also has a crucial development role to play.

But quite apart from these developmental benefits of alternation between modes, everyday life would seem to depend, if it is to be lived fully, on a kind of experiential dialectic in which each mode gives way to its opposite and then reasserts itself in a process of continuing self-contradiction.

It is ironic that the term 'stability' has generally become synonymous with mental health. The reversal theory view is that a certain kind of instability is essential for a full and happy life: one should be able to pursue the satisfactions of serious achievement, but also at other times the more frivolous joys of play; one should be able to feel the warm agreeableness of being a 'good citizen', but also from time to time the keen pleasures of defiance and independence; one should be able to experience the pride of personal strength as well as, on other occasions, the comforts of modest humility. The person who can only be serious, can only conform, and can only be modest, displays a stability which is maladjusted, not adjusted. The person who can never be serious, is always awkward and difficult, and continually strives to dominate others, is someone who is equally stable and equally unhealthy. Change and inconsistency cannot of themselves guarantee happiness or fulfillment, but the ability to reverse between metamotivational opposites would appear to be a prerequisite – provided such reversals, generally speaking, occur at suitable times and in suitable places, and in such a way that the individual is in harmony with the potentialities of each new situation as it arises. The watchwords for reversal theory, unlike most theories of personality and mental health, are not 'stability' and 'equilibrium' but rather 'change' and 'harmony'. From the reversal theory perspective, the healthy person is seen as less like a statue and more like a symphony.

10

The Experience of Stress

The suspense is terrible. I hope it will last.

The Importance of Being Earnest (Act III)
Oscar Wilde (1854–1900)

Suppose (which may even be true) that you have an important examination to sit in the near future. Further suppose (which may also be true) that you feel that the work which you have done in preparation for this examination is insufficient. The likely effect of this unfortunate combination of circumstances is that you will experience distress, especially in the form of anxiety. Now this anxiety will be different from the kind of neurotic anxiety discussed in the previous chapter in that it will be an appropriate reaction to a genuine threat. To use the term which counsellors are so fond of these days, you face a 'crisis'. Crises may be big or small, expected or unexpected, deserved or undeserved, but they have this in common: they are real, and something has to be done about them.

There is another word which has been used widely for even longer in connection with these sorts of events and situations: namely 'stress'. Examples of major stressors might be job loss, illness, financial insecurity, or divorce, and of minor stressors, having an argument, misplacing a book, cutting your finger, or breaking a shoelace. There are, actually, a number of conceptual difficulties with this notion of stress (and we shall return to some later in the chapter), but it has become so much a part of everyday speech that we all understand pretty well what is meant by it. For present purposes the point is that the upset caused by stress is different from that which arises from the kinds of psychological problems which were at the focus of the previous chapter: we all experience stress in different degrees and at different times, whereas not everybody is neurotic or suffering from a personality disorder. And the initial cause of stress may be something entirely outside one's control (like being robbed or catching a cold), whereas the problems discussed in the previous chapter were all essentially to do with a person's own psychological functioning or, more precisely, malfunctioning.

Over the years, an enormous research literature has grown up on the question of what it is, psychologically, that makes some people better able to resist the effects of stress than others – that is, what it is that enables them to be, as one notable researcher (Kobasa 1979) has put it, more 'hardy'. For the most part, as the word 'hardiness' suggests, this mainstream research assumes that the effects of stress are basically bad: that the individual will experience distress to some degree or another in response to life problems and may eventually develop somatic complaints if the problems persist. The main research question is then what it is that allows some people to feel less distress than others, and what it is that enables some to cope better than others with the effects of stress.

Clearly, the emphasis here is different from that which would be implied by reversal theory. Reversal theory would suggest that not only do some people respond less badly than others to the problems of everyday life, but that many people actually enjoy and seek out such problems. The rationale for this is that paratelic-dominant people are frequently in a state of mind in which they enjoy high arousal; if stressors increase felt arousal, then they will bring about exactly what these people so often want. Distress for them will arise when life *fails* to present such stressors, but a diet of threats and difficulties and crises is one on which they will thrive and flourish. Can this reversal theory view be sustained in the light of empirical data? It was this that Professor R. Martin and his colleagues at the University of Western Ontario set out to investigate, and it is to their research studies on this topic that I shall now turn (Martin 1985; Martin, Kuiper, and Olinger 1988; Dobbin and Martin 1988; Martin, Kuiper, Olinger, and Dobbin 1987; Martin-Miller and Martin 1988).

THE MARTIN ET AL. STRESS STUDIES

All these studies involve investigating the relationship between degree of telic dominance on the one hand and reaction to stress on the other. This means that there are always three terms: telic dominance, degree of stress, and the psychological effects of this stress – the basic hypothesis being that the first of these moderates the relationship between the second two. Telic dominance is measured throughout by means of the Telic Dominance Scale (total score), but different measures are used for severity of stress, and for the psychological effect of stress, in each of these pieces of research.

In the first study which Martin et al. reported (in which the subjects were 48 students of both sexes), stress was assessed by means of the Recent Stressful Event Questionnaire (based on Folkman and Lazarus' Ways of Coping Scale, 1985). In this questionnaire, subjects are asked to provide a written description of their most stressful event in the past month. These descriptions are then assessed by a judge in terms of whether the event has been resolved or is still ongoing. In some cases this information is spontaneously volunteered by the subject in his or her written description, but more usually it can be estimated in terms of whether the event is described in the past or present tense, or whether it is described as having taken place at a particular time or not. In this study, these assessments were made by three independent judges who generally showed acceptable agreement. What this all means, effectively, is that the stress variable is dichotomized into a low-stress, or no-stress, category on the one hand (where the problem has been resolved), and a high-stress category on the other (where the problem remains unresolved).

Reaction to stress was measured in this study by the Beck Depression Inventory (Beck, Ward, Mendelson, Mock, and Erbaugh 1961). Martin et al. argue that since all the scores on this inventory were well below the clinically depressed range, the results could be seen as indicative of dysphoria (unpleasant hedonic tone) rather than clinical depression.

The question now becomes one of how current hedonic tone levels relate to whether the principal stressor in the subject's recent life has been resolved or not. In these terms, reversal theory would suggest that telic-dominant subjects would show high negative hedonic tone if the stressor is continuing, and that paratelic-dominant subjects would be more likely to show high negative hedonic tone if the stressor has been resolved – since this removes from their lives something which generates the arousal which they so often want.

The results were subjected to what is known as a hierarchical multiple regression analysis, but the general pattern of results can be most easily grasped by means of the graph shown in Figure 22. This depicts two regression lines (lines which give the best fit to the data), one of these representing the relationship between telic dominance and mood disturbance for subjects who report resolved problems (the discontinuous line) and one representing this relationship for those who report that their problems are still unresolved (the continuous line).

It can be seen from this that where stress is unresolved, the more telic-dominant the individual, the more negative the mood which is experienced. In contrast, where the stressful problem is resolved, the relationship is inverted: now the more *paratelic* the individual, the more negative the mood. Putting this another way, if we look at the right-hand end of the graph, we see that telic-dominant subjects are much more disturbed if the stressor is unresolved than if it is resolved, whereas if we look at the left-hand end of the graph, we see that paratelic-dominant subjects (i.e. subjects who are low on telic dominance, which means the same thing) experience matters the opposite way: they find the situation more unpleasant when the stressor has been resolved. In fact, the two lines representing resolved and unresolved stressful events have crossed over each other, and diverge increasingly as we move to the extremes of telic and paratelic dominance. So we see that telic- and paratelic-dominant subjects do experience stress in opposite ways, and the paratelic-dominant subjects are unhappy with a comparative *lack* of stress.

Not content with this, however, Martin and his colleagues decided to see

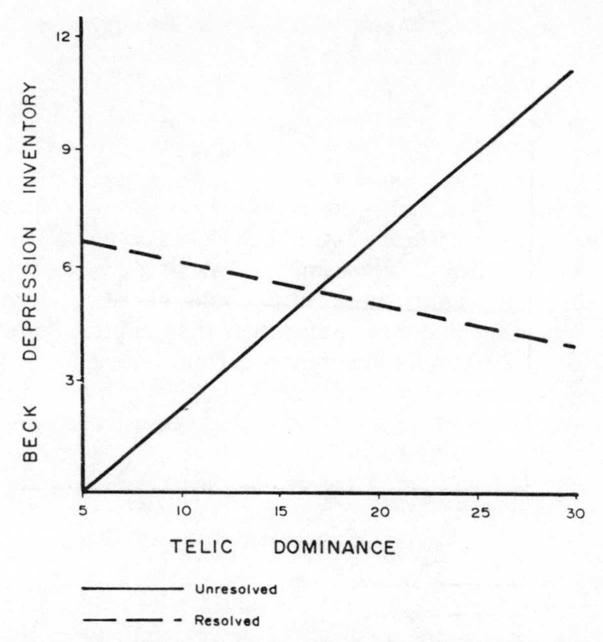

Fig. 22 Regression curves showing the relationship between telic dominance and depression (as measured by the Beck Depression Inventory), for subjects with resolved and unresolved recent life stressors. (After Martin, Kuiper, Olinger, and Dobbin 1987).

whether the same kind of pattern would hold up if a more objective index of the effects of stress were to be used. They therefore repeated this study (this time with 42 undergraduates of both sexes), but instead of using the Beck Depression Inventory they substituted for it a biochemical index of stress response, namely the amount of cortisol in a standard amount of saliva. This was obtained by asking subjects to salivate into a test tube immediately before they took the Telic Dominance Scale and the Recent Stressful Event Questionnaire. The saliva was subsequently tested for cortisol using standard procedures.

Again, the results of a multiple regression analysis showed that the effect of stress varied for telic- and paratelic-dominant subjects, depending on whether the main stressor which they had experienced during the previous month had been resolved or was still continuing. The nature of this relationship is shown by the regression lines in Figure 23. This graph discloses that when the stressful event has been resolved (shown by the discontinuous line in the graph), then the more paratelic the subject is, the higher the cortisol levels, and in this sense the more negative the effects. As it turned out, in this case there was no relationship between degree of telic dominance and cortisol levels for unresolved problems. None the less

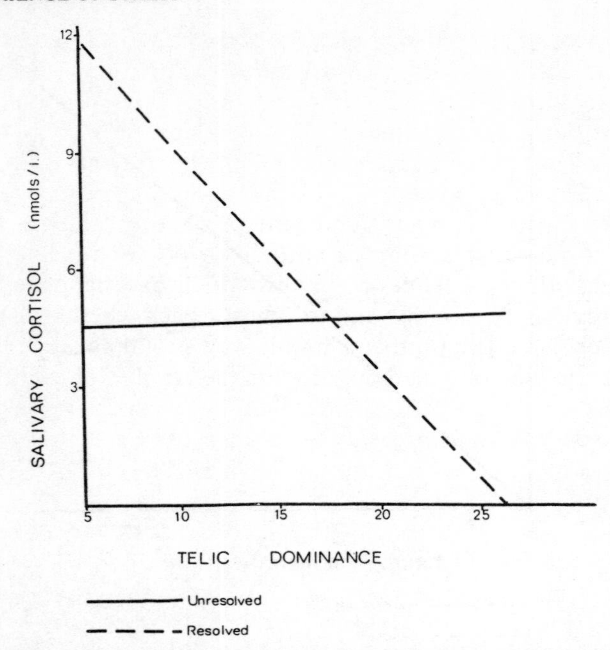

Fig. 23 Regression curves showing the relationships between telic dominance and salivary cortisol, for subjects with resolved and unresolved recent life stressors. (After Martin, Kuiper, Olinger, and Dobbin 1987.)

something of the same pattern emerges here as in the previous study: the two lines representing resolved and unresolved stress cross over each other and diverge increasingly towards the extremes of high telic and high paratelic dominance, showing again the contrasting ways in which telic- and paratelic-dominant people respond to stress.

There are limitations, however, on both of these studies. One of these is that in reducing the stress variable to a dichotomy it was not possible to see how different *degrees* of stress might be reacted to by telic- and paratelic-dominant subjects. In any case, by dichotomizing in this way subjects might have been grouped together who were rather different. Thus, some subjects in the resolved category may nevertheless have had various stressors to contend with other than their principal stressor, and the principal stressors chosen by subjects in the unresolved group may have varied considerably in seriousness. Clearly a measure of degree of stress, ranging from zero to very high levels, would be preferable. Second, the measure of the psychological effect of stress in both these studies was only sensitive to degrees of negative reaction, so although there were opposite reactions by telic- and paratelic-dominant subjects, there was no opportunity for these subjects to report positive hedonic tone. Therefore, it was not possible to test fully the original hypothesis that paratelic subjects might respond to stress with pleasure rather than displeasure. Both of these problems were overcome in the next study to be described.

The subjects here were 74 students of both sexes. Severity of stress was measured by means of the Life Events of College Students Scale (Sandler and Lakey 1982). This consists of a list of potentially stressful events of the kind which might well happen to students – such as failing a course or breaking up a relationship with a girlfriend or boyfriend. Subjects were asked to check off the events on this list which had happened to them during the previous 12 months, and to rate for each whether it had had a negative or positive effect on them. In this way a total negative life events (stress) score could be obtained by counting the number of events checked off which were also rated as negative. Finally, the psychological effects of these life events were measured by means of a scale which assesses negative *or* positive mood, the Profile of Mood States (POMS; McNair, Lorr, and Droppleman 1971).

In summary, then, it was possible to see whether subjects who scored high or low on telic dominance were affected in different ways, negative or positive (as measured by a mood scale representing hedonic tone), in relation to different levels of stress (as measured by number of negative life events). For the reasons we have seen, reversal theory would predict not only a difference between telic- and paratelic-dominant subjects in their response to stress, but an *inversion* of response. That is, the mood state of telic-dominant subjects would be expected to deteriorate in a linear way as stress mounted. In contrast, the mood of paratelic-dominant subjects would be expected to *improve* with increasing stress, at least up to a certain point, beyond which it would be reasonable to assume that a reversal into the telic state would take place under the combined onslaught of the various stressors.

In fact, the results were in exact conformity with these predictions. Telic- and paratelic-dominant subjects did not differ significantly in their reported overall levels of negative life events; that is, they experienced the same amount of stress on average. Nor were there overall differences between them in terms of the mood measure. But the *way* in which their moods differed as a function of the number of stressful events was very different, as was disclosed by a statistical analysis using multiple regression techniques. The nature of the difference can be shown most clearly by means of a graph (Figure 24) comparing the responses to different levels of stress of those selected subjects who scored more than a standard deviation above the mean TDS score with those who scored more than a standard deviation below; that is, by comparing a group of clearly telic-dominated with a group of clearly paratelic-dominant subjects. The lines in the graph are regression (best-fit) lines, as in the earlier graphs, but in this case it is the telic dominance variable which has been dichotomized (into telic-

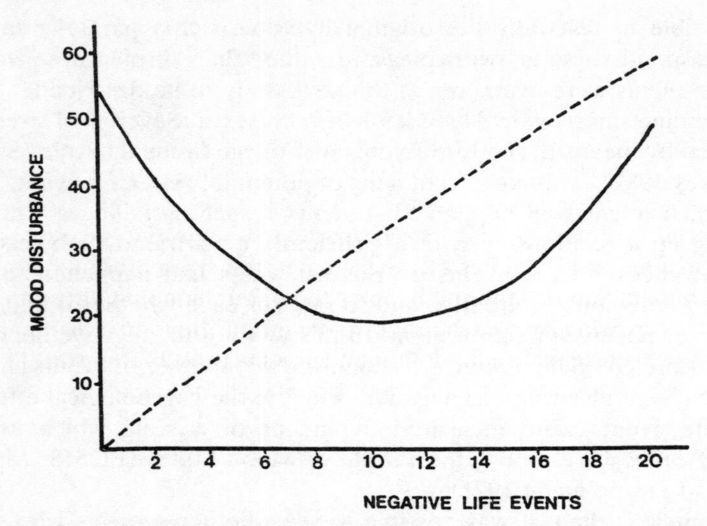

Fig. 24 Regression curves showing the relationship between level of stress as measured by number of 'negative life events' and mood disturbance, for telic-dominant and paratelic-dominant subjects. (After Martin, Kuiper, Olinger, and Dobbin 1987.)

versus paratelic-dominant groups) and which the two lines represent – rather than, as in the earlier graphs, stress (resolved versus unresolved).

It can be seen from this graph that the relationship of stress to mood is indeed, for telic-dominant subjects, a linear one in the direction expected: the worse the stress, the worse the mood. For paratelic-dominant subjects, however, the reverse is the case, at least initially as stress increases from zero. The line which represents the relationship in their case moves in the opposite direction to that of the telic-dominant subjects and actually crosses over the latter. Here, the worse the stress the better the mood. It is only as stress increases beyond a certain point that this trend for the paratelic-dominant subjects changes, the line curving round and moving more into alignment with that of telic-dominant subjects. This, of course, is in accordance with the prediction that sooner or later the mounting stress will 'get to them' and trigger a reversal to the telic state in an increasing proportion of the paratelic-dominant group.

Now, it could be argued that the measure of stress used here was still not ideal since it extended backwards in time over a full year, whereas the mood scale indicated current and recent mood (subjects were asked to assess their mood over the previous month). However, the researchers also included another stress scale in this study: the Daily Hassles Scale (Kanner, Coyne, Schaefer, and Lazarus 1981). This scale comprises, as the title suggests, a list of relatively minor everyday problems and irritations – losing things, having rows with people, and the like. Subjects are instructed to check off the 'hassles' on the list which have happened to them, and to rate the severity of each on a scale from 1 to 3. A total 'hassles' score is then obtained for each subject by simply adding these values. In this case, unlike the life events schedule, the choices and ratings are made in terms of the previous month, thus exactly coinciding with the time range of the mood scale.

The results still stubbornly display the same basic pattern. This is shown graphically in Figure 25, which compares the same two groups as those shown in Figure 24. As before, the greater the stress, the unhappier the telic-dominant subject and the happier the paratelic-dominant subject, the two curves crossing over each other on the graph. Beyond a certain level of stress, however, as paratelic-dominant subjects presumably start to switch into the telic state, so the curve moves back in the unpleasant direction, eventually catching up with the telic curve (and in this case even passing it).

Summarizing the results of these studies, then, it has been demonstrated that telic- and paratelic-dominant people are affected by stress in very different ways, and that over moderate levels of stress their reactions are not only different but opposite. It is worth emphasizing that this prediction that some people will react to stress not only with less displeasure than other people, but with actual pleasure, is one which derives from a key argument of reversal theory. These results therefore provide strong supportive evidence for the theory.

Martin et al. (in press) also report on a laboratory experiment they carried out in which stress itself was manipulated as an experimental

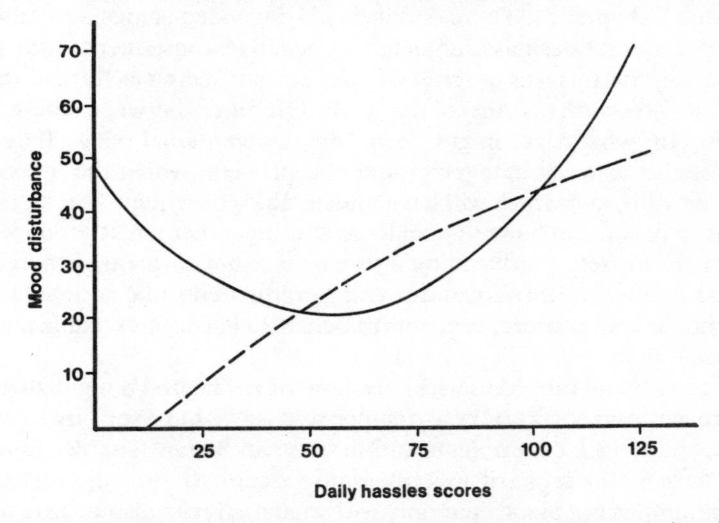

Fig. 25 Regression curves showing the relationships between level of stress as measured by the number and severity of 'daily hassles' and mood disturbances, for telic-dominant and paratelic-dominant subjects. (After Martin, Kuiper, Olinger, and Dobbin 1987.)

condition. They did this by having subjects (27 students of both sexes) perform the experimental task (a video game lasting ten minutes) either 'as fun' or after being told that their performance was going to be evaluated in comparison with that of other subjects. Clearly, the amount of stress involved in such social comparison was rather mild, and yet differences did emerge even here between telic- and paratelic-dominant subjects. On a set of rating scales, telic-dominant subjects reported feeling more unpleasant, more dissatisfied with their performance, and perceived the experimenter as more hostile in the stress than in the non-stress condition, all these differences being statistically significant. In contrast, the paratelic-dominant subjects did not differ between conditions on any of these variables. Furthermore, and this was the central interest of the researchers in setting up this particular experiment, telic-dominant subjects performed significantly better on the task in the non-stressful than the stressful condition, whereas paratelic-dominant subjects did the opposite, obtaining significantly higher performance scores under conditions of stress. Once more we see the contrasting effects of stressful circumstances on telic- and paratelic-dominant people.

RECONCEPTUALIZING STRESS

The final experiment of Martin et al. which I have just described will have reminded you of Svebak's laboratory research which was discussed earlier in this book (Chapter 5). There, subjects playing video games were also, in some experimental designs, subjected to negative consequences for poor performance, but this was described in Svebak's research as 'threat' rather than as a 'stressor'. Is there really a difference between these two concepts? In what one might term the conventional view they are essentially the same. Whatever produces a problem which the individual has to cope with, and which will have undesirable consequences if he or she is unable to do so, can be seen equally as causing either stress produced by a stressor, or anxiety produced by a threat. It is not surprising, therefore, that these two terms, *anxiety* and *stress*, have tended to be coupled in the titles of books and conferences, and to be used almost interchangeably by many researchers.

There are several problems with this, however. The first is highlighted by the inference from reversal theory, supported as we have seen by Martin's research, that a *lack* of problems and threats can be undesirable. In other words, stress, in the sense of an unpleasant reaction to some unsatisfactory state of affairs, is not associated only with anxiety; it can also be associated with its opposite, boredom. This means that there must be at least two different – and incompatible – types of stress. The second is that there is an obvious sense in which certain problems and pressures can produce stress without necessarily creating anxiety. The person working hard all day on a production line – and perhaps doing overtime as well – may feel stressed but not anxious. The student working hard for his or her examination may feel quietly confident about the outcome, but stressed by the long hours of concentration and self-discipline.

If we put these two problems together, we see that it is evident that a new and broader concept of stress is needed that will cover both (1) arousal-seeking *and* arousal-avoidance stress, and (2) the stress that comes with such unpleasant feelings as anxiety or boredom *and* the stress that comes with work and effort.

The first of these, the distinction between arousal-seeking and arousal-avoidance, is already explicit in reversal theory. The second may be assimilated to the reversal theory framework by making a distinction between two different sorts of stress. These may be termed 'tension-stress' and 'effort-stress' (Apter and Svebak, in press; Svebak, in press). The term 'tension' was introduced in its reversal theory sense in Chapter 2, where it was defined as the uncomfortable experience of a discrepancy between the preferred and actual level of some variable like felt arousal. In this sense, both anxiety and boredom are forms of tension-stress, since they both represent deviations from the level of arousal desired at the time. Effort-stress can now be defined as the experience of expending effort in order to avoid or reduce tension-stress. Thus, if one exerts effort to overcome anxiety or boredom, one will in doing so experience some degree of effort-stress. An analogy to these two different forms of stress would be the infection of the body by some disease, which would be equivalent to tension-stress, followed by the body's defence against the infection, which would be equivalent to effort-stress. In fact, this is a particularly apt analogy since both aspects of infection, the infection itself and the body's defence against it, involve upsetting the body in some way.

Experientially, tension-stress is a feeling of unease or discomfort, an impression that things are not as they should be and that something needs to be done. Effort-stress is then the feeling of doing something about such unease. It can be experienced as working at a problem, or coping with a crisis, or of striving to improve an unsatisfactory situation.

Putting things this way implies that effort-stress is a possible consequence of tension-stress, but it may also be the consequence of the perceived *possibility* of tension-stress. In other words, the person may take avoiding action before tension-stress actually arises. So the worker on the production line may not feel anxiety at all, but if he failed to expend the effort needed to keep on top of his job he might start to feel anxiety, and it is in part to avoid this feeling that he is working so hard.

It is clear that tension and effort are antagonistic and that, generally speaking, the greater the tension, the more the effort that will be needed to overcome it. This is represented schematically in Figure 26. Here we see an

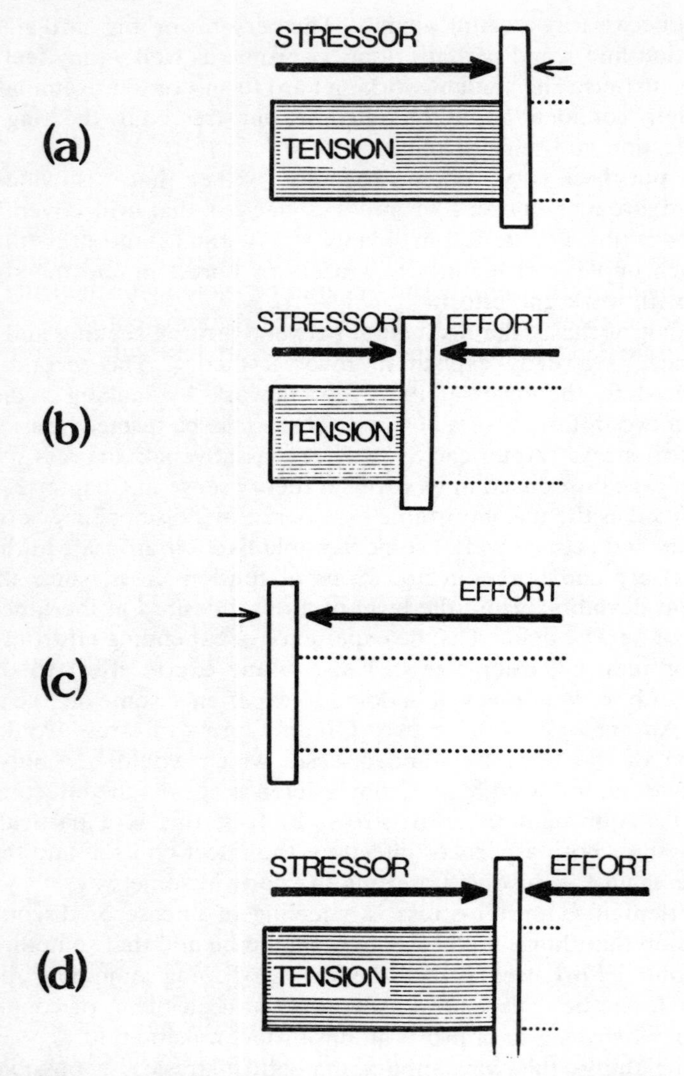

Fig. 26 A schematic representation of the relationship between tension-stress and effort-stress. The intensity of experienced tension is represented by the area of the rectangle to the left of the bar. The size of this area is a reflection of the relative strength of the stressor and the effort expended to oppose it, these two forces acting in opposite directions on the bar which we may imagine as sliding to left or right under their combined impact. At (a) the stressor is strong enough to produce high tension; at (b) there is a balance between them; at (c) the effort is strong enough to reduce tension to zero; and at (d) there is both high tension-stress and high effort-stress (due to the effort being expended inefficiently or inappropriately).

upright bar being pushed in a rightward direction by the force of a stressor and in a leftward direction by the force of effort. Where the stressor is stronger than the effort (as shown at *a* in the figure), then tension will be experienced. Where the effort is stronger, then tension will be overcome (as shown at *c* in the figure). And where there is balance between the two, there will be a moderate amount of tension-stress to go with the moderate amount of effort-stress (as shown at *b* in the figure). We may suppose that where sufficient effort is expended, and is expended early enough, tension need not be experienced at all. It must also be added, on the other hand, that expending effort in itself does not guarantee avoiding or reducing tension, and in some cases, where the individual is incompetent or uses inappropriate strategies, he may expend great effort and still not remove the causes of tension, thus suffering both types of stress at the same time and having the worst of both worlds (shown at *d* in the figure).

We are always faced with choices, then, each time it comes to the periods of tension-stress which we all face regularly in the course of our everyday lives. On each occasion we can either accept the unpleasant feeling that goes with the tension, or try to remove the causes – as we see them – of that tension. In other words, we always have a choice: we can either 'get up and go' or 'sit and suffer', but even if we do something about a situation which generates tension we do not, on this analysis, avoid stress: we simply substitute one form of stress for another, effort-stress for tension-stress. In a less than ideal world, stress will therefore always be part of our lives, but it seems that we have some freedom in choosing the form in which we take it. Imagine that you have an overdraft building up at the bank. This naturally makes you feel anxious every time you think about it or are made aware of it. But you have a choice. Either you can go out of your way to do something about the situation, perhaps by taking on extra work, or you can just put up with the worry and do nothing about it. In the industrial West, the first option is generally regarded as more praiseworthy, but in some cultures where a more 'fatalistic' attitude is taken to life's inevitable problems, the second option is acceptable. Either way, stress will be experienced, but it will be of a different kind. And within a culture such as ours, some people seem generally more inclined to strive and be effortful and others to take life more easily, meaning that some people will tend to experience effort-stress more often than tension-stress and others will tend to experience tension-stress more than effort-stress.

Since two different, and opposite, types of tension-stress have been identified – anxiety and boredom – then effort will also need to be expended in two different directions at different times, depending on which of these types of tension-stress is prevailing. In one case, the aim of the effortful striving will be to increase felt arousal levels, thus overcoming the tension of boredom; in the other the aim will be to lower arousal in order to avoid the tension of anxiety. What all this comes to is that there would appear to be four basic and contrasting types of stress. That is, both tension-stress and effort-stress can be experienced in the arousal-seeking metamotivational mode, and the same is true of the arousal-avoidance mode.

Putting this in the wider context of the telic and paratelic modes, we can say that there would appear to be both telic and paratelic tension-stress and both telic and paratelic effort-stress. These can be contrasted as follows:

1. Telic tension-stress will be experienced as arising from threats, serious problems, and unavoidable duties, with the anxiety which tends to go with them.
2. Telic effort-stress will be experienced as the effortful attempt to cope with such stressors.
3. Paratelic tension-stress will be experienced as arising from a lack of threats or problems, with the boredom which is associated with this.
4. Paratelic effort-stress will be experienced as the active setting up and confrontation of some challenges.

Table 5 Four contrasting ways of experiencing stress.

	TENSION-STRESS	EFFORT-STRESS
TELIC	Threat/Anxiety	Effortful coping
PARATELIC	Lack of threat/Boredom	Responses to challenge

This is summarized, with some slight simplification, in Table 5, which depicts the four contrasting types of stress which have been suggested here. One implication of this is that telic-dominant people would be expected to experience stressors as 'threats' more frequently than paratelic-dominant people and the latter would be expected to be more likely to experience stressors as 'challenges' than telic-dominant people would. In fact, data exactly consistent with this prediction have been presented by Baker (1988), who found significant differences between telic- and paratelic-dominant subjects of both these kinds when they were asked to assess 'bothersome events' over a seven-day period.

I have used the word 'suggested' in the last paragraph and 'appeared' several times in the last few paragraphs where these four different types of stress have been described. The reason is this: if one of the essential features of stress is that it is unpleasant, then there are really only three types of stress. As reversal theory itself points out, and as the data of Martin described earlier in this chapter also indicate, paratelic effort-stress tends to produce a pleasant mood state. In other words, the paratelic response to a supposed stressor is, up to a certain level of stress, a positive one. Furthermore, the effortful paratelic response to a freely chosen challenge of some kind can obviously not be realistically thought of as dysphoric. On the contrary, it may even be joyful. The challenge and effort of contest in sport, of solving intellectual puzzles, of creating works of art, and of willingly taking on the problems posed by hobbies and leisure activities of all kinds, can provide keen pleasure – it is, after all, in the hope of this that they are generally undertaken in the first place. This is quite different from effort expended in the telic mode. Certainly there are pleasures in the telic mode, especially the pleasure of experiencing progress towards some important goal, but the effort which accompanies this is in itself regarded as something to be tolerated for the sake of these goals. And effortful telic coping, especially where it is in response to urgent or exigent needs, probably comes closest to what most people think of as stress in everyday life. In contrast, effortful paratelic activities are freely undertaken for their own sake and, typically, means are used to increase the amount of strenuous effort, physical or intellectual, which is needed in their pursuit. If we use the word *stress* to refer to paratelic effort, therefore, we should perhaps at least put it in inverted commas, as was done earlier for parapathic emotions like 'anxiety', and refer to it as 'stress'. This should not be taken to imply that the only pleasure of the paratelic mode comes from strenuous activity. Obviously there are excitements of a relatively passive nature, such as listening to music, being a spectator at sporting events, and the like. But where effort comes into the picture, it is high effort that seems to be enjoyed in the paratelic mode, along with high felt arousal.

For completeness, in this analysis of stress, we should also remember that tension arises not only in relation to the telic and paratelic modes, but also in the negativistic–conformist modes and the different combinations of mastery–sympathy and autocentric–allocentric modes. In each of these cases, the tension–stress has its own affective quality – for example, it is experienced as humiliation or guilt – and in each case effort is needed to overcome the tension. However, there is no reason to suppose that there are individual and special types of effort associated with each of these types of tension. For the moment, the most parsimonious way of looking at the situation is rather to assume that the only critical distinction in terms of types of *effort* is that between telic and paratelic effort. In this way, whether the effort is felt as desperate coping or joyous striving will depend on whether the telic or the paratelic mode is being experienced at the time, rather than upon whichever of the other modes are also being experienced.

THE CONSEQUENCES OF STRESS

One of the major reasons that stress has been studied by health psychologists, psychophysiologists, medical researchers, and others is that it is presumed to play a major part in the development of psychosomatic disease; that is, problems of bodily functioning. The reconceptualization of stress suggested in the previous section of this chapter allows us to ask whether it is *any* of the types of stress depicted there which are likely to lead to this kind of problem or whether it is one type alone.

Certainly, the telic mode would appear to be implicated on the basis of Svebak's data which were described in Chapter 5. Take muscle tension, for example. Svebak's data, in which increasing muscle tension is indicated by means of the steepness of EMG gradients, showed clearly, as we have seen, that it is in the telic rather than the paratelic mode that muscle tension builds up, and that this build-up occurs in muscles which are not directly involved in the task ('passive muscles') as well, presumably, as those which are. One may suppose, then, that someone working in the telic mode over a prolonged period might start to suffer muscle tension problems in different parts of the body: for example, he or she may come to experience such psychosomatic symptoms as backache or a headache. Turning to respiration, it was found that telic-dominant subjects under stress breathed more rapidly and more deeply than paratelic-dominant subjects, implying that such psychosomatic symptoms as dizziness and nausea are more likely to be experienced by telic-dominant subjects in everyday life. Again, Svebak's data shows that heart-rate increases in response to threats while the subject is performing a task are much greater for telic-dominant than for paratelic-dominant subjects, and that when Type A (coronary-prone) characteristics are added to telic dominance the heart rate reactivity becomes particularly pronounced (Svebak, Nordby, and Ohman 1987). Consistent with this is some further evidence from Gallacher and Beswick (1988) that, among other things, Type A subjects in the telic mode show significantly greater increases in diastolic blood pressure in response to mild stress (mental arithmetic) than the other combinations of telic/paratelic mode and Type A/B. It was argued in Chapter 5 that this combination of telic and Type A may represent a cardiovascular 'responder' type of person who might be particularly vulnerable to heart attacks. In fact, Svebak (1988a) has argued that the Type A person is someone who, from the combination reversal theory perspective, can be seen as negativistic, mastery- and autocentric-dominant (which he associates with Type A behaviour), and that it is this set of personality characteristics which, when combined with telic dominance, produce the individual who is most at risk of heart attack.

Whether particular psychosomatic symptoms are a sign of tension-stress or effort-stress in the telic mode, however, is more problematic. In

Svebak's experiments, any increased arousal may be accompanied by increased effort and it is often difficult to know to which to attribute physiological changes which occur in relation to different experimental manipulations. Similarly, in Martin's research it is unclear whether the mood disturbance reported by telic-dominant subjects in relation to stressors was related to the tension of anxiety or the effort of coping. However, in several of Svebak's studies the somatic effects of threat were not only related to telic dominance, but also *unrelated* to arousal, since levels of arousal in response to threat were the same in both telic- and paratelic-dominant subjects in these experiments. Thus, in the results reported by Svebak (1984), although EMG gradients were steeper in telic-dominant subjects, reported arousal levels were not significantly different from those of paratelic-dominant subjects. Likewise, in the research reported in Svebak (1986a) although heart-rate increases under threat were greater for telic-dominant subjects, again there was no significant difference between their scores on self-reported arousal and those of paratelic-dominant subjects. This implies that some other factor is at work. This could simply be the fact of being in the telic rather than the paratelic mode, but it is also possible that this factor is high effort.

Indirect evidence that telic-dominant people often do react to threats and stressors in a more effortful way than paratelic-dominant people comes from a set of three independent studies of the way in which telic- and paratelic-dominant individuals attempt to cope with the stresses of everyday life. (1) Murgatroyd (1985b) administered the Ways of Coping Inventory (Folkman and Lazarus 1980) to 100 students about to take a degree examination. (2) Howard (1988) administered a revised version of the same inventory to a group of telic-dominant ($N = 32$) and paratelic-dominant ($N = 35$) students who were asked to respond in terms of their most stressful encounter during the previous week. (3) Baker (1988) in a study mentioned above selected a group of extreme telic-dominant and a group of extreme paratelic-dominant subjects (15 in each) from a sample pool of 107 subjects with ages ranging from 17 to 70; she then asked them to appraise 'the most bothersome event of the day' every day for seven days, using a questionnaire adapted from Stone and Neale (1984). In each of these studies, despite the use of different designs and measures, the same main result came through. This was that telic-dominant subjects are significantly more likely than paratelic to use problem-focussed coping strategies involving direct action against the source of the stress. In contrast, paratelic-dominant subjects tended to use a variety of other strategies (which differed as between studies) such as wishful thinking or distraction. What this seems to mean, therefore, is that telic-dominant subjects are more likely to exert effort against the source of stress rather than taking any kind of easy way out. This does not, of course, mean that all telic-dominant subjects and paratelic-dominant subjects acted in these ways, and many acted in the opposite sense. But nevertheless, these studies do seem to point to a definite trend.

In the light of all this, it is possible to suggest in at least a preliminary way that it is telic effortful coping which might underlie the physiological effects demonstrated by Svebak. It is therefore the effortful telic-dominant individual who, especially if confronted by frequent and intense stressors, is sooner or later likely to pay the price of this coping style with psychosomatic illness of one kind or another, be it short-term and irritating, like a headache, or long-term and serious, like a heart attack.

There is another question which arises concerning the consequences of stress, and this is the part which stress may play in the generation of neurosis. Now, at the beginning of this chapter it was argued that stress is different from neurosis or personality disorder in that it occurs in normal people. But this does not mean that stress cannot *also* be experienced by neurotics, and that it may not, in at least some cases, play some part in precipitating or exacerbating a neurotic disorder, by unhelpfully feeding into some type of psychological malfunction. For example, the phobic individual may irrationally interpret certain types of events, like driving a car, as threatening. But if some genuinely stressful problem occurs while he has forced himself to drive – for example, a breakdown, or a minor accident – this may serve to validate his fears and support his irrational interpretations of the situation. Or someone who uses the inappropriate strategy of taking drugs of the stimulant type in response to the paratelic stress of a boring environment makes it more difficult to adjust in the long term, because increasing amounts of the drug are likely to be needed to bring about the same stimulating effects. Or if an individual fails continually over a period, perhaps through using inappropriate strategies, to overcome one or another form of tension-stress (e.g. anxiety, guilt, boredom), depression may be added to the continuing tension-stress. Again, it should be emphasized that the claim is not being made that neurosis is caused by stress – far from it. The point is rather that stressors may sometimes interact with psychological malfunctions of the type discussed in the last chapter in such a way as to precipitate symptoms or to make matters worse than they would have been.

Now this raises an interesting question: Why is it that stress in some people leads to psychosomatic complaints – even serious health conditions – while in others it may play a part in the development of neurotic symptoms? This is an important question, but one which is rarely asked because, generally speaking, those working on stress either work within the medical/physiological tradition – in which case it is simply assumed that stress leads to psychosomatic problems – or they work within the psychotherapy/counselling tradition – in which case it is effectively assumed that it is psychological problems which are brought on by stress.

The most obvious answer to this question would be that some people are inherently vulnerable somatically and others psychologically. But of what would such a vulnerability consist? A neat solution, in terms of the framework which has been set up in this chapter and the last, would be that people who develop psychological disturbances in response to stress are those who, by and large, have difficulty in avoiding or handling tension-stress and therefore experience unnecessary distress. It could then be suggested that those who develop somatic symptoms are those who attempt to cope with stressors in a highly effortful way which may well be effective in removing the tension-stress, but which has deleterious biological consequences. In brief: neurosis would tend to revolve around tension-stress and psychosomatic pathology around effort-stress. (This would not, of course, preclude some people being vulnerable to both types of stress.)

It is possible to adduce various findings from the enormous research literature on stress, both medical and psychological, which could be considered consistent with this and other arguments which have been put here (and some of these are touched on in Apter and Svebak, in press; Svebak, in press). But the area of stress research is an unusually complicated and difficult one, and it is possible to find support for many different positions. Nevertheless, reversal theory does offer some novel conceptual distinctions which might provide a fruitful direction for future investigation. And it also not only draws attention to the phenomenon of 'stressors' which are enjoyed as stimulating challenges, but, more importantly, shows how this phenomenon can be fully incorporated within a systematic explanatory framework.

11

Motivation, Emotion and Personality

Life is an unequal, irregular and multiform movement.

Essays
Michel de Montaigne (1533–92)

There are a number of topics which have emerged in the growing body of reversal theory which it has not been possible to discuss at any length in this book. These include the reversal theory perspective on sport and games (Kerr 1985a, b, 1986, 1987a, c, d, 1988b, in press), religious experience (Fontana 1981b; Apter 1982a: Chapter 2, 1985; Hyers 1985), education (Fontana 1985; Boekaerts 1986) and creativity (Fontana 1985), as well as the relationship of the theory to the psychology of self and identity (Fontana 1988), to learning theory (Cowles and Davis 1985; Van der Molen 1985, 1986b; Brown 1987, 1988, in press; Boekaerts 1988), and to evolutionary biology (Apter 1982: Chapter 13; Van der Molen 1984, 1986a). Rather than pursue these varied themes here, the aim of this final chapter will be to take stock by looking briefly at each of the three principal areas to which the theory is addressed – motivation, emotion, and personality – and highlighting the distinctive characteristics of the theory in each area.

MOTIVATION

The significance of the reversal theory approach to motivation can be appreciated most clearly if it is placed in the context of a historical movement towards greater complexity in motivational theories (Apter 1984b).

During the first half of this century a basic assumption in such theories was that the organism is always engaged in attempts to reduce one or another motivational variable to as low a level as possible. Thus, underlying all the complexities of Freudian theory, and remaining constant through all the changes which occurred in it over the years, is the idea that excitation is basically unpleasant, is experienced as anxiety if it becomes too great, and is avoided wherever possible. In drive-reduction theory – Clark Hull's mammoth edifice which dominated learning theory for so long

– the aim of the organism is seen as keeping drives at a low level and therefore taking such actions as are needed to reduce each drive whenever it exceeds this level (e.g. Hull 1943). In ethological theories, such as that of Lorenz (1950), the organism is regarded as engaged in a perpetual struggle to find ways of releasing 'action-specific energy' whenever it builds up. All three of these classical theories are not only important in their own right but represent the whole tenor of motivation theory until the 1950s. Their spirit can be captured by the graph at (a) in Figure 27; if we wanted to express this in terms of motivational experience we could say that such theories account very well for the unpleasant feeling of anxiety and the pleasant feeling of relaxation.

Unfortunately, these formulations began to lose conviction as researchers became increasingly aware of the fact that the organism sometimes performed in ways which appeared to heighten rather than lessen excitation or drive, and that monotonous environments (such as those used in sensory deprivation experiments) produced boredom rather than relaxation. The initial response was to attempt to assimilate these unhappy findings to extant theory by postulating such drives as a curiosity drive or an exploratory drive – which would be reduced by increased stimulation.

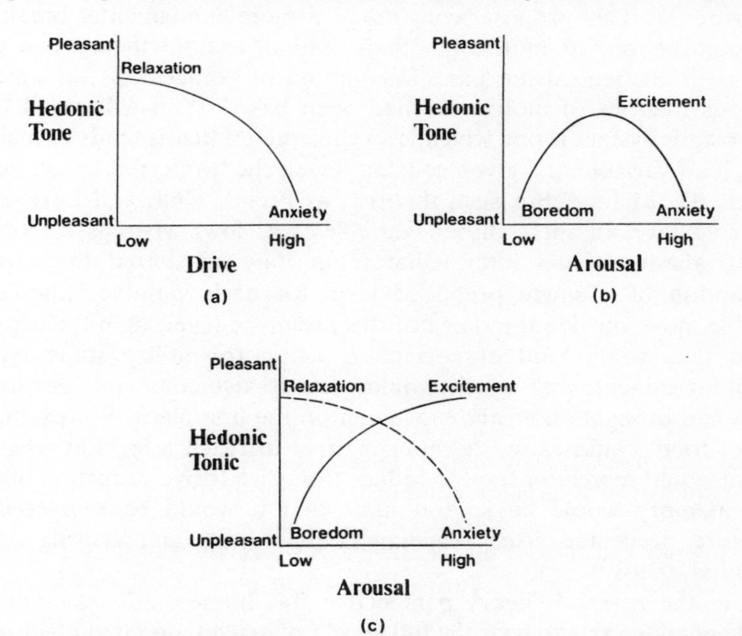

Fig. 27 The hypothetical curves in these three graphs typify alternative accounts of the relationship between the value of motivational variables and hedonic tone. The graph at (a) represents theories of the drive-reduction type; (b) represents optimal arousal theory; and (c) depicts reversal theory. (After Apter 1984b.)

But soon a newer and better idea took over: the idea of optimal arousal (e.g. Hebb 1955). As we saw in Chapter 2, this theory postulated a preferred intermediate, rather than low, level of arousal, the variable which it took as its key motivational construct. This meant that both very low and very high levels of arousal would be aversive, while intermediate levels would be pleasant. In this way, the organism would sometimes behave in such a way as to increase arousal (up to the optimal intermediate level from a lower level) and at other times to decrease arousal (down to this same optimal level from a higher level). This certainly seemed to capture more of the experimental facts, to do so elegantly, and to tie in better with everyday experience. Furthermore, as shown at (b) in Figure 27, it was able to extend the range of emotions which could be accounted for, although the exact position of relaxation and excitement was problematic and only excitement is shown on the curve in this figure.

For the numerous reasons we examined in Chapter 2, this approach also turned out to be unsatisfactory. It was argued in that chapter that the problems inherent in the optimal arousal approach could only be overcome satisfactorily by postulating two arousal systems instead of one, and the resulting formulation is shown graphically for comparative purposes at (c) in Figure 27. This proposal constituted a more fundamental break with previous theories of motivation than optimal arousal theory had done, because it challenged the basic assumption of homeostasis on which all previous theories of motivation had been based. You will recall that a homeostatic system is one which is so constructed that it tends to maintain a specified variable at a given constant level, the 'preferred level', despite outside disturbance. For such theorists as Freud, Hull, and Lorenz, this preferred level of their chosen variables was low, whereas for optimal arousal theory it was intermediate; but they all shared the common assumption of a single preferred level for each variable. Should the variable move outside the range of this preferred level, then the organism would take some kind of corrective action (or utilize some type of psychological defence) which would tend to overcome the disturbance which had brought about the movement in the first place. For example, a lack of food would cause the hunger drive to reach a level at which the animal would search for food to reduce this drive (drive-reduction theory); or a memory would be so traumatic that it would be repressed and therefore prevented from reaching consciousness and causing anxiety (Freudian theory).

From the reversal theory perspective this homeostatic assumption is simply not adequate to bear the full weight of explanation that is called for, or to do justice to the complexity, changeability, richness, and sheer perversity of human experience and behaviour. Instead, therefore, reversal theory suggests that, at least for certain key motivational variables, there is more than one preferred level towards which, under different circumstances and at different times, the organism will tend to return. Specifically, as we have seen, it suggests that there are two preferred levels at, or towards the ends of, each of the dimensions concerned so that, as one replaces the other, there is on each occasion a dramatic switch in the direction of the organism's intentions. In this way, reversal theory substitutes the principle of bistability for that of homeostasis, and opens the way to more sophisticated multistable models in the area of motivation research. In this respect it is ironic to note how statistical sophistication has increased enormously in psychological research from univariate to multivariate methods. But at the same time, and certainly in the area of motivation, the sophistication of theory-building has progressed hardly at all and remained based firmly on the notion of unistability rather than opening itself to the possibility of multistability.

Not only is reversal theory a multistable theory of motivation, it is also a multilevel theory since it insists on the distinction between motivation and metamotivation. In contrast, all other theories deal with the level of motivation alone and, generally speaking, change is seen in these theories to occur only on this level: hunger drive increases and decreases; anxiety is felt and then repressed, and so on. Admittedly, there are some elaborations of optimal arousal theory, for example that of Fiske and Maddi (1961), which do allow that the optimal point may itself shift to some extent as a function of the sleeping–waking cycle, and in this sense a second level of change is introduced. But certainly there are no other theories which suggest that the higher level of change is one which involves totally different systems which can only be adequately represented in the arousal/hedonic-tone space by separate curves. Another way of putting this harks back to the distinction between control and regulation made earlier in this book (Chapter 2). This is that most theories of motivation are really theories of regulation alone (since they assume that control remains constant for all practical purposes), whereas reversal theory is a theory of both control and regulation. In other words, in most theories what the organism wants remains the same (the control setting), but how successful it is at getting it (regulation) varies under a variety of circumstances. In reversal theory, in contrast, what the organism wants in some fundamental respect also changes and changes radically as reversals occur between metamotivational modes.

In all theories of motivation, regulation may be more or less successful, depending on the resources and disturbances of the environment. Thus a given animal in a given environment may be able to satisfy its hunger drive more or less readily, and be facilitated or hindered in its search for food by a variety of environmental factors which are outside its powers of determination. In reversal theory, matters are seen as more difficult for the organism because not only are regulatory (motivational) processes insufficient to command complete success at all times, but change at the level of control (metamotivation) is also subject to circumstantial environmental events which the organism cannot always foresee or determine. That is, the reversal process which decides the setting of the controller (i.e. which metamotivational mode in each pair is operative) is also, at least in part, affected by environmental processes. And, to make matters even worse, in the reversal theory account this control setting is additionally influenced by internal processes over which the organism also has no direct voluntary control (i.e. satiation).

If we put all this in everyday human terms we can see why it is, in the reversal theory account, that we have so much difficulty in achieving or maintaining a state of pleasure or happiness for very long. It is not just that our environment does not always provide us with what we need at a given time (such as stimulation, sympathy, or important goals), or that we do not always have the ability to make the most of such environmental 'resources' as are available; it is that as soon as we get what we want, or even before we get it, we often find that we want something entirely different and incompatible. For example, on getting to the disco we find that what we really want is peace and quiet; on getting to a quiet spot in the countryside for a picnic we find that we want some excitement. In concluding an advantageous financial deal we feel none of the expected pleasure, but guilt at having profited from someone else; on attempting to feel virtuous by being selfless we finish up instead feeling humiliated at not having stood up for ourselves. This, or something like it, occurs so often in even the best-regulated lives that we must conclude that it is part of the human condition. Our conscious self may be compared to a sailor in a small dinghy on a stormy sea. Staying happy, or in a state of pleasurable enjoyment, is like holding course in the face of unpredictable cross-currents and fluctuating winds, in which each action may only compound whatever error has been made by the time it comes into effect, and in which the effect of any deliberate action may in any case be suddenly swamped by larger natural forces.

EMOTION

If the significance of the reversal theory approach to motivation can best be appreciated in a historical context, the same is true of the reversal theory orientation towards the emotions. We shall here be focussing on the relationship of the emotions to each other rather than on emotional function, since the latter is really part of the field of motivation which we have already been looking at.

Some of the earlier theories of the emotions were content simply to produce lists of the different types of affect. Watson (1924), for example, suggested that there were three primary emotional reactions, these being fear, rage, and love. McDougall (1923), in one version of his famous instinct theory, proposed that there were fourteen different emotions, each associated with its own underlying instinct. While there have also been later lists of emotions, such as the list of eight basic emotions provided by Tomkins and McCarter (1964), and Izard's (1977) list of ten emotions, the tendency has been to introduce a greater degree of structure into accounts of emotional life.

One way of doing this has been by organizing the emotions into pairs of opposites. Plutchik (1962), in particular, proposed that there were eight pairs, and he organized these into a circle in such a way that each emotion faced its opposite. Another organizing principle was that of placing emotions in unique positions in two-dimensional space. Schlosberg (1952), for example, showed how a wide variety of emotions could be placed in different positions in relation to the two orthogonal dimensions of pleasant/unpleasant and accept/reject. De Rivera (1977), in an interesting theory which is otherwise more complicated than Schlosberg's, has suggested that emotions could be placed in a two-dimensional space defined by person-as-subject/person-as-object and subject-moves/object-moves.

What reversal theory does is to take this search for structure a great deal further by introducing a new and powerful structural principle – that of reversal itself. By means of this principle a whole range of emotions can be generated from a small set of binary oppositions. In other words, reversal theory goes much further than simply placing individual emotions in pairs of opposites. To be sure, there are such pairs in reversal theory, like relaxation and anxiety, or modesty and shame, these contrasting with each other by virtue of the fact that they are situated at the opposing ends of a given dimension. But reversal theory discloses a deeper opposition underlying these contrasts. This is the opposition of the *emotional dimensions themselves*. That is, each pair of emotions is itself opposed by another pair, for example relaxation–anxiety by boredom–excitement.

If we look at the nature of such dimensional oppositions more closely we see that what it consists of is this: around a fixed dimension, like that of felt arousal, there are two opposite dimensions in terms of hedonic tone. As the result of a reversal, the hedonic tone dimension is inverted around the arousal dimension. The result is that the pleasant becomes unpleasant and the unpleasant pleasant. (This was illustrated clearly in Figure 2 in Chapter 2.) An analogy would be that of inverting the polarity of a magnet: the magnet remains in the same orientation in space, but the poles swap position, the positive becoming the negative and the negative becoming the positive. What reversal theory refers to as a 'reversal' therefore is an inversion through 180° of an emotional dimension. And the structure of emotional life is made up of pairs of such symmetrically opposite emotional dimensions between which reversal is possible. It should be noted that this relationship between dimensions is quite different from that of such theorists as Schlosberg. Rather than a pair of dimensions being placed at right angles to each other, in reversal theory they are parallel but in opposite directions. In other words, rather than being unrelated, they are closely related mirror-image forms.

The effect of this is that each individual emotion has two opposites rather than one. It has an opposite on its own dimension, and it also has an opposite on the reversed dimension. Thus anxiety is opposite to relaxation on its own dimension, and opposite to excitement in the sense that excitement is what replaces it in its own position on the arousal dimension following a reversal. The result is that we have not just a pair of opposites, or even two unrelated pairs of opposites, but an integrated pattern consisting of a pair of pairs of opposites. That is, there is a tight nexus of relationships which can generate a set of four contrasting but related primary emotions.

In the course of this book, a number of such 'pairs of pairs' of emotions have emerged. First of all, we saw that there was also a negativistic pair of pairs, which contrasted with the conformist pair. By combining these two into a single set, a 'pair of pairs of pairs' was produced. Then we saw that there was another equivalent set of emotions mirroring the first set, but involving the fixed dimension of 'felt transactional outcome' rather than 'felt arousal'. If we put all these together we find that there is a 'pair of pairs of pairs of pairs' of emotions. In other words, there are eight emotional dimensions made up of four pairs of opposite dimensions, and producing between them sixteen primary emotions. This complete set of emotions and emotional dimensions is shown in Figure 28, which could be said to represent the basic structure of emotional life as seen from the reversal theory perspective.

This is not a static structure. Rather, it represents a deep structure of relationships which generates a surface structure of individual emotions. This is made clearer by Figure 29, which shows the underlying hierarchy of 'decisions' which determine which particular emotions will be experienced at a particular moment. The most basic dichotomy represented by level I in the figure is that between somatic emotions (based on felt arousal) and transactional emotions (based on felt transactional outcome). These are complementary in the sense that at a given time *both* will be in operation, producing one somatic *and* one transactional emotion. At the next level of the hierarchy (level II) we have the metamotivational pairs: arousal-avoidance/arousal-seeking, mastery/sympathy and the rest. These are also complementary in that each pair plays a part in the determination of the emotion which will actually be felt. The crucial choice point comes at level III where, through the principle of reversal, one mode from each metamotivational pair will be chosen to be operative. These modes combine to produce the emotional dimension which will be operative (level

SOMATIC

	1 CONFORMIST	2 NEGATIVISTIC
AROUSAL-AVOIDANCE	Relaxation ← Anxiety	Placidity ← Anger
AROUSAL-SEEKING	Boredom → Excitement	Sulleness → 'Anger'

TRANSACTIONAL

	3 MASTERY	4 SYMPATHY
AUTOCENTRIC	Humiliation → Pride	Resentment → Gratitude
ALLOCENTRIC	Modesty ← Shame	Virtue ← Guilt

Fig. 28 This shows how the combination of four pairs of metamotivational modes gives rise to eight different emotional dimensions and sixteen different 'primary' emotions. The arrows show the preferred direction of movement on each dimension. For the somatic emotions the underlying variable is felt arousal (low to the left in each case); and for the transactional emotions it is felt transactional outcome (showing loss to the left in each case and gain to the right).

IV). For example, negativism combines with arousal-avoidance to produce the anger–placidity dimension. (Since one cannot easily represent combinations in a hierarchy, I have arbitrarily placed one pair, e.g. arousal-seeking/arousal-avoidance, above the other, e.g. negativism/conformity; but this arrangement could as easily have been the other way round.) Finally, the particular somatic and transactional emotion which is experienced from each of these dimensions will depend on the actual value of the felt arousal or felt transactional outcome variable at the time in question.

In this way, reversal theory provides a kind of 'generative grammar' of the emotions which would have pleased William James. Writing in the late nineteenth century of works on the psychology of emotion he stated: 'I should as lief read verbal descriptions of the shapes of the rocks on a New Hampshire farm as toil through them again. They give nowhere a central point of view, or a deductive or generative principle' (James 1890).

There are several points about this account of the emotions which may have occurred to the reader and which it might be useful to address briefly at this final stage, while we are looking at the emotions as a whole. The first concerns an apparent contradiction. Felt arousal was defined from the beginning as the experience of emotional intensity. And yet transactional emotions can also be experienced in different degrees of strength. How can it be, then, that any value of the felt transactional outcome variable can, as I have been implying, be combined with any degree of felt arousal? Surely it must be the case that high arousal must go with strongly felt transactional emotions and low arousal with weakly experienced emotions of this kind. The answer is that we are here talking about two different kinds of strength, so that it is perfectly possible to feel highly aroused but only moderately humiliated, or highly guilty but only moderately aroused. An analogy may be helpful here. If we think of a transactional emotion as being like a colour, then the strength of this emotion (e.g. how guilty one feels) is like the *saturation* of the colour. The degree of arousal which is associated with the emotion is then like its *brightness*. Thus, in the same way that it is possible to have a saturated colour with little brightness, or a colour low in saturation which is bright, so it is possible to experience a strong form of a transactional emotion with little arousal, or a weak version with strong arousal.

The second point concerns the completeness of reversal theory, as it stands, as a theory of the emotions. Now obviously the set of sixteen emotions which can be generated in accordance with the principles discussed here do not contain among them every conceivable emotion. Nevertheless, it is possible to regard this set as a core structure into which most types of emotion can, in one way or another, be assimilated. This can be done in a number of ways. For example, love and hate may be related to this structure, and jealousy and envy, in the ways discussed in Chapter 7.

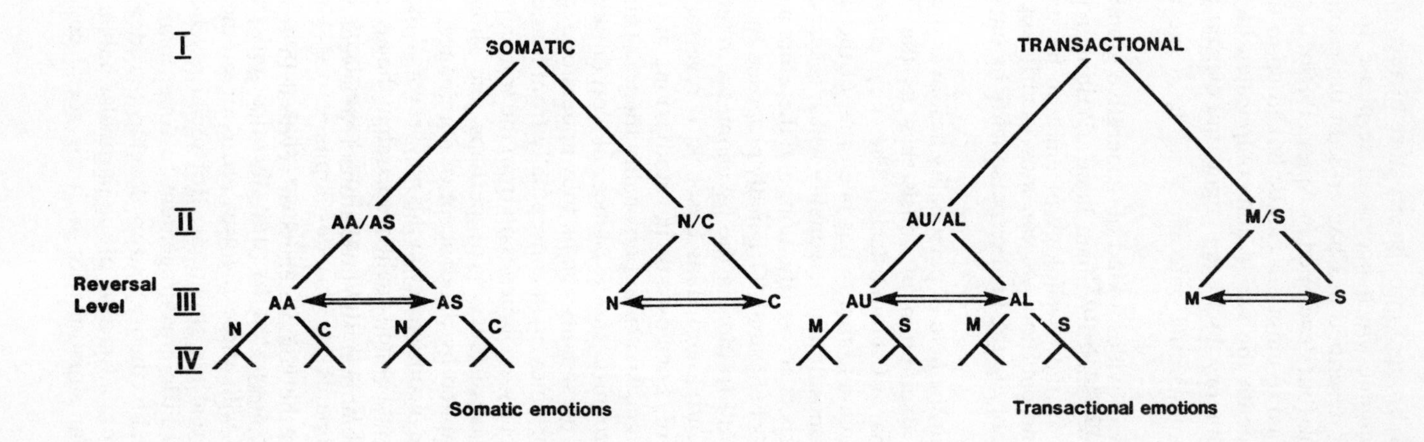

Fig. 29 The deep structure underlying the generation of sixteen 'primary' emotions. AA stands for 'arousal-avoidance', AS for 'arousal-seeking', N for 'negativistic', C for 'conformity', AU for 'autocentric', AL for 'allocentric', M for 'mastery', and S for 'sympathy'.

The feeling of humour may be brought into the structure by recognizing it as a form of paratelic excitement which occurs in response to certain definable types of synergy, as described in Chapter 8. In these and other ways not dealt with in this book (but developed in Apter (1988b, in press)), something like the full spectrum of emotions can be linked up to the core structure presented here. Beneath the varied and complicated life of the emotions, therefore, reversal theory discloses a 'tight' and elegant pattern of symmetrical contrasts.

PERSONALITY

Finally, as with motivation and emotion, we can most clearly appreciate the significance of reversal theory in the field of personality by once again taking a historical perspective.

It is probably true to say that the field of personality has, over the years, been as dominated by the assumption of consistency as the field of motivation has been by that of homeostasis. The key concept in mainstream personality research and theory has been that of the trait – a form of regularity or stable disposition in personality which is supposed to lead to consistency in some respect across situations and therefore a certain predictability in an individual's behaviour. Originally proposed by Allport (1937), the concept reached full fruition in the psychometric research of such major figures as R. B. Cattell and Hans Eysenck. If reversal theory challenges the assumption of homeostasis in motivation, it equally challenges the assumption of consistency in personality theory. This is not to say that it does not recognize the existence of certain kinds of consistency, but it denies that personality can be fully understood in terms of them. Just as reversal theory moves on conceptually from homeostasis to more complex forms of stability, so it moves on from the trait concept to the more complex form of consistency – or perhaps one should say consistency/inconsistency – implied by the concept of dominance.

In placing more emphasis on inconsistency in this way, reversal theory is, on the face of it, following a trend in personality research in the last several decades which has attempted to substitute situational specificity for the trait concept. Part of the impetus for this development was Mischel's (1968) argument, based on a variety of evidence, that people do not behave with the consistency suggested by trait theories and that the measuring devices associated with these theories are poor predictors of people's actual behaviour in real life situations. But social psychologists and learning theorists needed little encouragement to come more to the centre of the stage in personality theory and to develop the idea that a person's behaviour is much more a function of the particular habits he has learned to deal with particular situations, or with the social codes and expectancies which apply in relation to the activities he finds himself involved in, than to internal regularities. Such 'situationism' or 'contextualism' or 'interactionism' – to use three terms which apply to this same general approach – emphasizes that to predict someone's behaviour it is more important to know about the immediate context, especially the social context, of that behaviour than some nebulous personal disposition. Thus, if you want to predict if someone will be punctual for work it is better to find out if he is usually punctual for work than to attempt to assess whether he is, generally, a 'punctual type of person'. He may, after all, be inconsistent in his punctuality, usually being on time for work but late for parties.

Certainly, as Fontana (1983) has pointed out, reversal theory does have something in common with this approach. It sees personality processes as more flexible than they are generally conceived to be from the trait perspective, and it does not expect people to behave in similar ways under different circumstances. In this respect both situational theories and reversal theory recognize inconsistency in people's lives.

The inconsistency which is recognized by reversal theory, however, goes much deeper than that of situationism. In reversal theory terms, as we noted in Chapter 4, the individual can be inconsistent not only across situations of different types (e.g. work and parties), but also across different occurrences of the same situation (e.g. work). That is, the person can experience the *same* situation in different ways at different times and respond differently to it. One day he may be in the telic mode on the way to work and arrive on time; the next he may be in the paratelic mode, stop to enjoy watching an argument in the street, and be late. Another way of putting this is to say that situationism is still in one important respect a form of consistency theory: the individual is at least consistent from one situation to other occurrences of the same situation. In reversal theory, in contrast, even this type of consistency is lost. So although in one respect reversal theory develops the tendency in personality theory to pay greater attention to the way in which the same person 'differs from himself' over time, in another respect, by introducing the notion of regular internal change due to satiation, the theory marks a sharp break with all other theories of personality, be they of the trait or situationist type.

A further respect in which the inconsistency of reversal theory is different from that of situational theories arises in the following way. There is a sense in which the variable of mode, that is, which mode from each pair is operating at a given moment, is what is known in personality research as a 'moderator variable'. By a moderator variable is meant one which modifies the degree of relationship between two other variables. For example, Kogan and Wallach (1964) found that correlations between different measures of risk-taking were high for anxious individuals but not for low anxiety individuals; anxiety was therefore a moderator variable for different aspects of risk-taking. In these terms we could say that, in general, metamotivational mode moderates the relationship between the situation and behaviour. A given hypothesis about what behaviour to expect in a given situation may turn out to be supported in one metamotivational mode, but not in another. For example, as Svebak found (see Chapter 5), EMG gradients are steep in reaction to a threatening situation in the telic mode but not the paratelic mode. However, if mode is a moderator variable, it would appear to act in many situations as a special kind of moderator variable which has not previously been recognized in the literature on personality research. We could call it a 'radical moderator variable' because its effect is not so much to raise or lower the size of a correlation, but rather to change its sign. We saw this particularly clearly in the work of Martin et al. (the previous chapter) which showed how the relationship between stress and mood was moderated not so much in strength as in direction by the telic and paratelic modes. It is this which underlines the radical nature of the inconsistency to which reversal theory draws attention: people do not just behave differently at different times, but in ways which can be construed as opposite and even self-contradictory. In this too, the reversal theory 'principle of inconsistency' is stronger than the inconsistency allowed by situational theories.

There is a broad sense in which all personality theorists, of whatever persuasion, find common ground in seeing behaviour as a function of individual and situational characteristics. The difference between trait and situational theorists is then that the former lay more emphasis on the individual and situationists on the situation, in trying to explain and predict behaviour. But this 'dual-factor' assumption is also one which is challenged by reversal theory. From the reversal theory perspective there is a third factor which needs to be included in any predictive equation, and this is that of the metamotivational modes which are in force at the time in question.

The point may be made most sharply by means of an analogy. Suppose that we wanted to predict the speed and direction of a yacht. To do so we would need to know certain things about both the yacht (analogous to the individual) and the prevailing conditions (analogous to the situation). In particular we would need to know about the yacht such things as its weight, length, sail dimensions, and type of keel. And about the conditions we would need to know at least the speed and direction of the winds and currents. But given all this, we would still make a poor job of prediction unless we also knew something else: we would also need to know which 'mode' the yacht was being made to sail in: was it running before the wind, or reaching (attempting to move obliquely against it). This third piece of information is not 'situational' because the yacht can be made to do either in any given conditions. Neither is it a 'trait' because it will change from time to time – sometimes it will be running and sometimes reaching, sometimes going with the wind and sometimes doing the opposite and going against it.

Likewise, in predicting an individual's behaviour at a given time, we would need to know not only his or her dispositions and the nature of the situation, but also which mode was actually in operation at that time from each pair of modes. However playful a situation might seem to be, and however paratelic-dominant the individual in it, if for some reason he is not in the paratelic mode at that moment then he will not behave in a playful way. Similarly he will not behave angrily if he is not in the negativistic mode or guiltily if he is not in the allocentric sympathy mode combination.

In fact, of course, things are more complicated than suggested by the yacht analogy, because which mode from each pair of modes is operative is itself influenced by both individual dispositional factors (dominance) and situational factors (those that influence contingent reversals and those which constitute frustrations). Other things being equal, someone who is telic-dominant will be more likely to be in the telic than the paratelic mode at a given moment. And other things being equal, a situation which would appear from the outside to be serious, stressful, and threatening will be likely to induce the telic mode. But we cannot reduce mode to these two terms, dominance and situation, because each pair of modes also has to some extent a life of its own, governed by the process of satiation. This means that there is a natural rhythm of alternations from one mode to the other in each pair. Although dominance may tell us something about the balance of these underlying alternations over time, it cannot in itself tell us where, on this cycle, the individual is at a given moment of time. This may not matter: environmental factors may swamp the influence of satiation at a particular moment; but also they may not.

None of this should be taken to imply that, from the reversal theory perspective, the individual's experience and behaviour are unpredictable. If, as the theory suggests, inter-individual differences are a reflection of intra-individual differences – specifically, the way in which the individual tends to be characterized by different mode combinations over time – then this certainly makes personality more complex than might be supposed from the more static trait conception, or the more straightforward situationist viewpoint. But it does not in any way make individual differences inherently unpredictable or less amenable to scientific investigation.

One final point in relation to personality is that the reversal theory approach has some serious implications for the methodology of psychological experimentation. If the way in which people experience and behave is influenced by which metamotivational modes are in operation, and if people can switch modes even during the course of the same activity, then it may be crucial to know which modes subjects were actually in at each stage of an experiment if the results of the experiment are to be interpreted meaningfully. This raises the general issue of whether it is ever safe to match subjects for personality on the assumption that personality is invariant, or to use subjects as their own controls by comparing their performance at different stages of an empirical study.

SIMPLICITY AND COMPLEXITY

Much has been made in this chapter of the greater complexity of reversal theory than other theories in the fields of motivation, emotion, and personality. Multistability is more complex a concept than homeostasis, inversion structures are more complex than lists, the dominance notion is more complicated than that of the trait. Furthermore, reversal theory adds a new level of analysis to psychological theorizing – the metamotivational level – and it proposes a new principle of change – reversal – to add to the two main principles of change on which psychology has so far been based, namely learning and maturation. But are good theories not supposed to be simple?

In the fourteenth century William of Occam (or Ockham as his name is also spelled) put forward a well-known principle for theological argument to the effect that 'entities should not be multiplied needlessly'. (What he actually said was that 'It is vain to do with more what can be done with less.') Carried over into science, and referred to as 'Occam's razor', the principle suggests that a scientific theory should make as few assumptions as possible and be as simple as is necessary to account for the facts. Everything else should be cut away with his metaphorical razor. In the attempt to make psychology into a respectable science, the principle was followed assiduously over the years. Unfortunately, in the process many psychologists seemed to forget that it is perfectly proper, when one theory breaks down, to propose a more complicated theory to replace it – albeit only moving into greater complexity to the minimum extent that seems to be necessary to overcome the problems which emerge. By 'more complicated' here is meant starting with more complex assumptions in order to account for all the known facts in a way which is ultimately more elegant. Kepler's assumption that planets move in ellipses was undoubtedly more complicated than the medieval assumption that they must move in circles, and was generally treated with some horror when it was first proposed. But by means of the newer assumption, it was possible to do away with the increasingly ungainly system of epicycles added to cycles in order to explain the known facts of planetary motion with greater parsimony. The result was a theoretical system which was considerably more convenient to use and even, when astronomers had become used to it, more intellectually pleasing.

In the areas of perception, learning, attention, memory, language, and thinking, this need for more sophisticated premisses became evident in the 1960s and led to the renascence of these areas, which have gone by the collective appellation 'cognitive psychology'. Ideas were drawn in from linguistics, artificial intelligence, systems theory, and elsewhere to add to the rather simple, largely associationist, notions which were prevalent before, to produce an explosion of new and exciting research. Meanwhile, the study of motivation, emotion, and (to a lesser extent) personality was left, comparatively speaking, in something of a backwater. The view which led to the development of reversal theory was that the time for re-examining assumptions in these latter areas was also long past. There was a need to take the next step into complexity and replace the circle with the ellipse. If this could be done, it might be possible for these topics to take their rightful place again in the forefront of the development of psychology.

It would, of course, be presumptuous to claim that the premisses of reversal theory – multistability, dimensional inversion, and so on – might represent the ellipse, or to deny that some of the other approaches mentioned in this chapter are also beginning to break out in new directions. Also, because ideas are more complex, this does not, in itself, guarantee that they are better. But whatever the strengths and weaknesses of reversal theory it does at least draw attention to some of the most important unexamined assumptions of present-day research in these fields. In this way it can play its own part in raising a number of critical issues and stimulating new thinking. What its substantive contribution will turn out to be beyond that only time can tell.

No doubt in the light of further research and clinical experience the theory will need to be thoroughly revised; and, if it survives, it may even need to become more complex in certain respects. But this is one of the ways in which science progresses. Occam's razor is an essential piece of methodological equipment, but it has to be wielded properly. In psychology, especially in the areas which have been of central concern to the present book, we have perhaps been in danger of using it to cut our own throats.

Bibliography

Allport, G. W. (1937) *Personality: a Psychological Interpretation*, New York: Holt.

Anderson, G., and Brown, R.I.F. (1984) 'Sensation seeking and arousal in real and laboratory gambling', *British Journal of Psychology* 85:401–10.

—— (in press) 'Some applications of reversal theory to the explanation of gambling and gambling addictions', *Journal of Gambling Behaviour*.

Apter, M. J. (1976) 'Some data inconsistent with the optimal arousal theory of motivation', *Perceptual and Motor Skills* 43:1209–10.

—— (1979) 'Human action and the theory of psychological reversals', in G. Underwood and R. Stevens (eds), *Aspects of Consciousness, Volume I: Psychological Issues*, London: Academic Press, pp. 45–65.

—— (1981a) 'The possibility of a structural phenomenology: the case of reversal theory', *Journal of Phenomenological Psychology* 12, no. 2:173–87.

—— (1981b) 'Reversal theory: making sense of felt arousal', *New Forum* (now *Changes*) 8 (December):27–30.

—— (1981c) 'On the concept of bistability', *International Journal of General Systems* 6:225–32.

—— (1982a) *The Experience of Motivation: the Theory of Psychological Reversals*, London and New York: Academic Press.

—— (1982b) 'Fawlty Towers: a reversal theory analysis of a popular television comedy series', *Journal of Popular Culture* 16, no. 3:128–38.

—— (1982c) 'Metaphor as synergy', in D. S. Miall (ed.), *Metaphor: Problems and Perspectives*, Sussex: Harvester Press, pp. 55–70.

—— (1983) 'Negativism and the sense of identity', in G. Breakwell (ed.), *Threatened Identities*, London: Wiley, pp. 75–90.

—— (1984a) 'Reversal theory, cognitive synergy and the arts', in W. R. Crozier and A. J. Chapman (eds), *Cognitive Processes in the Perception of Art*, Amsterdam: North-Holland, pp. 411–26.

—— (1984b) 'Reversal theory and personality: a review', *Journal of Research in Personality* 18:265–88.

—— (1985) 'Religious states of mind: a reversal theory interpretation', in L. B. Brown (ed.), *Advances in the Psychology of Religion*, Oxford: Pergamon Press, pp. 62–75.

—— (1988a) 'Beyond the autocentric and the allocentric', in M. J. Apter, J. H. Kerr, and M. Cowles (eds), *Progress in Reversal Theory*, Amsterdam: North-Holland.

—— (1988b) 'Reversal theory as a theory of the emotions', in M. J. Apter, J. H. Kerr, and M. Cowles (eds), *Progress in Reversal Theory*, Amsterdam: North-Holland.

—— (in press) 'Reversal theory and the structure of emotional experience', in Z. Kulcsar, J. Strelau, and C. D. Spielberger (eds), *Stress and Emotion*, Budapest: Hungarian Academic Press, and New York: Hemisphere/Harper & Row.

Apter, M. J., Fontana, D., and Murgatroyd, S. (eds) (1985) *Reversal Theory: Applications and Developments*, Cardiff, Wales: University College Cardiff Press, and New Jersey: Lawrence Erlbaum.

Apter, M. J., Kerr, J. H., and Cowles, M. (eds) (1988) *Progress in Reversal Theory*, Amsterdam: North-Holland.

Apter, M. J., and Smith, K. C. P. (1977) 'Humour and the theory of psychological reversals', in A. J. Chapman and H. C. Foot (eds), *It's a Funny Thing, Humour*, Oxford: Pergamon Press, pp. 95–100.

—— (1978) 'Sexual dysfunction – depression, anxiety and the reversal theory', *British Journal of Sexual Medicine*, Part 1: 5, no. 38:23–4; Part 2:5, no. 39:25–6.

—— (1979a) 'Sexual behaviour and the theory of psychological reversals', in M. Cook and G. Wilson (eds), *Love and Attraction: an International Conference*, Oxford: Pergamon Press, pp. 405–8.

—— (1979b) 'Psychological reversals: some new perspectives on the family and family communication', *Family Therapy* 6, no. 2:89–100.

—— (1985) 'Experiencing personal relationships', in M. J. Apter, D. Fontana, and S. Murgatroyd (eds), *Reversal Theory: Applications and Developments*, Cardiff, Wales: University College Cardiff Press, and New Jersey: Lawrence Erlbaum, pp. 161–78.

—— (1987) 'Reversal theory', in B. McGurk, D. Thornton, and M. Williams (eds), *Applying Psychology to Imprisonment: Theory and Practice*, London: HMSO.

Apter, M. J., and Svebak, S. (1986) 'The EMG gradient as a reflection of metamotivational state', *Scandinavian Journal of Psychology* 27:209–19.

—— (in press) 'Stress from the reversal theory perspective', in C. D. Spielberger and J. Strelau (eds) *Stress and Anxiety*, Vol. 12, New York, Hemisphere/McGraw Hill.

Baker, J. (1988) 'Stress appraisals and coping with everyday hassles', in M. J. Apter, J. H. Kerr, and M. Cowles (eds), *Progress in Reversal Theory*, Amsterdam: North-Holland.

Bateson, G. (1958) *Naven*, Stanford, CA: Stanford University Press.

Beck, A., Ward, C., Mendelson, M., Mock, J., and Erbaugh, J. (1961) 'An inventory for measuring depression', *Archives of General Psychiatry* 4:53–63.

Becker, A. T. (1967) *Depression: Clinical, Experimental and Theoretical Aspects*, London: Staples Press.

Beebe-Center, J. G. (1932) *The Psychology of Pleasantness and Unpleasantness*, New York: Van Nostrand.

Binet, A., and Simon, T. (1905) 'Méthodes nouvelles pour le diagnostic du niveau intellectuel des anormaux', *Année Psychologique* 11:191–336.

Blackmore, M., and Murgatroyd, S. (1980) 'Anne: the disruptive infant', in S. Murgatroyd (ed.), *Helping the Troubled Child: Interprofessional Case Studies*, London: Harper & Row.

Boekaerts, M. (1986) 'Arousal, telic dominance and learning behaviour', in R. Gupta and P. Coxhead (eds). *Cultural Diversity and Learning Efficiency: Recent Developments in Assessment*, London: Macmillan.

—— (1988) 'Are there two types of arousal avoidance?' in M. J. Apter, J. H. Kerr, and M. Cowles (eds), *Progress in Reversal Theory*, Amsterdam: North-Holland.

Boekaerts, M., Hendriksen, J., and Michels, C. (1988a) 'The assessment of telic dominance in primary school pupils', in M. J. Apter, J. H. Kerr, and M. Cowles (eds), *Progress in Reversal Theory*, Amsterdam: North-Holland.

—— (1988b) 'The Nijmegen Telic Dominance Scale for Primary School Pupils (N-TDS)', in M. J. Apter, J. H. Kerr, and M. Cowles, *Progress in Reversal Theory*, Amsterdam: North-Holland.

Bowers, A. J. (1985) 'Reversals, delinquency and disruption', *British Journal of Clinical Psychology* 25:303–4.

—— (1988) 'Telic dominance and delinquency in adolescent boys', in M. J. Apter, J. H. Kerr, and M. Cowles (eds), *Progress in Reversal Theory*, Amsterdam: North-Holland.

Braman, O. R. (1982) *The Oppositional Child*, Guam: Isle of Guam Publishers.

—— (1988) 'Oppositionalism: clinical descriptions of six forms of telic self-negativism', in M. J. Apter, J. H. Kerr, and M. Cowles (eds), *Progress in Reversal Theory*, Amsterdam: North-Holland.

Brown, R. I. F. (1987) 'Classical and operant paradigms in the management of gambling addictions', *Behavioural Psychotherapy* 15: 111–22.

—— (1988) 'Reversal theory and subjective experience in the explanation of addiction and relapse', in M. J. Apter, J. H. Kerr, and M. Cowles (eds), *Progress in Reversal Theory*, Amsterdam: North-Holland.

—— (in press) 'Gambling addictions, arousal and an affective decision making explanation of behavioural reversions or relapses', *International Journal of Addictions*.

Cannon, W. (1932) *The Wisdom of the Body*, New York: Norton.

Clarke, D. and Crossland, J. (1985) *Action Systems*, London: Methuen.

Cooper, R., Osselton, J. W., and Shaw, J. C. (1980) *EEG Technology*, 3rd edn., London: Butterworth.

Cowles, M., and Davis, C. (1985) 'Strength of the nervous system and reversal theory', in M. J. Apter, D. Fontana, and S. Murgatroyd (eds), *Reversal Theory: Applications and Developments*, Cardiff, Wales: University College Cardiff Press, and New Jersey: Lawrence Erlbaum, pp. 129–43.

De Rivera, J. (1977) 'A structural theory of the emotions', *Psychological Issues*, Monograph 40, 10:4.

Dobbin, J. P., and Martin, R. A. (1988) 'Telic versus paratelic dominance: personality moderator of biochemical responses to stress', in M. J. Apter, J. H. Kerr, and M. Cowles (eds), *Progress in Reversal Theory*, Amsterdam: North-Holland.

Doherty, O., and Matthews, G. (1988) 'Personality characteristics of opiate addicts', *Personality and Individual Differences*, 9, 171–2.

Du Plat-Taylor, K., and Hourizi, S. (1985) 'Managing a disruptive child using reversal theory', *Newsletter of the Reversal Theory Society*, 1, no. 1:1–6.

Ellis, A. (1962) *Reason and Emotion in Psychotherapy*, New York: Lyle Stuart.

Fiske, D. W., and Maddi, S. R. (1986) 'A conceptual framework', in D. W. Fiske and S. R. Maddi (eds), *Functions of Varied Experience*, Homewood, Ill: Dorsey, pp. 11–56.

Folkman, S., and Lazarus, R. S. (1980) 'An analysis of coping in a middle-aged community sample', *Journal of Health and Social Behaviour* 21:219–39.

Fontana, D. (1981a) 'Obsessionality and reversal theory', *British Journal of Clinical Psychology* 20:299–300.

—— (1981b) 'Reversal theory, the paratelic state, and Zen', *Self and Society* 9, no. 5:229–36.

—— (1983) 'Individual differences in personality: trait based versus state based approaches', *Educational Psychology* 3, nos. 3/4:189–200.

—— (1985) 'Educating for creativity', in M. J. Apter, D. Fontana, and S. Murgatroyd (eds), *Reversal Theory: Applications and Developments*, Cardiff, Wales: University College Cardiff Press, and New Jersey: Lawrence Erlbaum, pp. 72–88.

—— (1988) 'Self-awareness and self-forgetting: Now I see me now I don't', in M. J. Apter, J. H. Kerr, and M. Cowles (eds), *Progress in Reversal Theory*, Amsterdam: North-Holland.

Foster, M. LeCron (1988) 'Cultural triggering of psychological reversals', in M. J. Apter, J. H. Kerr, and M. Cowles (eds), *Progress in Reversal Theory*, Amsterdam: North-Holland.

Frankl, V. (1973) *Psychotherapy and Existentialism: Selected Papers on Logotherapy*, Harmondsworth: Penguin.

Gallacher, J. E. J., and Beswick, A. D. (1988) 'Telic state, Type A behaviour and blood pressure', in M. J. Apter, J. H. Kerr, and M. Cowles (eds), *Progress in Reversal Theory*, Amsterdam: North-Holland.

Girodo, M. (1985) 'Telic and paratelic modes in operational undercover and field narcotics agents', paper presented at the Second International Conference on Reversal Theory, York University, Toronto, May 1985.

Harré, R., Clarke, D., and De Carlo, N. (1985) *Motives and Mechanisms*, London: Methuen.

Hart, J. (1987) 'Why not more phenomenology and less structure?' in J. Norcross (ed.), *Casebook of Brief Psychotherapy*, New York: Brunner/Mazel.

Hebb, D. O. (1955) 'Drives and the C.N.S. (Conceptual Nervous System)', *Psychological Review* 62: 243–54.

Howard, R. (1988) 'Telic dominance, personality and coping', in M. J. Apter, J. H. Kerr, and M. Cowles (eds), *Progress in Reversal Theory*, Amsterdam: North-Holland.

Hull, C. L. (1943) *Principles of Behaviour*, New York: Appleton-Century-Crofts.

Hyers, C. (1985) 'Reversal theory as a key to understanding religious diversity', in M. J. Apter, D. Fontana, and S. Murgatroyd (eds), *Reversal Theory: Application and Developments*, Cardiff, Wales: University College Cardiff Press, and New Jersey: Lawrence Erlbaum, pp. 117–28.

Hyland, M. E., Sherry, R., and Thacker, C. (1988) 'Prospectus for an improved measure of telic dominance', in M. J. Apter, J. H. Kerr, and M. Cowles (eds), *Progress in Reversal Theory*, Amsterdam: North-Holland.

Izard, C. E. (1977) *Human Emotions*, New York: Plenum Press.

James, W. (1890) *The Principles of Psychology*, New York: Holt.

Jones, R. (1981) 'Reversals, delinquency and fun', *Self and Society* 9, no. 5:237–41.

Kanner, A. D., Coyne, J. C., Schaefer, C., and Lazarus, R. S. (1981) 'Comparison of two modes of stress measurement: daily hassles and uplifts versus major life events', *Journal of Behavioural Medicine* 4:1–39.

Kaplan, H. S. (1978) *The New Sex Therapy: Active Treatment of Sexual Dysfunctions*, Harmondsworth: Penguin.

Kerr, J. H. (1985a) 'A new perspective for sports psychology', in M. J. Apter, D. Fontana, and S. Murgatroyd (eds), *Reversal Theory: Applications and Developments*, Cardiff, Wales: University College Cardiff Press, and New Jersey: Lawrence Erlbaum, pp. 89–102.

—— (1985b) 'The experience of arousal: a new basis for studying arousal effects in sport', *Journal of Sports Sciences* 3:169–79.

—— (1986) 'Play: the reversal theory perspective', in R. van der Kooij and J. Hellendoorn (eds), *Play, play therapy, play research*, Proceedings of the International Symposium, Amsterdam, September 1985. PAOS Series, no. 6. Berwyn: Swets North America and Lisse: Swets & Zeitlinger, pp. 67–76.

—— (1987a) 'Differences in the motivational characteristics of "professional", "serious amateur" and "recreational" sports performers', *Perceptual and Motor Skills* 64:379–82.

—— (1987b) 'The theory of psychological reversals: implications for future work in behavioural medicine', in J. L. Sheppard (ed.), *Advances in Behavioural Medicine*, Vol. 4, Sydney: Cumberland College of Health Sciences.

—— (1987c) 'Structural phenomenology, arousal and performance', *Journal of Human Movement Studies* 13:211–29.

—— (1987d) 'Cognitive intervention with elite performers: reversal theory', *British Journal of Sports Medicine* 21, no. 2:29–33.

—— (1988a) 'Soccer hooliganism and the search for excitement', in M. J. Apter, J. H. Kerr, and M. Cowles (eds), *Progress in Reversal Theory*, Amsterdam: North-Holland.

—— (1988b) 'Play, sport and the paratelic state', in M. J. Apter, J. H. Kerr, and M. Cowles (eds), *Progress in Reversal Theory*, Amsterdam: North-Holland.

—— (in press) 'Anxiety, arousal and sport performance: an application of reversal theory', in D. Hackfort and C. D. Spielberger (eds), *Anxiety in Sports: an International Perspective*, series in Health Psychology and Behavioural Medicine, New York: Hemisphere Publishing.

Kobasa, S. C. (1979) 'Stressful life events, personality and health: an inquiry into hardiness', *Journal of Personality and Social Psychology* 37:1–11.

Kogan, N., and Wallach, M. A. (1964) *Risk-Taking: a Study in Cognition and Personality*, New York: Holt, Rinehart and Winston.

Kruger, D. (1981) *An Introduction to Phenomenological Psychology*, Pittsburgh, PA: Duquesne University Press.

Kuhn, M. H., and McPartland, T. S. (1954) 'An empirical investigation of self attitudes', *American Sociological Review* 19:58–67.

Lachenicht, L. (1985a) 'Reversal theory: a synthesis of phenomenological and deterministic approaches to psychology', *Theoria*, 1–27.

—— (1985b) 'A reversal theory of social relations applied to polite language', in M. J. Apter, D. Fontana, and S. Murgatroyd (eds), *Reversal Theory: Application and Developments*, Cardiff, Wales: University College Cardiff Press, and New Jersey: Lawrence Erlbaum, pp. 144–60.

—— (1988) 'A critical introduction to reversal theory', in M. J. Apter, J. H. Kerr, and M. Cowles (eds), *Progress in Reversal Theory*, Amsterdam: North-Holland.

Lafreniere, K., Cowles, M., and Apter, M. J. (1988) 'The reversal phenomenon: reflections on a laboratory study', in M. J. Apter, J. H. Kerr, and M. Cowles (eds), *Progress in Reversal Theory*, Amsterdam: North-Holland.

Lorenz, K. (1950) 'The comparative method in studying innate behaviour patterns', in *Symposia of the Society for Experimental Psychology*, Vol. 4, Cambridge: Cambridge University Press, pp. 221–68.

Lowen, A. (1975) *Pleasure: a Creative Approach to Life*, New York: Penguin.

Malmo, R. B. (1965) 'Activation: a neurophysiological dimension', *Psychological Bulletin* 64:225–34.

Martin, R. A. (1984) 'Telic dominance, humour, stress and moods', paper given at the International Symposium on Reversal Theory, Gregynog, Wales, September 1983. Abstract in *Bulletin of the British Psychological Society* 37(1984):A45.

—— (1985) 'Telic dominance, stress and moods', in M. J. Apter, D. Fontana, and S. Murgatroyd (eds), *Reversal Theory: Applications and Developments*, Cardiff, Wales: University College Cardiff Press, and New Jersey: Lawrence Erlbaum, pp. 59–71.

Martin, R. A., Kuiper, N. A., and Olinger, L. J. (1988) 'Telic versus paratelic dominance as a moderator of stress', in M. J. Apter, J. H. Kerr, and M. Cowles (eds), *Progress in Reversal Theory*, Amsterdam: North-Holland.

Martin, R. A., Kuiper, N. A., Olinger, L. J., and Dobbin, J. (1987) 'Is stress always bad? Telic versus paratelic dominance as a stress moderating variable', *Journal of Personality and Social Psychology* 53:970–82.

Martin-Miller, L., and Martin, R. A. (1988) 'Metamotivational state and emotional response to false heartrate feedback', in M. J. Apter, J. H. Kerr, and M. Cowles (eds), *Progress in Reversal Theory*, Amsterdam: North-Holland.

Matthews, G. (1985) 'Personality and motivational trait correlates of the Telic Dominance Scale', *Personality and Individual Differences*, 6, no. 1:39–45.

McDermott, M. (1987) 'Rebelliousness in adolescence and young adulthood', unpublished Ph.D. thesis, University College Cardiff, Wales.

—— (1988a) 'Measuring rebelliousness: the development of the Negativistic Dominance Scale', in M. J. Apter, J. H. Kerr, and M. Cowles (eds), *Progress in Reversal Theory*, Amsterdam: North-Holland.

—— (1988b) 'Recognising rebelliousness: the ecological validity of the Negativism Dominance Scale', in M. J. Apter, J. H. Kerr, and M. Cowles (eds), *Progress in Reversal Theory*, Amsterdam: North-Holland.

McDermott, M., and Apter, M. J. (1988) 'The Negativism Dominance Scale (NDS)', in M. J. Apter, J. H. Kerr, and M. Cowles (eds), *Progress in Reversal Theory*, Amsterdam: North-Holland.

McDougall, W. (1923) *An Outline of Psychology*, London: Methuen.

McNair, D. M., Lorr, M., and Droppleman, L. F. (1971) *The Profile of Mood States*, San Diego, CA: Edits.

Miller, W. R. (1985) 'Addictive behaviour and the theory of psychological reversals', *Addictive Behaviors* 10:177–80.

Mischel, W. (1968) *Personality and Assessment*, New York: Wiley.

Murgatroyd, S. (1981) 'Reversal theory: a new perspective on crisis counselling', *British Journal of Guidance and Counselling* 9, no. 2:180–93.

——(1985a) 'Introduction to reversal theory', in M. J. Apter, D. Fontana, and S. Murgatroyd (eds), *Reversal Theory: Applications and Developments*, Cardiff, Wales: University College Cardiff Press, and New Jersey: Lawrence Erlbaum.

—— (1985b) 'The nature of telic dominance', in M. J. Apter, D. Fontana, and S. Murgatroyd (eds), *Reversal Theory: Applications and Developments*, Cardiff, Wales: University College Cardiff Press, and New Jersey: Lawrence Erlbaum, pp. 20–41.

—— (1987a) 'Depression and structural phenomenological eclectic psychotherapy: the case of Gill', in J. Norcross (ed.), *Casebook of Brief Psychotherapy*, New York: Brunnel/Mazel.

—— (1987b) 'Humour as a tool in counselling and psychotherapy: a reversal theory perspective', *British Journal of Guidance and Counselling*, 15, no. 3:225–36.

—— (1987c) 'Reversal Theory and Psychotherapy', Ph.D. thesis, Open University, Britain.

—— (in press), 'Combatting truancy: a counselling approach', in K. Reid (ed.), *Combatting School Absenteeism*, London: Hodder and Stoughton.

Murgatroyd, S., and Apter, M. J. (1984) 'Eclectic psychotherapy: a structural phenomenological approach', in W. Dryden (ed.), *Individual Psychotherapy in Britain*, London: Harper & Row, pp. 389–414.

—— (1986) 'A structural-phenomenological approach to eclectic psychotherapy', in J. Norcross (ed.), *Handbook of Eclectic Psychotherapy*, New York: Brunner/Mazel, pp. 260–80.

Murgatroyd, S., Rushton, C., Apter, M. J., and Ray, C. (1978) 'The development of the Telic Dominance Scale', *Journal of Personality Assessment* 42, no.5:519–28.

Nowlis, V. (1970) 'Mood: behavior and experience', in M. B. Arnold (ed.), *Feelings and Emotions*, New York: Academic Press.

O'Connell, K. A. (1988) 'Reversal theory and smoking cessation', in M. J. Apter,

J. H. Kerr, and M. Cowles (eds), *Progress in Reversal Theory*, Amsterdam: North-Holland.

Perls, F. S., Hefferline, R. F., and Goodman, P. (1973) *Gestalt Therapy: Excitement and Growth in the Human Personality*, Harmondsworth: Penguin.

Piaget, J. (1971) *Structuralism*, London: Routledge and Kegan Paul.

Plutchik, R. (1962) *The Emotions: Facts, Theories and a New Model*, New York: Random House.

Rhys, S. (1988) 'Mastery and sympathy in nursing', in M. J. Apter, J. H. Kerr, and M. Cowles (eds), *Progress in Reversal Theory*, Amsterdam: North-Holland.

Rimehaug, T., and Svebak, S. (1987) 'Psychogenic muscle tension: the significance of motivation and negative affect in perceptual-cognitive task performance', *International Journal of Psychophysiology* 5:97–106.

Sandler, I. N., and Lakey, E. (1982) 'Locus of control as a stress moderator: the role of control perceptions and social support', *American Journal of Community Psychology* 10:65–80.

Sandler, J., and Hazari, A. (1960) 'The obsessional: on the psychological classification of obsessional characteristics and symptoms', *British Journal of Medical Psychology* 33:113–22.

Schachter, S., and Singer, J. (1962) 'Cognitive, social and physiological determinants of emotional state', *Psychological Review* 69:78–99.

Schlosberg, H. (1952) 'The description of facial expressions in terms of two dimensions', *Journal of Experimental Psychology* 44:229–37.

Scott, C. S. (1985) 'The theory of psychological reversals – a review and a critique', *British Journal of Guidance and Counselling* 13, no. 2:139–46.

Seldon, H. (1980) 'Patricia: a problem of adjustment', in S. Murgatroyd (ed.), *Helping the Troubled Child: Interprofessional Case Studies*, London: Harper & Row.

Seligman, M. E. P. (1975) *Helplessness: on Depression, Development and Death*, San Francisco, CA: Freeman.

Smith, K. C. P., and Apter, M. J. (1977) 'Collecting antiques: a psychological interpretation', *Antique Collector* 48, no. 7:64–6.

Sollod, R. N. (1987) 'Is there truth in psychotherapeutic packaging?' in J. Norcross (ed.), *Casebook of Brief Psychotherapy*, New York: Brunner/Mazel.

Stone, A., and Neale, J. (1984) 'New measure of daily coping: development and preliminary results', *Journal of Personality and Social Psychology* 46, no. 4:892–906.

Stroop, J. R. (1935) 'Studies of inference in serial verbal reactions', *Journal of Experimental Psychology* 18:643–62.

Svebak, S. (1982) 'The significance of motivation for task-induced tonic physiological changes', D.Philos. thesis, University of Bergen.

—— (1983) 'The effect of information load, emotional load and motivational state upon tonic physiological activation', in H. Ursin and R. Murison (eds), *Biological and Psychological Basis of Psychosomatic Disease: Advances in the Biosciences*, vol. 42, Oxford: Pergamon Press, pp. 61–73.

—— (1984) 'Active and passive forearm flexor tension patterns in the continuous perceptual-motor task paradigm: the significance of motivation', *International Journal of Psychophysiology* 2:167–76.

—— (1985a) 'Psychophysiology and the paradoxes of felt arousal', in M. J. Apter, D. Fontana, and S. Murgatroyd (eds), *Reversal Theory: Applications and Developments*, Cardiff, Wales: University College Cardiff Press, and New Jersey: Lawrence Erlbaum, pp. 42–58.

—— (1985b) 'Seriousmindedness and the effect of self-induced respiratory changes upon parietal EEG', *Biofeedback and Self-Regulation* 10:49–62.

—— (1986a) 'Cardiac and somatic activation in the continuous perceptual-motor task: the significance of threat and seriousmindedness', *International Journal of Psychophysiology* 3:155–62.
—— (1986b) 'Patterns of cardiovascular-somatic-respiratory interactions in the continuous perceptual-motor task paradigm', in P. Grossman, K. Janssen, and D. Vaitl (eds), *Cardiorespiratory and Cardiosomatic Psychophysiology*, New York: Plenum.
—— (1988a) 'Cardiovascular risk', in M. J. Apter, J. H. Kerr, and M. Cowles (eds), *Progress in Reversal Theory*, Amsterdam: North-Holland.
—— (1988b) 'Psychogenic muscle tension', in M. J. Apter, J. H. Kerr, and M. Cowles (eds), *Progress in Reversal Theory*, Amsterdam: North-Holland.
—— (in press) 'The role of effort in stress and emotion', in Z. Kulcsar, J. Strelau, and C. D. Spielberger (eds), *Stress and Emotion*, Hungarian Academic Press and Hemisphere/Harper & Row.
Svebak, S. and Apter, M. J. (1984) 'Type A behavior and its relation to seriousmindedness (telic dominance)', *Scandinavian Journal of Psychology* 25:161–7.
—— (1987) 'Laughter: an empirical test of some reversal theory hypotheses', *Scandinavian Journal of Psychology* 28:189–98.
Svebak, S., and Grossman, P. (1985) 'The experience of psychosomatic symptoms in the hyperventilation provocation test and in non-hyperventilation tasks', *Scandinavian Journal of Psychophysiology* 26:327–35.
Svebak, S., Howard, R., and Rimehaug, T. (1987) 'P300 and quality of performance in a forewarned "Go-NoGo" reaction time task: the significance of goal-directed lifestyle and impulsivity', *Personality and Individual Differences* 8:313–19.
Svebak, S., and Murgatroyd, S. (1985) 'Metamotivational dominance: a multi-method validation of reversal theory constructs', *Journal of Personality and Social Psychology* 48, no. 1:107–16.
Svebak, S., Nordby, H., and Ohman, A. (1987) 'The personality of the cardiac responder: interaction of seriousmindedness and Type A behaviour', *Biological Psychology* 25:1–9.
Svebak, S., Storfjell, O., and Dalen, K. (1982) 'The effect of a threatening context upon motivation and task-induced physiological changes', *British Journal of Psychology* 73, no. 4:505–12.
Svebak, S., and Stoyva, J. (1980) 'High arousal can be pleasant and exciting: the theory of psychological reversals', *Biofeedback and Self-Regulation* 5, 4:439–44.
Thomas-Peter, B. A. (1988) 'Psychopathy and telic dominance', in M. J. Apter, J. H. Kerr, and M. Cowles (eds), *Progress in Reversal Theory*, Amsterdam: North-Holland.
Thomas-Peter, B. A., and McDonagh, J. D. (1988) 'Motivational dominance in psychopaths', *British Journal of Clinical Psychology* 27:153–8.
Tomkins, S.S., and McCarter, R. (1964) 'What and where are the primary affects? Some evidence for a theory', *Perceptual and Motor Skills* 18:119–58.
Twain, Mark (1959 edn) *The Adventures of Tom Sawyer*, New York: Signet Classics from the New American Library.
Van der Molen, P. P. (1984) 'Bi-stability of emotions and motivations: an evolutionary consequence of the open-ended capacity for learning', *Acta Biotheoretica* 33:227–51.
—— (1985) 'Learning, self-actualisation and psychotherapy', in M. J. Apter, D. Fontana, and S. Murgatroyd (eds), *Reversal Theory: Applications and Developments*, Cardiff, Wales: University College Cardiff Press, and New

Jersey: Lawrence Erlbaum, pp. 103–16.
—— (1986a) 'The evolutionary stability of a bistable system of emotions and motivations in species with an open-ended capacity for learning', in J. Wind and V. Reynolds (eds), *Essays in Human Sociobiology* Vol. 2, Brussels: V.U.B. Study Series No. 26, pp. 189–211.
—— (1986b) 'Reversal theory, learning and psychotherapy', *British Journal of Guidance and Counselling* 14, no. 2:125–39.
Walters, J., Apter, M.J., Svebak, S. (1982) 'Colour preference, arousal and the theory of psychological reversals', *Motivation and Emotion* 6, no. 3:193–215.
Watson, J. B. (1924) *Behaviorism*, New York: Acton.
Wicker, F. W., Thorelli, I. M., Barron, W. L., and Willis, A. C. (1981) 'Studies of mood and humor appreciation', *Motivation and Emotion* 5, no. 1:47–59.

Index